MAKING THE ECONOMY WORK

Also edited by Jon Shields and published by Macmillan for the Employment Institute

CONQUERING UNEMPLOYMENT: The Case for Economic Growth

Making the Economy Work

Edited by
Jon Shields

M
MACMILLAN in association with the EMPLOYMENT INSTITUTE

First published 1989

Published by
THE MACMILLAN PRESS LTD
Houndmills, Basingstoke, Hampshire RG21 2XS
and London
Companies and representatives
throughout the world

Printed in the People's Republic of China

British Library Cataloguing in Publication Data
Making the economy work
1. Great Britain. Unemployment. Implications
of theories of economics
I. Shields, Jon II. Employment Institute
331.13'7941
ISBN 0–333–47132–6 (hardcover)
ISBN 0–333–47133–4 (paperback)

COUNCIL OF THE EMPLOYMENT INSTITUTE

(as at 1 June 1988)

cont. overleaf

The Employment Institute is a research organisation promoting study and debate about the best methods of reducing unemployment without setting in motion an inflationary upsurge. Its staff conduct in-house research on barriers to employment growth and arrange for the publication and discussion of pamphlets by distinguished outside contributors.

The Trustees and advisory Council of the Employment Institute are listed on the previous page.

The Employment Institute's series of pamphlets and other publications are available to the public on payment of a yearly subscription. Requests for further information about the Institute should be addressed to:

Employment Institute
Southbank House
Black Prince Rd
London SE1 7SJ
Tel: 01–735–0777

Contents

List of Tables

List of Figures

Preface

This book and its companion volume *Conquering Unemployment: The Case for Economic Growth* portray major aspects of the Employment Institute's published output in its first three years. The books draw on the series of policy pamphlets produced by the Institute to explain why alternative prescriptions to 'monetarism' could have avoided the massive rise in unemployment in the early 1980s. If implemented now, these policies could ensure that recent reductions in unemployment would be hastened and sustained.

The policies recommended cover both 'macroeconomic' and 'microeconomic' solutions. Broadly speaking, the contributions in this book look at microeconomic or structural issues, whilst those in *Conquering Unemployment* concentrate on the macroeconomic side, including theoretical arguments for and against monetarism, guidelines for the government's budgetary and financial policies and why mass unemployment returned to the United Kingdom with such a vengeance.

This book is about possible structural reforms which would permit the economy to be expanded further without rekindling inflation and make it possible for a permanently lower level of unemployment to be sustained. Two innovations are explored in the field of wage-setting: profit sharing between employees and share-holders and the use of either tax incentives to employers or agreements with unions to restrain wage increases. A fresh look is taken at regional policy and the case for concentrating help on small firms is subject to critical evaluation. Most importantly, a new approach to reabsorbing the million long-term unemployed back into the labour market is outlined and costed.

The aim throughout has been to tackle complex economic issues in as readable and non-technical a manner as possible. This does not mean that jargon has been wantonly jettisoned where it actually helps the reader, nor that arguments are only superficially displayed. The contributions are intended to be meaty, but not tough.

Many people have had a hand in the production of these readings. The authors themselves toiled willingly but without financial reward and often under uncomfortable pressure from myself, Richard Layard and other trustees of the Institute. Brenda Haddou, Sandra Cox,

Michelle Bailleux and Harbans Chana processed various of the manuscripts with remarkable patience. Mark Cornelius provided invaluable support and advice. Errors no doubt remain and, where I can't blame individual authors, fall on me.

May 1988 JON SHIELDS

Notes on the Contributors

Harvey Armstrong is Senior Lecturer in the Department of Economics at the University of Lancaster. He edits, with Jim Taylor, *Regional Studies* the Journal of the Regional Studies Association.

Lord Basnett (David Basnett) was General Secretary of the General, Municipal, Boilermakers and Allied Trades Union until December 1985, and Chairman of the TUC Economic Committee until April 1986. He was a Council Member of the Employment Institute.

Saul Estrin is a Research Fellow at the London School of Economics.

Richard Jackman is Senior Lecturer in Economics at the London School of Economics and a Trustee of the Employment Institute.

Stephen Johnson is Research Associate at the Centre for Urban and Regional Development Studies, University of Newcastle-upon-Tyne.

Richard Layard is Professor of Economics at the London School of Economics and Head of the Centre for Labour Economics. He is Chairman of the Council of the Employment Institute.

Stephen Nickell is Professor of Economics at the University of Oxford and Director of the Institute of Economics and Statistics. He is a Council Member of the Employment Institute.

David Storey is Director of Research, Small Business Centre, University of Warwick.

Jim Taylor is Professor in the Department of Economics at the University of Lancaster. He edits, with Harvey Armstrong, *Regional Studies*, the journal of the Regional Studies Association.

Sushil Wadhwani is a Research Fellow at the London School of Economics.

Martin L. Weitzman is Mitsui Professor of Economics at Massachusetts Institute of Technology.

1 Introduction

Jon Shields

A startling success story of the postwar world in industrialised countries seemed to be the eradication of mass unemployment. After the privations of the early 1930s, when unemployment in Britain affected nearly a fifth of the population, the unemployment rates registered in the 1950s and 1960s seemed miniscule. Nearly everyone who wanted to work could find work. Developed nations were encouraging immigration to cover hard-to-fill vacancies.

Until the late 1960s, the dangers of inflation also seemed to have been contained. Occasional price surges were quickly subdued and although signs of balance of payments difficulties or mounting wage pressures sometimes forced politicians to put the brakes on the economy and allow some rise in unemployment, the increases that occurred were very small by today's standards.

Without appreciating this background, it is difficult now, from the perspective of Britain in the 1980s and an unemployment level that remained at around the three million level for five years, to appreciate the horror that greeted the apparent ending of this period of unparalleled success with the breaching of the one million figure in 1971. Even then, few saw it as other than a temporary blot on the economic record, reflecting distortions caused by incipient inflation and harsh or misconceived policy reactions to it.

Yet events now show that this was just one milestone on a long upward climb. By the mid-1970s advocates of alternative approaches to economic policy were able to show how each successive cycle in the economy was delivering higher peak rates of both unemployment and inflation. The economic downturn of 1980–1 was to prove further vivid evidence of the steepening upward drift in the unemployment rate even if the peak in the inflation rate did not quite attain previous levels.

As the accompanying volume (*Conquering Unemployment: The Case for Economic Growth*) shows, the peculiar savagery of the 1980–1 downturn and the enormous rise in unemployment in the United Kingdom can to a large extent be explained by misconceived economic policy actions taken by the government. But *some* rise in unemployment was probably inevitable and these policies would not have been so doggedly pursued, nor their effects have been so disastrous, had there not been serious underlying deficiencies in the economy that prevented an easy return to the 'low unemployment, low inflation' days of the fifties and sixties.

What were these deficiencies? Were they products of the 1970s or had they always been present, muted in their impact in the first two postwar decades, but now exacting their toll on economic performance? Are they now capable of correction? These are the fundamental issues which the works in this volume address. Each chapter examines a specific concern – profit-sharing, wage-bargaining, unions, regional disparities, small firms, the long-term unemployed – and blends a practical approach with a coherent theoretical framework. Neither the specification of nor justification for idealised models of the economy is on their agenda. Indeed, their major contributions lie in demonstrating the deficiencies of existing models and in showing how changes in institutional structures or economic policies can yield equally attractive results to those promised by theoretically elegant artefacts.

Liberation from the world of free competition demanded by neoclassical economists, with its impersonal, harsh and increasingly unrealisable system of perfect markets in commodities, industrial products, labour and finance, has allowed the authors to show how modern economies, ailing as they are, can be made to bounce back from setbacks and shocks without resort to the sort of painful medicine recently inflicted on the British economy. The health of the whole patient is the aim rather than the amputation of limb after limb in the desperate hope that, by eliminating all those parts which are not working according to expectations, the rest of the body will be cleansed and reborn.

As Martin Weitzman eloquently points out in his introduction to Chapter 2 the major economic problem lurking behind apparent success stories in both the United Kingdom and the United States, is the 'two-headed monster: stagflation'. We know, within reasonable limits, how to reduce unemployment by expansionary measures; and we know how to reduce inflation by contractionary ones. What we still do not know how to do on a sustained basis is to reduce unemployment and inflation simultaneously. Our failure is evidenced by the gyrations in economic policy we have seen in the last twenty years and the continual presence of one problem or both. Although

Reaganomics in the United States has certainly produced superior performance in terms of both unemployment and inflation than has Thatcherism in the United Kingdom – and a respectable one in general postwar terms – it would be a foolhardy individual who did not see some pain round the corner as the budgetary and trade imbalances in the US economy are corrected.

Much of the debate about what should be achievable through economic policy action centres round the notion of what Milton Friedman called the 'natural' rate of unemployment or the currently-fashionable derivative, the 'non-accelerating-inflation rate of unemployment' (NAIRU). As an expository device, there can be little doubting the usefulness of this concept. The realisation that below some minimum level of unemployment (or rate of utilisation of another scarce factor of production) an increase in demand will result in an upward spiralling of wages or other prices is a crucial reminder that there are physical limits to what can be achieved by economic policy. But the implications of the NAIRU concept are frequently taken too far. With the labour force as geographically, educationally and industrially dispersed as in the United Kingdom, much will obviously depend on where any additional demand is spent. If a national unemployment rate of 8 per cent conceals (as now) an absolute shortage of skilled labour in parts of the South East of England with no obvious means of replenishment through migration or training, then clearly a new computer facility in Reading for the armed forces will lead to higher wage pressure amongst computer engineers. But there is no reason to expect a similar increase in wage pressure if the money is spent instead on a barracks in Liverpool.

Many of the schemes presented in this volume can be seen as proposals for reducing unemployment rates by 'lowering the NAIRU'. But they are actually more than that. Their proponents mostly took as read that some stimulus to the economy was and probably still is needed. What they sought to do was to ensure that when a stimulus was imparted to the economy it would both result in an immediate boost to output and employment rather than inflation and ensure that in the longer term the structural balance of the economy would be improved and the labour market would respond more flexibly to changed demand conditions. This alone would permit the postwar golden combination of low unemployment and low inflation to become realisable once again.

PROFIT-SHARING

The first proposal under consideration is that firms should break away from fixing total levels of remuneration in advance for their employees and then reserving profits (or losses) either for retention or distribution to shareholders. Instead workers, too, should get a share of the profits in return for accepting a lower 'base' wage. That would give them a stake in the performance of the company and decrease their cost to employers when times were bad.

The main advocate of profit-sharing has been Professor Martin Weitzman. Whilst making radical claims for its impact on the economy, Weitzman is at pains to point out that it is not a new invention. Indeed, some 15 per cent of American firms are said already to carry out 'profit-sharing' with their employees in some form or another and virtually all Japanese employees currently enjoy profit-related bonuses.

In Britain, too, profit-sharing is not new (the John Lewis Partnership has been operating schemes since 1929) but its impact had been extremely limited until tax concessions in the late 1970s and, recently, government interest and specific tax incentives, began to spur companies to experiment. Even so, initial response to the government's advocacy of profit-sharing and the tax reliefs announced in the 1987 budget has been way below hopes and expectations.

This must be disappointing to those who see in Weitzman's ideas a way of breaking out of two of Britain's most serious economic problems: the tendency of employment rather than real earnings to respond when there is a downturn in the economy and a perceived lack of motivation among many workforces which inhibits productivity growth and innovation. But Weitzman's claims go way beyond these benefits. To him, profit-sharing holds 'the key to non-inflationary full employment'. The key is the tying of part of an employee's remuneration to a firm's actual profits. If a firm makes lower profits, it pays lower wages. So it can afford to take greater risks in hiring people. The marginal cost of employment will go down. Which means that employment levels will rise.

Weitzman's model is an attractive one. Some of the risk associated with an employee's future profitability is shifted from the firm to the employee. More people can safely be taken on in an upswing and fewer laid off in a downturn. The real wages of those in employment will be more volatile, but extremes of wage loss – unemployment – will become less frequent.

These arguments may impress the policy maker and the unemployed. What about workers who currently see their employment as secure? Why should they voluntarily accept greater risk and the prospect of their remuneration being diluted as employers take on more, less profitable workers who will be entitled to a share of 'their' profits? Weitzman has two answers to this. Firstly, they should perceive that it is to their good also that output and employment levels be higher because this increases demand for their firms' products and reduces their share of the burden of state finances. Secondly, just in case they do not, existing employees should simply be denied any say in the hiring policies of their firm.

These arguments do not convince Sushil Wadhwani (Chapter 3). He foresees collusion between firms and their existing workforces to prevent the mechanisms outlined by Weitzman from ever working. If all that happens under profit-sharing is that remuneration is formally split between wages and a profit-share element, without any change in the total, there will be no permanent effect on employment either. Tax incentives, in particular, will simply encourage 'cosmetic' schemes in which both sides agree a forecast for profits and then agree a synthetic formula which looks like profit-sharing but does not in fact change the total sum of wages being paid out.

Wadhwani also finds the empirical evidence unconvincing. Japanese bonuses may or may not produce the type of profit-sharing arrangement described by Weitzman, but the Japanese economy does not seem any less prone than European ones to 'stagflation' when one takes into account the effects that the 'lifetime employment system' have on disguising unemployment.

On incentives, Saul Estrin (Chapter 4) finds some evidence in favour of greater employee involvement in profits, shares or decision making. Industrial relations, organisational efficiency, factor productivity and profitability can all be shown to have been better in firms with higher levels of participation. The experience has however by no means been universal and the differences compared with firms not practising participation have often been only marginal. Furthermore, it is by no means clear that schemes in which workers get a cash share of the overall profits of the firm, but no share in company decisions, are as effective as those where group incentive schemes operate or workers have shares or responsibilities in the company.

It is not necessary, however, to refute either the theoretical objections raised by Wadhwani or the relative inferiority of profit-sharing compared with other forms of participation implied by Estrin to support Weitzman's overall case. Compared with the rigidities currently experienced in major parts of the United Kingdom's wage-bargaining structure, no harm and perhaps some considerable good could come from moves to experiment with profit-sharing. Whether this justifies the government stepping in with tax reliefs which could otherwise finance direct employment creation is another matter.

COLLECTIVE BARGAINING

Weitzman's proposals would shake the whole structure of collective bargaining, forcing unions to accept greater volatility in wage levels and precluding any restrictions on new hiring. While blaming the wage system rather than unions *per se* for the problems of stagflation, his solution would result in their role being much diminished.

Not surprisingly, for a man whose life was devoted to the Trade Union movement, Lord David Basnett (Chapter 5) took a very different view. He took the government to task for what he saw as an unjustified and destructive assault on trade unionism and collective bargaining, aided and abetted by high unemployment and some aggressive employers. Were the trade union movement instead to have been restored to a position of responsibility, he believed that it would be able to deliver the goal that the government say they want: lower inflation. But it would also be able to couple this with higher output and employment.

Basnett believed that trade unions did in fact survive fairly well during the 1980s. Although membership has dropped, most of the fall has simply reflected the overall decline in employment. Shop stewards are relatively more numerous and most employers, embarking on structural change, have chosen to use existing union procedures and opt for negotiated solutions.

The problem is that the levels at which bargaining takes place have become fragmented. This has given rise to a whole set of anomalies which threaten cohesion and stability. Attempts to compartmentalise union interests and power have failed to recognise the interrelationship of shop-floor issues to those affecting the firm, the sector and in fact the whole economy. Not just health and safety issues, but the distortion of differentials, prevalence of low pay and impact of part-time work need to be considered right the way up through the industrial structure.

Basnett wanted to see a return of the unions to the national negotiating table through the setting-up of a 'National Economic Summit'. In response to greater involvement in the framework of social policy (issues such as minimum wage) the unions could play their part in ensuring that an expansionary economic policy did not see the fruits of higher demand dissipated in higher inflation. For a short period, while the economy was subject to a stimulus from the public sector – or presumably in the high demand conditions of recent years – he would have been prepared to see the specification of a wages norm which resulted in incomes rising only marginally higher than inflation. This would clearly imply some restrictions on collective bargaining, but in return there would be a greater freedom for real improvements to be made at the work-place.

INCOMES POLICIES

Basnett's principal message was thus for a return to some form of incomes policy. Indeed, if wages threaten to take off whenever demand is increased and this pressure cannot be dissipated through Weitzman's profit-sharing, formal agreements to limit earnings growth seem to offer the only hope of achieving a generalised and sustained non-inflationary expansion.

Not everyone, however, shares Basnett's optimism that the co-operation of the trade union movement would either guarantee success or would not involve too high a price. Against the undoubted success story of the 1975–77 period, when wage inflation declined from 28 per cent a year to 8 per cent, can be set numerous examples of 'wage creep' or (as in 1978–9) breakdown under either compulsory or voluntary agreements.

Such considerations prompt Richard Layard and Steve Nickell (Chapter 6) to opt for a new strategy. If strict controls tend to be cumbersome and inflexible and voluntary agreements often prove to be ineffective at the level of the bargaining unit, their answer would be to invent a financial incentive to encourage co-operation. Their chosen incentive would be a hefty tax on employers who increased average wages in their establishments by more than a specified amount. This would avoid any question of compulsion. Some flexibility would be retained because those employers who were particularly profitable could still pay above-average wage increases to attract and retain staff. The tax would be large enough, however, to ensure that the general level of wage increases did not rise by much more than the specified norm.

Layard and Nickell doubt whether the scheme would be difficult to enforce. They would restrict it to firms with over 100 employees and use the existing PAYE mechanism for collection and monitoring. Against the risk that it could discourage profit-sharing by forcing higher profits within the tax net, they propose a special 'gateway' for increases in remuneration that arise from higher company profits. Productivity increases would thereby be encouraged and rewarded.

Such a scheme may seem well directed towards private sector wage payments, but what about the public sector and dividends and prices? The authors would be prepared to see parallel policies adopted in these areas also but stress that, because of their central role in the inflationary process, it is primarily the earnings of employees in private sector firms that need to be constrained. Other elements in the spiral will follow.

REGIONAL POLICY

Success in restraining the overall level of wage increases would mean that an expansion of demand could take place without inflation being reignited, but only if the workers were available to do the additional jobs that could be created. With unemployment rates still running at 12 per cent in the North of England whilst they are below 6 per cent in the South-East, how can we be sure that the jobs will be in the right places for those so keenly looking for them?

In the fifties and sixties, the answer would have been clear. An effective regional policy, that prevented or penalised employers setting up new plants in congested areas and gave them incentives to move North, would bring jobs to the workers. Now, however, regional policy, like incomes policy, has become discredited. Memories of thousands of pounds spent on unprofitable or unnecessary plants or public sector projects are powerful reminders of misplaced zeal or political deals. Because regional economic policies did not succeed in eliminating (or in some cases even reducing) regional disparities they are widely assumed to have failed.

Such judgements, which have served to justify a substantial run-down in regional economic policies over the last decade, are, however, far too sweeping. As the evidence accumulated by Harvey Armstrong and Jim Taylor in Chapter 7 shows, both location decisions and employment have been powerfully influenced in the past by government inducements and regulations. Estimates of the initial costs to the public sector of each job created may look high, but if these jobs were permanent and if they sustained other jobs, it is easy to show that they could have paid for themselves. Simply by working against the tide and slowing up the drift to congested areas, policies which created jobs in the regions allowed a higher national level of employment to be achieved and thereby brought gains in national output and government revenues.

Armstrong and Taylor provide a depressing survey of the extent of current disparities between the regions. More recent signs of recovery in the North, as the benefits of the 'boom' in the South have spread outwards, simply point up even more powerfully the failures of corrective market mechanisms in the early 1980s. Added to that, so many different agencies seem to be involved in assisting specific areas and sectors that the dangers of overlap and mutually offsetting effects seem to be enormous.

The problem now is to devise a structure for regional policy that builds on lessons painfully learned in the past and is consistent with the government's general market-oriented approach to economic policy. The main message advanced by Armstrong and Taylor is that better co-ordination is needed between existing agencies, with the European Community now a central actor in the process. But the authors also call for the creation of new development agencies, on the lines of the successful Scottish Development Agency, for all the English regions and a better monitoring of the effects of all government activities (like the location of defence establishments).

SMALL FIRMS

One of the main aims of these new regional development agencies would be to attract new sources of capital into the regions, with a particular emphasis on the provision of venture capital. This would help to correct the problem identified by David Storey and Steve Johnson in Chapter 8 that the less developed regions tend to exhibit much lower levels of 'entrepreneurship' than does the prosperous South. Thus any national rather than regionally directed schemes aimed at encouraging the growth of small firms serve to exaggerate rather than reduce regional disparities.

Even so, Storey and Johnson are sceptical about the role played by small firms in generating employment and critical of the policies that have been put in place to encourage them. They show that many of the statements made about their contribution to employment growth both here and in the United States have been exaggerated or downright misleading. In particular, it is unlikely that small firms have in fact been the 'major contributors' to employment growth in either country. Much of the relatively superior growth performance in the early 1980s can be attributed to the savage effects of the recession on established firms. It is even probable that some of the growth in small firms has resulted directly from the decline of larger ones as functions have been split off or transferred to outside contractors. Most importantly, if we are looking for clues to full employment, there seems to be nothing in international evidence to support the view that a high proportion of employment in small firms promotes low levels of unemployment.

The merits of small firms have been exaggerated and (as the authors show) policies to assist them may have been relatively ineffective. But it does not follow that all efforts to foster their development should be abandoned. The defeat of unemployment necessitates the encouragement of fast-growing, employment-intensive companies. The risk is that many apparently successful start-ups become hindered by shortage of capital, information, specialist advice or just by red tape. What the authors require is a policy to spot the real high-fliers on their way up. This should be done on the evidence of at least a limited track record rather than in blind faith before the business is even created. Cost-effectiveness requires that small firms be helped by selective entry to state kindergartens rather than general entry to maternity wards.

A JOB GUARANTEE

Selectivity, or targeting, also emerges as the major theme in the final chapter of this volume. Here, however, the target is not a particular region or type of firm that is likely itself to promote employment, but the unemployed themselves. Such targeting tends to be viewed very much as a last resort. Everyone would prefer to see the long-term unemployed taken into regular employment as part of a general upturn in the economy. Indeed, the evidence compiled by Richard Jackman and his associates in Chapter 9 confirms that there is little that is 'special' about the long-term unemployed as a group except for long-term unemployment itself. They have a variety of skill levels and come from all regions and all ages. But the longer an individual is unemployed, the smaller are their chances of finding a job. If it is not their own motivation that goes or their skills or health that decays, it is employers' reluctance to choose them rather than someone with more recent work experience.

It is this last factor which may explain why long-term unemployment has emerged as a much more severe factor in this recession than in previous downturns. Employers have had a long time to be choosy. Once off the employment ladder, it has become harder and harder for an individual to return to it. Similar phenomena have emerged in other European countries.

There is however one country where both unemployment as a whole and long-term unemployment within it have remained at low levels. Sweden achieved unemployment levels in the early 1980s consistently around 3 per cent with the long-term unemployed accounting for little more than 10 per cent. By contrast, figures for the United Kingdom showed plateaus of 13 per cent and over 40 per cent respectively.

There are doubtless many ingredients which account for Sweden's success. Not least is the sort of consensus approach to wage bargaining called for in the United Kingdom by David Basnett. But one crucial factor must be Sweden's active and well-co-ordinated labour market policies. Not only is there a nation-wide emphasis on training and retraining but the Labour Market Board is given the duty of ensuring that no person should remain unemployed for more than ten months without being offered a job or a place on a training scheme. In practice, the Labour Market Board steps in long before this, but the emphasis is on finding the right opportunity for the individual rather than pressurising them into taking the first vacancy. Unemployment is a time for redirection rather than a desperate search for income.

Some of the messages of the Swedish approach now seem to be being assimilated by the UK government. The programme of 'Restart' interviews for anyone who has been receiving unemployment benefit for six months gives the Department of Employment the opportunity to advise claimants of courses and schemes that might help them back into employment. The new 'Employment Training' initiative promises a useful mixture of work experience and training. But there are still strong signs that the government is concerned more about reducing the unemployment count itself – and at minimum cost

– than about providing high quality training and long-term career assistance (see Employment Institute, 1988). It looks as if the unemployed will be given little financial incentive to participate and the training element will be skimpy.

What still seems to be lacking in the government's approach is a forward-looking attitude to what the labour market could achieve at full employment and an easily-understood and trusted commitment to the worst victims of the 1980s recession. That is where the recommendations of Jackman and his colleagues have their greatest force. The concept of a *guarantee* of a job or a training place has been deemed useful in the context of young people. It now needs to be extended to all those whose working life is (or should be) far from over.

But there is also useful work that many of those people could be doing now. Even in conditions of a construction 'boom' in the South of the country, there are still many Northern cities where large unemployed labour forces, containing skilled construction workers, exist side-by-side with housing that is dilapidated and decaying. Jackman presents a viable scheme for putting the two together. He also points out areas where the public sector could usefully take on more staff from the ranks of the long-term unemployed and even ultimately integrate some into their permanent structure.

He also opts for a general recruitment subsidy for any private employer who expands their labour force by taking on a long-term unemployed person. This would not involve the government in breaking any new ground. Wage subsidies have already been offered in the case of new, young workers and anyone who has been unemployed for a short while is entitled to £40 per week if they start their own business. It is not clear why this incentive should not also be paid to a prospective employer, particularly in the light of David Storey's findings about the relatively limited potential to create jobs of small rather than growing or large firms.

THE NEXT STEPS

The danger now is one of complacency. Unemployment in 1988 fails to attract the headlines in the way it did in the early 1980s. Two years of declining unemployment figures and stories of labour shortages in some areas are encouraging the belief that the problem is over. It is not. Much of the reduction in the figures has been achieved by tightening the conditions under which individuals can claim unemployment benefit (see, for example, Charter for Jobs, 1987). Even if the figures are taken at face value, the level of unemployment is still nearly twice what it was at the end of 1979. With benefit levels falling well behind the growth in wages, it takes a wide stretch of the imagination to believe that this additional unemployment has been voluntary.

Yet there is a strong risk that unemployment could, in time, actually start rising again. Although the economy has at last achieved the sort of growth rates that were being called for when unemployment was at its peak (Charter for Jobs, 1985) the growth has been unbalanced and unsustainable. Demand in the regions did not start picking up until inflationary pressures in the South-East threatened. Earnings growth has been much higher than could be consistent with the government's inflation targets. A poorly trained labour force and creaking infrastructure have constrained the ability of domestic companies to compete at high exchange rates.

The response of the government, under strong pressure from the markets, has been to restrain demand, initially by raising interest rates. But the fact that relatively few firms actually see either capital or overall labour shortages as a constraint on their output suggest that it is the balance of growth that is the problem, not over-rapid growth *per se*. Once again, measures are being taken to attack demand without addressing the underlying structural issues. Once again, the unemployed stand to suffer.

There are alternatives. The challenges thrown down in this volume on wage setting, regional policy and training for the long-term unemployed suggest some ways forward.

2 The Case for Profit-Sharing[1]

Martin L. Weitzman

INTRODUCTION

I come from a state in the United States – Massachusetts – where the unemployment rate averaged 4 per cent in the mid-1980s, and from a metropolitan area – Boston – where the unemployment rate has been even lower. Furthermore, this is a region of the country which not such a very long time past bore roughly the same relation to the rest of the United States as Northern England does to Southern England today. In the early 1970s Massachusetts was a place with one of the worst unemployment rates in the United States, with empty textile or shoe factories and run-down blighted areas all over the landscape. How the economic turn-around occurred is a story that must be saved for another time. The point I wish to make here is this. Massachusetts today bears witness to the fact that there is no reason in principle why unemployment rates of 4 per cent or less should be unattainable.

When I buy computer equipment, or go out to eat in a restaurant, or carry on any other economic transaction, I am not aware that the service is slower or the product inferior than in other places or other times with much higher unemployment. The system seems to be working well even though unemployment is 4 per cent. The only thing in short supply is labour. Some companies actually offer to bus in workers from outlying regions or inner city locations. Employees in many firms get a bonus if they can bring in an acceptable new co-worker.

Why cannot this regional story be repeated on a national level? Why cannot the United States as a whole have such a tight labour market? And, more to the point, why cannot Great Britain get down to such low unemployment levels, to the levels taken for granted two decades ago? The answer is the two-headed monster – stagflation. Illusions of being able to fine tune aside, we know how to get unemployment down and output up by the usual expansionary monetary and fiscal measures. We also know how to break inflation by policy-induced recessions. What we do *not* know – and this is the central economic dilemma of our time – is how *simultaneously* to reconcile reasonably full employment with reasonable price stability. Expansionary policies dissipate themselves, to an excessive degree, in too large wage and price increases rather than expanded employment and output.

STAGFLATION

Why this has occurred in general, more so in European economies than in America or Japan, and with particular vengeance in Britain, is a subject of some dispute. Here I can only deal somewhat casually with the two main contending explanations. One school of thought blames the adverse economic situation on a high 'natural rate of unemployment'. A standard explanation at one time relied on 'demographic factors', but they have mostly been going the other way lately. A different story emphasises the 'revenge of the welfare state'. A theory now popular contends that long-term unemployment is largely inertial or hysteresis-like – once unemployment continues long enough, no matter how it started, it almost gets built into the system, perhaps because the long-term unemployed outsiders do not or cannot act effectively as a disciplining force in wage setting, perhaps because of the rise of an 'unemployment culture', perhaps owing to other factors. Anyway, for whatever reasons it might be, the 'non-accelerating-inflation rate of unemployment' (NAIRU) has apparently deteriorated. That this has actually occurred is undeniable, both from commonsense observations and from the formal statistical approaches which, in effect, practically make the NAIRU a weighted average of past unemployment rates. In practice the 'high NAIRU' explanation almost amounts to a tautology: the unemployment rate is high because the unemployment rate is high. I think the more honest practitioners of this approach admit they are close to a tautology in terms of actual explanatory power.

Another approach is the *au courant* explanation that European-style unemployment is of the classical rather than Keynesian variety, caused by 'too high' *real* wages. A problem with this line of argument is that real wages no more 'cause' employment levels than the other way around. Both are simultaneously determined within the economic system. Given money wages and aggregate demand, companies *choose* employment levels and prices. Hence, the aggregate *real* wage (money wage divided by the price level) is no less determined by the decisions of firms than is employment. The germ of truth this approach is trying to capture, I think, by artificially compressing an inherently dynamic story into a static framework, is that the too-high real wage *aspirations* of workers, coupled with too-great insider power in wage setting and a too-compliant tendency of employers to give in, ultimately causes a form of unemployment that cannot be reduced by ordinary macroeconomic policies. But I am not sure the workers ever actually *attain* the higher real wages they aspire to because the effect of higher money wages is mostly to push up the prices of goods workers buy. Somewhat ironically, real wages would probably end up higher in the kind of full employment boom-economy that is attainable in practice only when there is greater money wage restraint.

What, then, is causing the unemployment? There is only one answer. But, like a coin, the answer has two sides. Side one is that unemployment is caused by insufficient aggregate demand (relative to money wages). Side two is that unemployment is caused by too-high money wages (relative to aggregate demand). Sometimes it is useful to stress one side of the coin; sometimes the other. But it is always the same coin. In either case, the key to non-inflationary full employment is an economic expansion that holds down the marginal cost to the firm of acquiring more labour. Pure macroeconomic policy alone – the purposeful manipulation of financial aggregates – is no longer sufficient to guarantee full employment without inflation because labour costs begin to rise well before the economy starts to strain at full capacity.

At this point the honest Keynesian puts in the awkward if obligatory footnote about the need for some form of incomes policy. But this phrase is usually added rather mechanically, as an afterthought, with little enthusiasm or follow-up. I think it may be time to reverse the emphasis. In countries like Britain and France (or, for that matter, Argentina and Israel) today the main operational issue is how to introduce greater wage restraint and 'flexibility' into the labour market, especially as it starts to become tight. Compared with this issue the nuances of how best to reflate the economy are relatively straightforward. Although the dilemma being described is currently seen most starkly in some European economies, the same basic issues are involved almost everywhere. Things have reached a point where a surprising number of macroeconomists of Keynesian or classical persuasion have essentially abandoned the hope that traditional macroeconomic policies can do a great deal to promote prosperity. I would argue, as a general proposition, that implementable structural changes in the labour market should be a relatively more pressing concern than the demand management policies currently occupying the attention of most macroeconomists.

There should be more focus on the labour market itself, on measures to build in automatic flexibility and to reform structural rigidities away – not so much to replace traditional macroeconomic policies as to enable them better to deliver non-inflationary full employment. Such measures must be applied uniformly throughout society, not just loaded on blue-collar workers. What is required is bold institutional changes in incentive structures to make it in employers' strong self-interest automatically to maintain high levels of output and to keep prices low. There are many possibilities here – including tax-based incomes policies, multi-tiered pay systems, employee ownership or control, profit-sharing, and several others. I am in favour of maintaining a positive, constructive attitude towards all measures that might improve the employment–inflation trade-off. But, in my opinion, profit-sharing is the most solidly based of the alternatives and, I believe, holds by far the most promise.

PROFIT-SHARING IN PRACTICE

Profit-sharing is not an exotic innovation, untried and unknown. The largest private employer in the world, General Motors, currently shares profits with its employees under an agreement with one of the largest unions in the world, the United Automobile Workers. That agreement was explicitly hammered out at the bargaining tables of Ford and General Motors in the negotiations of autumn 1984 in order to ensure that more previously laid-off automobile workers could be put back on the payroll and that fewer automobile workers would lose their jobs in the future if there were an economic downturn in the US automobile industry. The record shows that both sides – union and management – understood quite clearly the trade-off between increased profit-sharing and increased jobs. (Incidentally, lady luck smiled on this endeavour because profits have been higher than expected and each worker is several thousand dollars richer than if a strict wage settlement had been negotiated.)

About 15 per cent of American firms, including some of the most advanced, practise some form of profit-sharing. These US profit-sharing firms include, in addition to General Motors and Ford, such big name companies as Texas Instruments, Hewlett Packard, Sears Roebuck, Procter & Gamble, Eastman Kodak, Xerox, Levi Strauss, Polaroid, Bank America, Chase Manhattan, Johnson's Wax, Kellogg, Standard Oil of California, Prentice Hall, Digital Equipment, and many, many others. Almost the entire Japanese economy, it can be argued, is in essence a profit-sharing system. Fully one-quarter of an average Japanese worker's pay is in the form of a twice-yearly bonus with strong profit-sharing overtones. Virtually any Japanese firm you have ever heard of is essentially a profit-sharing company. Korea and Taiwan operate with similar nationwide profit-sharing systems, although the bonus is a somewhat lower fraction of total pay, closer to 15 per cent on average. In Europe there is much less profit-sharing than in the United States, and *a fortiori* less than in Japan.

I will turn presently to the important issue of whether or not, or to what extent, such examples can be used to 'prove' that profit-sharing leads to better economic performance and particularly to higher and more stable employment levels. As might be guessed, this issue is difficult to resolve decisively without the ability to perform controlled experiments, although I think it is possible to build a reasonable case on circumstantial evidence that profit-sharing has lots of good effects, microeconomic and macroeconomic. For my purposes now, I want to state two strong, essentially indisputable propositions that follow from the record.

The record shows that the profit-sharing firm is an indigenous species in Japan, Korea, Taiwan, and, to a lesser extent, in the United States. Furthermore, at the very minimum, these economies do not appear to be suffering because of profit-sharing, nor do the profit-sharing firms or their workers seem to be doing poorly – if anything it is the other way around. I do not think such observations are trivial or irrelevant. To see why, contrast profit-sharing with some other proposals to improve labour market performance. For example, labour co-operatives or labour–capital partnerships (whether of the 'egalitarian' or 'discriminating' varieties), or various incomes policies (whether wage-price controls or tax-based incomes policies) in my opinion represent more radical and far-fetched mutations of a market economy that are basically just not out there making it on their own. With respect to improving the performance of European-style economies via profit-sharing, the issue is, through moral persuasion and financial incentives, to move towards an already existing variant of capitalism – not towards some artificially engineered creation. I think that is an important, if not decisive, distinction.

The case for widespread profit-sharing is like the case for free trade. It is not true that free trade benefits every individual. It is not even true, in a realistic world of increasing returns to scale and imperfect competition, that free trade must benefit the community as a whole. Yet, when all is said and done, when the possible costs and benefits of alternative trade policies have been calculated, weighted by the relevant probabilities, and added up, most economists agree that free trade is the best policy. The argument for profit-sharing is of this same form. It is possible to dream up unlikely counter-examples and to interpret the existing evidence perversely. But the bulk of economic theory, empirical evidence, and common sense argue that widespread profit-sharing will help to improve macroeconomic performance. The bottom line is that it is easy to envisage situations where profit-sharing helps economic performance while it is difficult to imagine scenarios where profit-sharing damages an economy, which is as much as can be claimed for any economic idea.

It is no mystery why profit-sharing makes the employer view things fundamentally differently. In a profit-sharing system the young school-leaver looking for work would come with an implicit message to the employer saying: 'Hire me. I am reasonable. Your only absolute commitment is to pay me the base wage. That is my marginal cost to you. The profit-sharing bonus is like a variable cost, depending to some extent on how well the company is doing. So you have a built-in cushion or shock absorber if something should go wrong.' By contrast, the young British school-leaver looking for work in a wage system now comes to a potential employer with the implicit message: 'Think very carefully before you hire me. I am expensive and inflexible. You will have to pay me a fixed wage independent of whether your company is doing well or poorly, and you will not easily be able to lay me off if your business goes badly.' Is it difficult to deduce in which situation companies might be expected to recruit new employees more eagerly and in which situation new hiring commitments are likely to be avoided when at all possible? The essence of the case for profit-sharing is the basic idea that, on the margin, the profit-sharing firm is more willing than the wage firm to hire new workers during good times and to lay off fewer workers during bad times.

So far I have outlined, in general form, the basic argument why, for a given level of aggregate demand and worker remuneration, profit-sharing tends to result in higher levels of employment and output with lower prices. The essential message is that widespread profit-sharing, operating within a sympathetic social and political climate (which, for Britain, unquestionably means some basic changes in attitudes), can serve as the operational centre-piece of a broadly based programme that, in conjunction with traditional macroeconomic policies, has a good chance of significantly reducing unemployment without increasing inflation. This message survives critical scrutiny. Furthermore any realistic economic recovery programme for Britain is going to have to confront the same basic issues and problems that the profit-sharing approach does, and I doubt that there is a programme that can do it as well or command the broad support it can.

I will not dwell further on this basic line of argument, in part because some of it is already familiar and in part because I want to move on to other matters. The technical aspects of modelling a profit-sharing economy have been treated in the academic literature. The formal mathematical models seem to bear out the contention that a profit-sharing economy tends to deliver superior macroeconomic performance compared to a wage economy. I would like now to deal with some of the major objections that have been raised against profit-sharing. The most effective format, I believe, is to answer the important questions in the way they are typically posed by astute critics.

UNDER-INVESTMENT

Question: A system that shares profits is analogous to the notorious share-cropping system in agriculture. As was pointed out by many of the classical economists, such a system reduces the incentives to invest because the capitalist must share some part of increased profits with the workers. Would not profit-sharing cause under-investment, too little capital, and too low labour productivity?

The classical economists were wrong about this point, or at least incomplete in their arguments. The issue is now well understood in the modern share-cropping literature. The critics had in mind a situation where pay parameters were more or less permanently frozen. In that case profit-sharing would, indeed, cause under-investment for the well-publicised reason that any incremental profits would have to be shared with labour. But over the longer time horizon relevant to decisions about durable capital investments, where either base wages or profit-sharing coefficients (or both) respond to the invisible hand of the market and the visible hand of collective bargaining, both wage and profit-sharing systems stimulate equal efforts towards output-increasing improvements – to the point where the marginal value of capital equals the interest rate. Even if this theoretical isomorphism between investment in wage and profit-sharing systems did not exist, the cost of capital is only one side of the picture, and probably the less important side. The more dominant consideration is the demand side. If profit-sharing results in a macro-economic environment where output is being stabilised at or near the full-employment, full-capacity level, while a wage economy results in erratic, fluctuation-prone output and capacity utilisation levels, there is bound to be more investment in a profit-sharing economy. And, as if these two arguments were not enough, interest rates, investment tax credits and the like could be used to influence investment decisions in any system. The really important distinction concerns the average level of unemployed resources.

RESISTANCE BY EXISTING EMPLOYEES

Question: A key part of the mechanism causing a profit-sharing firm to want to expand employment is that the marginal value of labour under such a system exceeds the marginal cost of labour. But this occurs because, in effect, the additional hired worker dilutes the profits per worker which the previously hired workers receive. Would not this cause the existing labour force to resent newly hired workers and, in extreme cases, lead to restrictions against new hiring?

First of all, it is important to keep things in perspective. Even a worst-case scenario where profit-sharing 'merely' dampens economic down-turns by encouraging employers to lay off fewer workers during recessions still represents an economic benefit of potentially enormous magnitude. If profit-sharing did nothing more than reduce downside risks to an economy, it would still be tremendously important. And when it comes to internal labour relations, let us not forget that the wage system is hardly a bed of roses. Younger, untenured workers are pitted against older high-seniority workers in the conflict between jobs and wages. Feather-bedding is widespread. Workers resist the introduction of new labour-saving technology and, more generally, take relatively little interest in the fortunes of the firm because they do not have any direct stake in its profitability. Worker alienation is widespread in an environment where the employer is essentially indifferent on the margin as to whether the worker stays or goes.

Any system where a substantial number of the major firms are operating with the marginal cost of labour lower than the marginal value of labour will have an inherent predilection towards providing more employment and expanding output. This tendency may take a long time to be fully realised. It may be frustrated by aggressive unions (where they exist) or voluntarily slowed by the employers themselves. But if the incremental, hardly-noticed decision at the margin has more of a bias than before to lean towards firing fewer workers during bad times and taking on more of them during good times, then gradually, perhaps imperceptibly, the system will ratchet itself towards an ever-tighter labour market. The point is not that widespread conversion to profit-sharing would instantly result in full employment by itself, thereafter rendering macroeconomic policy unnecessary. That kind of polarised way of posing the issue is a red herring. To help create a tight labour market and improve the employment–inflation trade-off so that macroeconomic policy can be used more effectively, it suffices that during downswings a few less workers than under a wage system are laid off and during upswings a few more workers than under a wage system, are hired.

Why is the employers' incentive to maintain or even slowly increase employment in a system of widespread profit-sharing likely to prevail over the insider workers' possible incentive to resist new hirings? First of all, in the situation where an entire economy of profit-sharing firms is geared up and functioning smoothly at full employment, there is a significant excess demand for labour as a whole and there are no long-term jobless people to be picked up easily. In that case, the image of hordes of labour out there about to be so rapidly brought into profit-sharing firms that they will cause significantly noticeable depreciation of per capita profitability, in the short period between labour contract negotiations, is ridiculous. New workers cannot be obtained except from other firms reluctant to part with them. The tenuous aftermath of hiring a few more workers in one profit-sharing firm will scarcely be noticed, disguised as it must be behind a myriad of more important economic changes that much more directly influence short-term profitability per worker. In a profit-sharing system, effort spent to enhance productivity and profits has a much higher pay-off for the already employed workers of a profit-sharing firm than effort spent on restricting new hirings.

The more relevant issue than what happens when there already is full employment concerns getting there from a situation of less than full employment. For this purpose I advocate strong tax incentives making it in workers' strong self-interest to want to take some significant fraction of their pay in the form of profit-sharing with no restrictions on new hirings. I would also hold out the hope of simultaneous gradual macroeconomic expansion as a *quid pro quo* for the widespread adoption of profit-sharing with no hiring constraints. I have calculated that even under very extreme assumptions a substantial tax reduction for profit-sharing income would break even and pay for itself as a tax reform if it reduced the unemployment rate by just one or two percentage points. That may sound rather too much like 'supply-side economics', but the fact is that unemployment is expensive, as well as immoral, so that virtually any measure which significantly reduced unemployment would yield enormous savings to society.

Those who argued at a time when Britain had an unemployment rate of 13 per cent that it had never had it so good for the 87 per cent with work were at best uttering a half-truth. The other half of the truth was that everyone could gain significantly, including the 87 per cent with jobs, if the far-too-high unemployment rate could be reduced. This is because the 13 per cent without work pay essentially no taxes. Yet they must be fed, they must be clothed, they must be housed, they must be kept warm in the winter, their children must go to school, and they must receive health benefits. These are paid for by real transfers of income from the 87 per cent of those who are working to support the 13 per cent who are not.

The tax benefits for sharing profits should only be granted in situations where the union and employer explicitly agree to forswear any restrictive hiring practices. No trade union is compelled to petition for the special tax status of a share plan. But if it chooses to participate, a union cannot enjoy the considerable tax benefits without reaffirming an already existing legal commitment to open its ranks to as many qualified members and apprentices as the company wishes to hire under the agreed-upon share contract. The normal expectation is that profit-sharing firms will wish to expand employment somewhat when there are unemployed workers available to be hired. If a trade union or an employer finds repugnant the idea of hiring unemployed workers, they should not sign up for the plan.

'No collusive restrictions on new hiring' is a logical requirement for the government to insist upon, since the basic reason the differential tax treatment is being granted in the first place is to encourage increased employment. I do not think such a plan can be fairly characterised as anti-labour. Instead, it works within the existing framework, asking only that trade unions play their fair role in helping to get unemployed workers into the company and producing output so that these much-too-high unemployment rates can be reduced to almost everyone's advantage.

It is best to be under no illusions about the political realities involved in making an economy-wide transition to a system based on profit-sharing principles. Any change hurts some people, and they will shout loudest to preserve the *status quo* even though, as with free trade, a share system is highly beneficial to the population as a whole. When all is said and done, no matter how well designed are the incentives, such change will require genuine consensus, a general agreement cutting across left–right political lines, that the broad social gains of full employment without inflation are worth more than the narrow private losses which inevitably will be incurred here and there. If people in Britain want to reduce unemployment, an obvious prerequisite is that they are going to have to create a climate where it is socially acceptable, even advantageous, to hire unemployed workers. This issue is going to have to be faced honestly by any employment-promoting scheme, not just profit-sharing.

I believe that pure self-interest based on strong tax incentives in favour of profit-sharing income will go a long way towards convincing unions and others to look favourably upon a system which holds out the promise that aggregate output will be produced, and consumed, at the full-employment level even if it erodes some part of the monopoly rent above competitive pay which they currently enjoy. If the tax incentives are strong enough, a unionised firm will not only be enticed to join the share economy, but in a sense will be driven to enrol. It will be compelled because, if many other firms adopt share plans and if the pecuniary advantages in the form of tax savings are significant enough (larger than the union premium), a union will be unable to compete for members without following suit. And the potential tax benefits could be made extremely attractive without doing fiscal harm to the government's budget since the increases in government revenues and decreases in outlays obtained from even moderate expansion of employment are so enormous.

In summary, then, it must be admitted that widespread profit-sharing will probably alter the nature of industrial relations: workers sharing profits with management represents a different way from the wage system of doing business in the labour market. It could even be argued that share bargaining is likely to prove healthy and invigorating for labour unions – calling for new expertise and an expanded role in working with firms to increase profitability. The relevant theory shows that, if the firm retains control of the employment decision, other things being equal a profit-sharing system results in greater output, higher employment, and lower prices. The trick is to make the transition to profit-sharing while preserving the employer's traditional right to decide, ultimately, the employment level, and at the same time allowing workers to bargain over base wages and profit-sharing coefficients. I do not think this trick is all that difficult to accomplish because, in contrast to other reform proposals, it builds on some already existing natural tendencies. Throughout the world, profit-sharing is not an exotic innovation or an externally-imposed artifice, but an existing reality for many tens of millions of workers. Since widespread conversion to profit-sharing will undoubtedly require government incentives anyway, the issue then reduces to reinforcing with such incentives, or at least not undermining, managements' traditional right to hire and fire as they see fit.

ROLE OF TRADE UNIONS

Question: What is the proper role of trade unions in a profit-sharing system? If labour is treated like more of a residual claimant, will not workers demand more of a say in how the firm is run?

First of all, labour as a whole is no more of a residual claimant under profit-sharing than under a wage system. In both cases, total labour income is variable. In a wage system, the employment level changes to absorb shocks, while in a share system it is more the nominal level of pay that adjusts. In one case the outsiders and fringe workers absorb all of the changes. In the other it is spread among the insider workers.

The right of labour to organise and bargain collectively is not a natural right like life, liberty, and the pursuit of happiness. It is a special monopoly privilege granted by the state to increase the general welfare. A framework of laws and traditions has grown up over the years which demarcates, to a tolerably usable approximation, what is the proper or traditional scope of collective bargaining agreements as opposed to the proper or traditional domain of management's right to control unilaterally certain other decisions. Under United States law, for example, unions simply do not have the right to bargain explicitly about the employment level. In technical parlance, employment is not a mandatory subject to bargaining. If management does not want to bargain about employment levels, the unions have no legal recourse. Mandatory subjects to bargaining include payment formulae, grievance procedures, rules about lay-offs and recalls, safety and working conditions, and so forth. Generally speaking, the union has a say about pay and working conditions, but no say about how the business is otherwise conducted, including the employment decision.

I would propose that this traditional demarcation of labour–management roles be preserved under a profit-sharing system, as it already is in most unionised profit-sharing firms in the United States or Japan. Typically it has been found that profit-sharing workers naturally take a greater interest in the profitability of the firm than do wage workers. But that does not necessarily mean that it is efficient for workers to serve on Boards of Directors or to be formally involved in decisions about new product lines, marketing strategies, and so forth. On the other hand it might not be such a bad idea for workers to get involved under certain circumstances. I do not think that hard and fast rules must be applied here. There are lots of cases where increased worker participation with the aim of raising company profits can be a good thing for both the workers and the company. The only absolute commandment is: 'Thou shalt not restrict thy unemployed brothers and sisters from taking a job'. In other words, co-determination is not a code word for collusive restriction of new hirings.

One natural and legitimate concern of a profit-sharing union will be the proper definition and verification of profits to be used in the pay formula. This should be spelled out in some detail in the pay agreement, and the union will want some means of verifiability. There is, for example, the issue of what measure of profitability is desired, and whether it should be based on company-wide figures or on the operations of a more narrowly-defined profit centre. In any case the profits should be accountable. A new and potentially constructive role for labour unions is thus created by a profit-sharing pay system. Under a wage contract any fool can determine whether he is being paid the specified amount. But under profit-sharing agreements, the average worker may need or want an advocate to make sure the contract is properly written, correctly specified and fairly enforced.

SHARING THE RISKS

Question: Under a wage system the firm bears all the risk, while under a profit-sharing system the worker bears some risk. Does not profit-sharing therefore represent a socially inefficient form of risk bearing, since the stockholder can naturally diversify risks more easily than the worker?

As this point is usually further developed, there is a good reason why capital should bear more risk than labour. Capital can be diversified in any portfolio, whereas labour tends to have but one job at a time. Therefore, the argument goes, it is better if the variable component of business income would accrue largely to capital, while the worker is paid a fixed wage. Right? Wrong! This argument, so widely parroted and seemingly so plausible, is in fact deep fallacious. A fallacy of composition is involved. What is a correct statement for the individual high-seniority worker who already has job tenure is patently false for the aggregate of all would-be workers. The problem of unemployment is in fact the largest income risk that labour as a whole, as opposed to the median tenured worker, faces, and it is concentrated entirely on the marginal or outsider worker. If more variable pay for the individual helps to preserve full employment for the group, while fixed pay for the individual tends to contribute to unemployment, it is not the least bit clear why overall welfare is improved by having the median worker paid a fixed wage. Actually, the correct presumption runs the other way around.

What is true for the individual tenured worker is not true for labour as a whole. When a more complete analysis is performed, which considers the situation not as seen by a tenured, high-seniority worker who already has job security, but by a neutral observer representing the entire population, it becomes abundantly clear that the welfare advantages of a profit-sharing system (which tends to deliver full employment) are enormously greater than a wage system (which permits unemployment). The basic reason is not difficult to understand. A wage system allows huge first-order losses of output and welfare to open up when a significant slice of the national income pie evaporates with unemployment. A profit-sharing system stabilises aggregate output at the full employment level, creating the biggest possible national income pie, while permitting only small second-order losses to arise because some crumbs have been randomly redistributed from a worker in one firm to a worker in another. It is extremely difficult to cook up an empirical real-world scenario, with reasonable numbers and specifications, where a profit-sharing system with a moderate amount of profit-sharing (say 20 per cent of a worker's total pay) does not deliver significantly greater social welfare than a wage system.

As if this argument alone were not enough, it would be a mistake to extrapolate the demand variability now observed in the firms of a wage economy to a share economy. Such cyclical industries as machine tools, metals, building materials, construction and the like would not fluctuate nearly so much, since the share economy is operating at or near full capacity. Every firm of a profit-sharing system would presumably exhibit significantly greater demand stability than we are now accustomed to because a budding recession cannot feed upon itself in a fully employed economy.

Any economy is full of uncertainty. There are no absolute guarantees, and if the uncertainty does not come out in one place, it will show up in another. I am saying that it is much better, much healthier, if everyone shares just a little bit of that uncertainty right at the beginning rather than lets it all fall on an unfortunate minority of unemployed workers who are drafted to serve as unpaid soldiers in the war against inflation. It is much better if people will agree that only 80 per cent of their pay is going to be tied directly to the funny-looking pieces of paper currency – which are themselves an illusion, although a very useful illusion – and 20 per cent will be tied to company profits per employee. Then the economy can be much more easily controlled to have full employment *and* stable prices. Society will be producing, and hence consuming, at its full potential. If people will face up to the uncertainty right at the beginning, and if everyone accepts some small part of it, then society as a whole will end up with higher income and less uncertainty overall.

The crucial thing to decide is whether or not profit-sharing would significantly reduce unemployment. The traditional 'insurance' argument in favour of a wage system is fallacious, being based on a partial equilibrium view which does not take into account the radically different macroeconomic consequences of the two systems for overall employment and aggregate output.

ROLE OF MACROECONOMIC POLICY

Question: Does widespread profit-sharing replace traditional macroeconomic policy?

Probably not. Probably the more realistic way to think of profit-sharing is as a way of making macroeconomic policies work more effectively in the sense of improving the underlying unemployment–inflation trade-off. With some tendency to hold the economy automatically at or near full employment, profit-sharing perhaps imparts somewhat more of a monetarist or classical flavour to economic policy, as opposed to a wage economy with its more closely associated Keynesian overtones.

But it must be said that we really do not know for sure. The most optimistic scenario imaginable would be that a significant dose of profit-sharing in an economy with strong free-market forces would almost make redundant the need for macroeconomic policy to stabilise the employment level, liberating it to perform other important functions. The most pessimistic scenario I can think of would improve macroeconomic performance only marginally, making perhaps a somewhat better, but not qualitatively different employment picture. The truth is probably somewhere in between. It is very difficult for me to imagine any realistic circumstances under which profit-sharing could actually worsen the unemployment–inflation trade-off.

CONTROLLING THE BASE WAGE

Question: What guarantee is there that a profit-sharing system will work the way you say it should? How can we be sure that tax breaks for profit-sharing income will not just dissipate themselves in increased pay for insider workers rather than new hiring of unemployed outsiders?

In a free market economy, the basic mechanism keeping wages from exploding towards infinity is the natural resistance of the employer to paying more than he wants to, backed, ultimately, by some of the checks and balances of competition throughout the system. British labour does not now have the power to dictate unilaterally whatever wage level they wish, irrespective of labour market conditions and product market conditions. I do not see why labour's bargaining power should suddenly increase under a profit-sharing system. The relevant theory shows that at the same labour payment level a profit-sharing system will have less unemployment than a wage system. The basic determinant of employment, aside from aggregate demand, is the base wage, not the profit share. In order to believe that increased profit-sharing would have no effect on employment one has to be prepared to believe that its introduction would be accompanied by an exactly offsetting increase in labour's bargaining power to secure just as high a base wage as under a wage system and, additionally, some share of profits to boot.

I believe that the introduction of a significant tax break for the profit-sharing component of a worker's income, under the conditions of free hiring of new workers I have previously described, would go a long way towards improving the unemployment–inflation trade-off in a fundamental way. But I am not so fanatical a believer in the power of the market, or of my own theories, that I would not take the extra precaution of writing into the tax legislation the additional condition that, in order for the tax advantages of profit-sharing income to be obtained, workers must agree to a base wage no higher than that of some arbitrary previous date, say one month before the tax concession was announced. Perhaps this extra stipulation is not needed, especially once the programme gets going. But why take chances? It could always be removed later.

USING AN EMPLOYMENT SUBSIDY INSTEAD

Question: In your scenario profit-sharing increases employment by making it in the self-interest of the firm to want to hire more workers during good times and lay off fewer workers during bad times. Could not the same end be accomplished more directly by giving firms an employment subsidy of some sort?

An employment subsidy amounts to a reduction in the payroll tax, on the margin. There is little doubt that such a measure would expand output and employment in the short run, just as would other Keynesian stimulative policies. An employment subsidy has the additional advantage of operating more directly on employment and output while putting less upward pressure on prices. But after the employment subsidy has been set in place, and the economy has adjusted to a new equilibrium, it will be just as vulnerable as before to contractionary shocks. An employment subsidy does not eliminate the fundamental problem that a sticky wage economy responds to insufficient aggregate demand or too-high wages by restricting output and employment.

Of course another employment subsidy could be added on to deal with the second contractionary shock, and so forth. But over time this would cumulatively increase the budget deficit, and inflation. An employment subsidy might be very worthwhile as a short-term expansionary measure essentially in the Keynesian tradition. But it does not eliminate the fundamental flaw of a wage economy.

REDUCING THE NAIRU

Question: Your arguments about profit-sharing having more favourable employment properties seem mostly to be based on short-run disequilibrium considerations, when pay parameters are quasi-fixed. But our unemployment problem in Britain is not so much a bad short-run disequilibrium, but rather a too-high non-accelerating-inflation rate of unemployment, or NAIRU. Would widespread profit-sharing lower the NAIRU?

Yes, it presumably would. Furthermore the short-run and long-run unemployment problems are probably related. In order to talk meaningfully about the effects of profit-sharing on the NAIRU, one has first to have some idea about what is causing such a high NAIRU in the first place. There are several theories. Some are more persuasive than others, and they are not mutually exclusive.

As discussed earlier, a leading theory views long-term unemployment as largely inertial or hysteresis-like. Whatever initial disequilibrium caused the increased unemployment in the first place, it holds that unemployment almost gets built into the economy once it has continued long enough. This may be because the long-term unemployed outsiders cannot or do not act effectively as a disciplining force in wage setting, or perhaps because working skills atrophy without work, or perhaps because the plight of the long-term unemployed gets forgotten by the electorate or perhaps for other reasons. In this view the rate of change of unemployment typically has a more powerful effect on wage settlements than the absolute level of unemployment.

If this kind of inertial effect lies behind the too-high NAIRU, then presumably widespread profit-sharing would lower or eliminate it. The long-term unemployment would have difficulty developing in the first place out of an initial contractionary shock because profit-sharing firms are reluctant to let go of workers. Taking as given this kind of NAIRU, leaving aside how it got started in the past, the natural expansionary bias of a profit-sharing system would act as a built-in counterforce to 'gobble up' the unemployed. The 'gobbling up' process could of course be speeded by traditional expansionary macroeconomic policies which, under profit-sharing, pose less danger of causing prices to accelerate because the unemployment–inflation trade-off has been improved. So any way you look at it, profit-sharing should definitely help to diminish long-term inertial unemployment.

Another theory as to why the NAIRU is so high is that labour has too much bargaining power. Whether a switch from a wage system to profit-sharing would lower this kind of NAIRU depends on what it is that labour and management bargain over. If they bargain over pay parameters, but management controls the employment decision, a switch to profit-sharing would lower the NAIRU. If labour and management bargain over both pay parameters and employment level, the NAIRU would be the same under either system. In-between bargaining would yield in-between results, with the NAIRU then being somewhat lower under profit-sharing than under a wage system.

A third class of theories, based on the so-called 'efficiency wage hypothesis', holds that long-term unemployment is caused by companies themselves choosing to pay above market-clearing wages because otherwise workers would shirk too much on the job. Within this kind of model, which has limited, if any, relevance for understanding the rise of European unemployment, the 'natural rate' would be the same under a wage or profit-sharing system.

To the extent that too-high unemployment in European-style economies is aided by overly generous unemployment and welfare benefits, which creates some voluntary unemployment, presumably the labour payment mechanism *per se* makes little or no difference. So 'the revenge of the welfare state' kind of unemployment would not be affected by a switch to profit-sharing.

Finally there is the long-standing identification of the 'natural rate' with semi-permanent frictional or structural unemployment, due to continuously occurring microeconomic changes. This kind of unemployment, it is usually said, cannot be reduced by policies which are purely macroeconomic except temporarily and at the cost of increasing inflation. As with inertial unemployment, however, the wage system is heavily implicated in frictional or structural concepts of the NAIRU. After all, both wage and profit-sharing systems respond to shifts in relative demand by sending a signal that eventually transfers workers out of a losing firm or sector and over to a winner. With a wage system the signal to a worker that his firm is a loser in the game of capitalist roulette, and it is time to look for a new job with a winning firm, is the boot – the worker is laid off and must suffer through an unemployment spell of some duration while searching for the new job. Under a profit-sharing system, the firm does not voluntarily let go of a worker because of weak demand. Instead it is the worker who chooses to leave because pay is too low relative to what is readily available elsewhere at successful firms eager to include new workers in their current profit-sharing payment plans.

Summing up, in none of the standard scenarios does a profit-sharing system cause a higher NAIRU than a wage system, and in most of the more reasonable descriptions a profit-sharing system generates a lower NAIRU than a wage system. In addition, of course, the profit-sharing system has better disequilibrium properties when pay parameters are sticky in the neighbourhood of the NAIRU unemployment rate. From all of these theoretical exercises considered together it seems difficult not to draw the conclusion that a profit-sharing economy is more likely to have lower unemployment than a wage economy.

PROFIT SHARING AND EXTERNALITIES

Question: If profit-sharing represents such a great idea for operating a market economy, why do we not see more examples of it arising spontaneously?

First of all, there are some significant examples of profit-sharing. In Japan, Korea, and Taiwan, it can be argued, steps have been taken in this direction. The performance of these economies hardly supports the view that widespread profit-sharing is likely to prove harmful to economic health. In the US economy, about 15 per cent of firms have what they call profit-sharing plans. Although the issue has not been carefully studied in a rigorous way, it is clear that many of these profit-sharing firms are among the most progressive, advanced companies in the economy. As just one informal indication, in a well-known book, *The 100 Best Companies to Work for in America*, over half of the cited companies have profit-sharing plans of some kind.

The reason profit-sharing is not more widespread despite its benefits involves an externality or market failure of enormous magnitude. In choosing a particular contract form, the firm and its workers only calculate the effects on themselves. They take no account whatsoever of the possible effects on the rest of the economy. When a firm and its workers select a labour contract with a strong profit-sharing component they are contributing to an atmosphere of full employment and brisk aggregate demand without inflation because the firm is then more willing to hire new 'outsider' workers and to expand output by riding down its demand curve, lowering its price. But these macroeconomic advantages to the outsiders do not properly accrue to those insiders who make the decision. Like clean air, the benefits are spread throughout the community. The wage firm and its workers do not have the proper incentives to cease polluting the macroeconomic environment by converting to a share contract. The essence of the public-good aspect of the problem is that, in choosing between contract forms, the firm and its workers do not take into account the employment effects on the labour market as a whole and the consequent spending implications for aggregate demand. The macroeconomic externality of a tight labour market is helped by a share contract and hurt by a wage contract, but the difference is uncompensated. In such situations there can be no presumption that the economy is optimally organised and society-wide reform may be needed to nudge firms and workers towards increased profit-sharing.

MOTIVATION AND PRODUCTIVITY

Question: You talk mostly about the favourable macroeconomic effects of profit-sharing. Why do you not put equal stress on the good microeconomic properties, the effects on motivation and productivity, which are aspects that many people identify with profit-sharing?

The microeconomic aspects are also important. The two biggest economic tasks of our time are to resolve the unemployment–inflation dilemma and to increase productivity growth. It is just possible that a well-designed profit-sharing economy has a big advantage in both of these important areas.

The few formal studies that have been carried out tend to show that greater profit-sharing in firms is positively related to increased productivity. One of the problems in interpreting this result is that it is not clear whether the profit-sharing is causing the higher productivity or whether some hidden third factor, call it superior management, tends to cause the more progressive firms to have both profit-sharing and high productivity.

Most economists would say that there are no grounds for subsidising profit-sharing on its possible productivity-enhancing merits because these are strictly internal to the firm. Firms do not need to be subsidised to take other productivity-enhancing measures, so why should they be especially subsidised for profit-sharing? I mostly agree with this interpretation, but I am not entirely sure, because in practice a labour payment mechanism may have large demonstration effects.

As for the employment-stabilising effects of profit-sharing on the level of the individual firm, these have only just begun to be studied in a formal way. My distinct impression from talking with representatives from a fair number of profit-sharing firms is that the built-in profit-sharing shock absorber protects jobs during bad times and that both labour and management understand this feature quite well, to the point of regarding it as self-evident.

TWO-TIER WAGE CONTRACTS

Question: Might not two-tier wage contracts help the unemployment problem? Are they not perhaps a better route to full employment than profit-sharing?

While most pay systems are based, at least in theory, on the egalitarian principle of 'equal pay for equal work', recently in the United States there have sprung up examples of inegalitarian two-tiered wage systems that explicitly pay new employees at a lower rate than previously hired workers were at first paid. Thus, a newly hired worker this year might be paid significantly lower than last year's new worker and be tracked onto a significantly lower pay ladder. Sometimes it is intended that such discriminations be 'temporary', for example, for five years, or until the company regains greater profitability, or whatever it might be, while in other instances the intended duration of the two different pay profiles is vague.

As a theoretical matter, could the two-tiered wage system we now see occasionally springing up in the United States serve as a kind of model approach to eliminating or greatly reducing unemployment on the macroeconomic level? Undoubtedly a more widespread use of two-tiered systems might somewhat reduce unemployment. (It would certainly be difficult to argue otherwise – how could it possibly *increase* unemployment?) One count against such approaches is their explicitly inegalitarian nature, which, with or without labour unions, could be viewed as unfair, repugnant, or inherently conflictual. As opposed to this view one must ask, as always, whether the alternative of greater unemployment is less unfair, less repugnant, or less inherently conflictual. Still I think there is a very fundamental difficulty with inegalitarian pay scales and with blatant violations of 'equal pay for equal work', at the same level of experience and job nature, that are not so easy to wave away. I am not sure that creating a second-class citizenry within the same work organisation will not lead to strong internal tensions, as it typically does in a wide variety of other contexts. Most two-tiered pay systems do not last long in practice. A job-creating two-tiered wage system in the US public sector had to be abandoned because of the antagonisms it created. The concept that all hired workers should be treated symmetrically by their employer, even if there is not a flat wage-earnings profile, is, to my mind, a very deeply rooted culture belief.

Suppose it were conceded, as I think it must be, that two-tiered wage systems are likely to reduce unemployment. It might legitimately still be wondered how far this effect is likely to go. The mainstream explanation of cyclical unemployment involves wage stickiness as a central ingredient. Why would not the second-tier wage also become sticky, even if not as sticky as the first-tier wage? The answer must depend greatly upon what one believes is behind the original first-tier wage stickiness. Whatever the ultimate explanation, it is difficult to envisage circumstances that would make the second tier of wages singularly free of stickiness. While I am prepared to believe that more widespread adoption of two-tiered wage systems might help somewhat to reduce unemployment, it is difficult for me to think of this as a breakthrough solution because the disequilibrium response of the two-tier wage firm will still be to lay off workers during an unexpected downturn.

The two-tiered wage idea merits attention, and we should not hesitate to turn to it if other, in my opinion better, constructs are not put in place. A major problem is that, whatever forces are causing first-tier stickiness, they are likely, although perhaps in somewhat attenuated strength, to cause second-tier wage stickiness. Of course one could go to three-tier wage systems, and so on, but the endeavour seems remarkably like trying to sneak through the back door a wage flexibility that simply will not pass through the front door. Far more desirable than the inegalitarian principle of unequal pay for equal work in the same work-place, I believe, would be a system that automatically preserves full employment even when sluggish pay parameters are frozen at the 'wrong' levels.

EMPLOYEE OWNERSHIP SCHEMES

Question: What is the relation between profit-sharing and various forms of 'employee-ownership', like employee stock ownership plans (ESOPs), worker co-operatives, labour-capital partnerships, and so forth?

'Employee ownership' is a term encompassing a broad spectrum of proposals for labour market reform. On the one hand, for some the term connotes a quite radical reorganisation of work relations – really some form of socialism or anarcho-syndicalism following loosely in the utopian tradition of, say, Robert Owen. Others see employee ownership as a variation on the prevailing capitalist theme, where workers own more of their company's stock, and thereby exert more control over its decisions. As might be expected, the kinds of suggestions for improving capitalism being considered here are often heavily tainted with ideological overtones. Indeed ideology, rather than strictly economic considerations, usually determines a typical proponent's attitude. At the one extreme, worker management represents to some a kind of idealised democratic socialism. At the other pole, those who strongly advocate employee stock ownership plans are frequently attached to some vision of peoples' capitalism. In between are often fuzzy images of workers' councils helping to create a more humane and more productive world. In this kind of potentially charged environment, I should perhaps make my own position clear. I am primarily interested in whether or not a proposed reorganisation increases employment without accelerating inflation. The bottom-line key operational question is whether or not, after a particular form of 'employee ownership' is put into place, forces are set in motion that tend to increase, or at least to facilitate, the hiring of currently unemployed workers.

A common, typically implicit, article of faith among those advocating increased employee ownership is that by eliminating the sharp distinction between 'us' who work for the company and 'them' who own or direct the company, economic performance will be bettered. After all, if the workers own or control the firm, the distinction between wages and profits largely vanishes, or at least becomes blurred. Is it not then reasonable to suppose that macroeconomic policies aimed at full employment in such an environment would be more effective because the push on wages, which bedevils current efforts to reconcile low unemployment with low inflation, would be greatly diminished? It is hard to have a problem of wage explosion, after all, when at least in the extreme case, there are no wages.

A major problem with this line of reasoning is that it is not supported by the relevant theory. Actually, the standard model of a labour co-operative whose members share an 'earned surplus' dividend (instead of a wage) has rather perverse employment properties. Turning traditional firms into worker co-operatives whose members control the employment decision is unlikely to result in new hiring. There is little basis for believing that labour co-operatives will aggressively attempt to integrate unemployed workers into their system. The absorption of unemployed outsiders would come about presumably through the creation of new co-operatives, which is, in my opinion, likely to prove at least as unreliable a stimulus to new hirings as wage cuts in the more conventional setting.

James Meade has proposed an imaginative variant of a labour-managed co-operative based on the 'inegalitarian principle' that new hirings are offered a different (presumably lower) number of shares than old hands. The proposal is somewhat of a hybrid between two-tiered (or multi-tiered) wage systems and worker co-operatives. The major problem I have with all multi-tiered payment systems (whether based on inegalitarian wages or inegalitarian dividends) is in wondering why the *n*th tier of an *n*-tiered system should be assumed to be a perfectly flexible subject of rational discourse when the heart of the macroeconomic problem, or so it seems to me, is the disequilibrium created when pay parameters (of whatever sort) are inflexible in the face of changed conditions. Virtually any system assuming perfect flexibility of pay parameters for the marginal worker will yield full employment. But is this a reasonable assumption? Perhaps it is. Perhaps society can be turned in this direction. But I think that a more promising line is not to abandon the egalitarian principle, and not to abandon the idea that the capitalist, when all is said and done, determines the employment level, but rather to motivate the same capitalist to hire more workers, expand output, and charge lower prices.

I must say I regard it as ironic that some critics have latched onto Professor Meade's proposal as a kind of shield from behind which they feel emboldened to sally forth and deplore profit-sharing as being flawed 'in practice'. For the facts are, as I have not been shy to emphasise, that over 80 million workers throughout the world are employed by profit-sharing enterprises, including many of the biggest and most advanced state-of-the-art companies in the United States and Japan. Worker co-operatives, by comparison, are a small, transient species that do not have an impressive record of dealing with high-tech, to put it generously. Professor Meade's discriminating labour–capital partnership, in particular, is non-existent. I do think the practical-minded critics might look a little more closely at practice.

What about the more openly capitalistic variants of 'employee ownership', like employee stock ownership plans, or ESOPs? Proponents of this approach typically adhere to the following philosophy. Capitalism, they believe, is basically a very fine system. But it is marred by a too-concentrated ownership of the means of production in too few hands. Corrective measures should be taken to spread capital around, so that the community becomes closer to a nation of capitalist–workers or worker–capitalists. Especially desirable would be a situation where the worker–capitalists essentially own the company they work for. Hence the motivation for a spate of tax gimmicks encouraging employers to pay workers stock in lieu of wages.

Whatever the possible political and social merits or drawbacks of a world of worker–capitalists, it is difficult to find a hard economic rationale in favour of worker capitalism as opposed to ordinary capitalism. When workers are paid so many pounds' worth of stock in lieu of wages, why does that encourage the company to hire the unemployed or to keep down prices? It is true that certain well designed stock payment plans are actually more like profit-sharing and do encourage additional employment on the margin. But the typical ESOP is not like this, although perhaps it could be made more like this, for example by automatically assigning the value of individual stock distributions in proportion to profits per worker. I would say that tax benefits should be granted only in these kinds of cases. In any event such considerations are not usually what the typical ESOP supporter has in mind. Perhaps the fact that workers 'own' a part of the company helps to moderate wage demands or motivates harder work, although the empirical evidence is mixed at best.

The idea that part of a worker's pay is linked to the well-being of the company seems like a good idea. What is typically lacking in such discussions when they are used vaguely to support ESOPs is any kind of hard economic theory that clearly identifies motives and behaviour under employee stock ownership that would result in improved macroeconomic performance. Perhaps such a connection can be made, but it is at the present elusive, at least for me. In this sense there is a strong contrast with profit-sharing, where a relatively much more tight economic theory can be used to argue that there might be favourable employment consequences.

Actually my general instinct is that worker ownership, or even worker control, is basically not a good idea under most circumstances. It is hard to believe that the modern corporation (especially in an internationally competitive environment) can be effectively run by a committee of workers. The relative scarcity of worker co-operatives, their inability to grow, their weak record in high-tech areas – all seem to me to be indirect evidence of this thesis. While there are bound to be specific exceptions, I fear that a worker-managed firm would generally have difficulty making the hard choices that need to be made quickly in a fast-moving environment where specific circumstances of time and place are important. Managers representing workers would also, I believe, have some difficulty keeping up the torrid pace of technological innovation upon which all economic growth and welfare is ultimately based. I think it is ultimately in the workers' own self-interest (just as it is ultimately in the consumers' self-interest) not to sit on committees that democratically vote for what is to be produced and how it is to be produced, but rather to be presented with so many viable alternative job opportunities in a tight labour market that the capitalist overseers simply have no choice but to provide high pay and good working conditions.

THE EXAMPLE OF JAPAN

Question: Is Japan an example of a share economy? What lessons can be learned from the Japanese experience?

Japan has an unusual labour payment system, where about one-quarter of an average worker's total compensation comes in the form of a twice-yearly bonus supplement added onto base wages. It has by now been firmly established that the Japanese bonus system can be viewed as a form of profit-sharing, even though only about 15 per cent of Japanese firms explicitly link the bonus to profitability via a prescribed formula. What I mean by saying that Japanese bonuses can be viewed as a form of profit-sharing is simply the statistical statement that the ratio of bonus payments to base wages varies positively with business condition indicators, including profitability per employee.

Japan has enjoyed the lowest average unemployment rate among the major industrialised capitalist economies over the last quarter-century or so. This comparatively outstanding employment record survives corrections for discouraged workers, relatively flexible hours, definitional differences, and so forth. Does the existence of a profit-sharing component of pay help in any way to account for the comparatively low, stable unemployment rate in Japan? This is an easy question to ask but a very hard one to answer. The whole Japanese system seems to be employment promoting, so it is not possible to isolate the precise contribution made by the bonus system. I think it is a fair statement to say that it would be more difficult for Japanese firms to maintain the full employment commitment without the automatic cushion that the bonus system provides. The Japanese experience is suggestive or supportive of the proposition that a profit-sharing system can be used to help promote full employment. But we cannot go much beyond such vague statements, at least at this stage.

CONCLUSION

I have attempted to deal with the major questions that have been raised about profit-sharing. No doubt the reader will have more. But there is a firm bottom line. The profit-sharing variant of a capitalist firm is a viable, healthy organism that has passed the market test for survival with flying colours. If European-style economies were to encourage this species to take hold by granting significant tax concessions to profit-sharing income, it is difficult to see how any great harm could be done and easy to see how a lot of good might come of it.

Note

1. This is an extended version of a lecture delivered on 7 July 1986 in the House of Commons. Martin Weitzman is Mitsui Professor of Economics at Massachusetts Institute of Technology.

3 Profit-Sharing and Employment: Some Doubts[1]

Sushil Wadhwani

WEITZMAN'S CASE

Let us begin with a concrete example of the case set out by Martin Weitzman in Chapter 2 and in Weitzman (1984). At present each worker gets, so to speak, a predetermined piece of the income pie, before it is out of the oven, indeed before even its size is known. It is argued that we should replace this with a system where, instead, a significant part of a worker's remuneration will be tied to the fortunes of the firm. In suggesting that a movement towards profit-sharing might be encouraged by tax incentives, HM Treasury originally envisaged a scheme where the current system might be replaced by one in which, say, 20 per cent of pay becomes profit-linked at the outset. This component of income will vary up and down with profits, while the base wage will remain fixed (during the contract period).

To illustrate the workings of Weitzman's system, suppose that 'Any Firm plc' pays wages equal to £200 per week and therefore has an incentive to employ workers as long as the *additional* value added per worker is equal to or in excess of £200. Assume also that the *average* value added per worker is £300 (to provide a cover for overheads, profits and so on) and that it actually employs ten people. Suppose that the firm adopts a profit-sharing scheme instead. It chooses a base wage of £160 per week (80 per cent of existing remuneration) and gives the employee a share of gross operating profits equal to £40 (see Annexe). This works out at two-sevenths of the profits per worker. As things stand, the worker is indifferent to the new arrangement. However, the firm now has an incentive to hire an extra worker because, if it did so, its value added goes up by £200 as before, but its cost of hiring the extra worker only increases by the base wage of £160, plus two-sevenths of the extra gross operating profits of £40 (=£200 − £160), or a total of £171.40.[2]

Therefore, if the company hires an extra worker, it stands to clear a profit of nearly £30. Under this new contract, Any Firm plc has an incentive to resist lay-offs and to expand production. When production is expanded, Any Firm's prices must come down, because more of the product can only be sold if the price is lowered. Therefore, if a large number of firms in the economy go over to profit-sharing, there will be a built-in bias towards eliminating unemployment, expanding output, and lowering prices.

Notice, though, that when an extra worker is hired, the total pay of each existing worker falls (in this case by about 1½ per cent). Therefore, existing workers in Any Firm plc will be made worse off. Weitzman points out that this does not necessarily follow if a large number of firms introduce profit-sharing, because as each firm expands and hires more workers, total workers' purchasing power rises, and so does the demand for Any Firm's products. However, if the wage is held artificially high by existing workers, we need to be told why they would be willing to accept lower pay. Also, we know that workers dislike too much variation in their income, often for good reasons such as mortgage commitments. Therefore it is likely that when profit-linked income falls employees will try to recoup these losses by demanding a higher base wage.

It is crucial for the success of the Weitzman scheme that employers feel able to reduce average total remuneration (in the first instance) for, if they were to feel that they must continue to pay the same total remuneration as in the existing wage system, introducing profit-sharing will not alter hiring behaviour. If, for instance, in the case of Any Firm plc, the firm felt that it must continue to pay its workers £200 per week (say, because this was the going rate for the job) then the extra cost of hiring an additional worker would remain £200. It no longer has an incentive to expand production. If firms felt committed to paying a certain total amount the manner in which this amount was divided into the two components – base wage and profit-linked pay – would become irrelevant. These would merely be labels, and would act as a veil. Nothing fundamental would have changed.

It is worth reminding ourselves that the wage and the profit-sharing systems have (in the terms of the Weitzman algebra) the same properties in the long run for precisely this reason. In the long run, full employment is assumed to prevail, and if the firm wishes to retain its workers (given the assumption of perfect mobility) it must pay them the existing 'going rate' for the job (where the 'going rate' is in terms of the total level of remuneration). Weitzman ignores this constraint on total compensation in the short run, by assuming that workers are glued to their existing firms. We are not, however, offered any description of the transition between the short run and the long run, and in the absence of that, must question the plausibility of the assumed behaviour in the short run.

Suppose that, in fact, wages are 'too high' today, and the reason they do not fall in spite of mass unemployment is that firms believe that lower wages would be counter-productive. This could occur if workers' productivity depends on the wage that they are paid. Firms may not then wish to lower the wage if doing so were to reduce productivity significantly. This intuition has been formalised in the so-called 'efficiency wage' theories, where wages are held to affect productivity for a variety of possible reasons. Employees might only work effectively if they receive what they consider to be a 'fair wage'. Hence wages must be set to at least match this notion. In recent years real wages have continued to rise in the United Kingdom despite high unemployment. This is, in part, a result of the fact that workers have been willing to end restrictive practices in return for pay rises. Alternatively, a cut in wages might be more than offset by an increase in costs associated with a greater turnover in employment. A cut in wages might also lead to a significant deterioration in the average quality of a firm's labour force, as all the better workers leave. For all these reasons firms might choose to pay a certain level of remuneration which, from their viewpoint, is optimal because it corresponds to a cost-minimising choice. Introducing profit-sharing should not affect this choice (since it is unlikely to affect the workers' notion of a 'fair wage'). Firms will continue to feel committed to paying a particular total amount and will not then alter their hiring behaviour. In this case, the wage and profit-sharing systems *will have the same properties in the short run*.

WILL PROFIT-SHARING LEAD TO WAGE MODERATION?

This brings us to the theoretical work which suggests that the reason that profit-sharing might reduce unemployment is that it will lead unions to demand lower wages. Note, however, that in a recent survey (EPIC, 1986) 81 per cent of managers and 84 per cent of trade unionists said that profit-sharing would have little effect on the rate of pay increases.

Weitzman has offered us one model (see Weitzman, 1985) in which he claims that profit-sharing leads to wage moderation. However, in order to avoid complexity, we shall consider the (more plausible) story told by Richard Jackman (see Jackman, 1985). He considers a world where the union wants more jobs and higher pay and chooses the level of pay by fully taking into account the implications of this decision for the level of employment, that is, it chooses the (from its viewpoint) optimal combination of jobs and pay. If in a wage economy the union cuts wages by 1 per cent to get, say, a K per cent rise in employment it will find that, in a profit-sharing economy, it only needs to cut the *base* wage (which is only 80 per cent of the total pay) by 1 per cent in order to secure the same increase in employment. Therefore in general it will choose a wage that yields higher employment than in a wage economy.

One might legitimately disagree with this view of the world and believe that unions have little to do with the current unemployment problem. Leaving that aside and dealing with the model as it stands, we are fundamentally sceptical that introducing profit-sharing will lead to wage moderation. This stems from the view that the individual union and firm prefer the wage system over the profit-sharing one. Indeed, this is why Weitzman thinks it is necessary to introduce tax incentives to encourage the spread of profit-sharing. However, even given tax incentives, it will always be in the interest of an individual firm and union to mimic the traditional wage economy. Workers and management would get together and agree on the total remuneration for each worker, as they do now. They would use an estimate of profits in the coming year to calculate the expected value of the profit-linked income. The base wage would then be set so that in combination with the profit-linked element it achieved the desired overall total (on average).

Workers would be better off under this arrangement as they would pay less tax. Firms could also end up better off if workers then agreed to accept a lower level of pre-tax remuneration. So it is true that there would be a reduction in wage pressure but it would not be qualitatively different from that which would arise from a cut in income tax thresholds. And a cut in income tax has the advantage of being rather simpler to implement.

It should be emphasised that the existence of a cosmetic profit-sharing scheme does not require the union to have the power to restrict new hirings. It merely requires the firm to understand that, on average, it must expect to pay a certain level of total remuneration and, given that, its incentive to hire and fire is no different from that in a wage economy. In other words, we continue to operate the system just as we do at present with the one difference that we attach labels to the two components of an individual worker's income. This difficulty will plague *any* attempt to encourage the growth of profit-sharing schemes through tax incentives.

THE INSIDER–OUTSIDER PROBLEM

Another possible problem arises from the fact that, if workers are to have a significant component of their remuneration related directly to a variable like profits, which depends in large part on management decisions, it is likely that they will wish to have a greater say in the decisions of the firm. We have already seen that insiders would not want the firm to employ more workers because the additional hired worker dilutes the profits per worker which the previously hired workers receive. Therefore, if they did have a say in the employment decision, insiders would vote against new hirings. In its first statement on profit-sharing, the Treasury recognised this danger and stated that if an agreement was to be deemed eligible for tax relief a necessary characteristic was that 'Employees would agree not to restrict the scope for employers to take on more labour' (National Economic Development Council, 1986). However this fails to deal with the possibility that an employer might perceive it to be in his interest to keep the insiders happy by not taking on these new workers. This might be owing to a variety of reasons – keeping the wage at its present level might be good for productivity or the employer might fear disruption from the insiders. It is for similar reasons that employers do not bring in the existing unemployed workers into the firm and pay everyone a lower wage. We suspect that the same influences might induce the employer to behave in an identical way in a profit-sharing economy.

Time and again we have seen that a fundamental problem with introducing profit-sharing is that it will be resisted because, in the first instance, it reduces the pay of the insiders. In order to improve matters, Professor James Meade has proposed an imaginative variant – that is, what he calls a Discriminating Labour–Capital Partnership (see Meade, 1986). A crucial feature of this scheme is that it would explicitly allow new entrants to be paid less than existing workers. However, since this two-tier pay system violates the principle of 'equal pay for equal work', it is difficult to see unions accepting it easily. Besides conflicting with deeply held notions of fairness, two-tiered wage systems amount to a phased-in wage cut in industries with a large turnover. In addition, if existing workers allow discriminatory pay for new workers, it is difficult to see why new workers, whose proportion is increasing over time, will defend the right of the existing workers to maintain this arbitrary differential in the future.

THE 'MEDIUM-BOILED' CASE

Until now we have only considered the so-called hard-boiled case for profit-sharing (that is, the Weitzman propositions). What though of the medium-boiled case that profit-sharing would improve the workings of the macroeconomy because it would make the wage more responsive to macroeconomic shocks? The Treasury appears to believe in this for they have argued that 'A business in which a profit-sharing agreement had been reached should become less vulnerable to adverse shocks' (National Economic Development Council, 1986). The argument here is that, although the total wage under profit-sharing will, on average, be the same as that under a system without profit-sharing, it will be more responsive to macroeconomic shocks during the contract period. This is predicated on the assumption that profit-linked pay is adjusted more often than the wage is. (At present, 95 per cent of private sector settlements occur on an annual basis.) There may be something to this argument, although we need to be careful about the measure of profit that we use. If we do use a measure of true economic income then, because labour's remuneration responds to shocks during the contract period, the macroeconomy is more stable. If we tie wages to historical cost profits this is no longer necessarily true. We should also emphasise that, unlike the United States case where many wage contracts run for three years, the practical difference between a system of this kind and the prevailing one cannot be expected to be very great in Britain, where we renegotiate every year.

It is difficult to believe that installing a system which dampens these output fluctuations will do much to reduce unemployment anyway. It is worth reminding ourselves that unemployment has been rising, almost without interruption in the UK (there were only three years between 1966 and 1986 when it did not rise). This relentless rise can hardly be attributed to unexpected cyclical fluctuations.

While we may argue about whether or not greater automatic wage flexibility is a good thing, it seems to us that if we want the workers to accept it they should be offered it as part of a package. Although there may be something in the argument that wages are not sufficiently responsive to changes in economic circumstances, it is equally possible to argue that something should be done to reduce the amplitude of these macroeconomic shocks. To take a concrete example, we would be the first to agree that wages should adjust to maintain Britain's competitiveness if there is a warranted change in the exchange rate. However it is difficult to resist the belief that a great deal of the exchange rate volatility that we have seen in recent years has not reflected changes in the economic fundamentals, but the whims and fancies of the speculators. Workers do think it unfair that they must bear the entire burden of adjusting to these wild swings in the rate – far better to attempt to reduce them.

Though the traditional medium-boiled argument emphasises the effect on output fluctuations, we think that one might actually be able to make a case for higher output using a rather different argument from that advanced by Weitzman. The Treasury certainly believe this in that they argue that a consequence of introducing profit-sharing would be to make '. . . employers less cautious about taking on new employees'. This might occur if we believe that employers take on fewer workers than would be warranted by a strategy to maximise expected profits, because they fear the risk of experiencing serious cash flow difficulties. By being less ambitious they are able to reduce this risk. However, were employees to share this risk (by agreeing to take a share of the profits) employers would become less cautious. Note, however, that, on this argument, introducing profit-sharing raises the firm's average profits because it need pay less attention to possible cash flow problems. However we do not observe many firms introducing profit-sharing autonomously. This might be because the additional costs associated with its introduction (which we do not fully understand) outweigh the benefit to the firm. It is sometimes argued that the present situation might be socially inefficient because the interests of the unemployed are ignored by the firm. While there may be something in this argument, it is also possible to argue that a government policy which cut, say, national insurance contributions in recessions would be just as effective in increasing employment. In addition, the latter would avoid the costs associated with the introduction of profit-sharing.

We now wish to deal with an argument that has always been advanced against profit-sharing (it was advanced by the classical economists against share-cropping), although we do not regard it as being terribly important. It is that the incentive to invest will be reduced. Clearly if the firm does perceive a reduction in the extra cost of hiring an extra employee it might, if it expected the pay parameters to remain fixed, use more labour relative to capital. Of course, if as we have argued the employer does not actually perceive a reduction in the cost of hiring labour, there will be no effect on investment. If, on the other hand, Weitzman turns out to be correct, we shall in any case have Heaven on Earth. There will be full employment and in this atmosphere firms are likely to invest more (owing to higher demand).

Much of the discussion above has been in the context of certain theoretical models of wage and employment determination. Yet these are things that we do not understand particularly well and there is in any case a plethora of inadequate models to choose between. Therefore it behoves us to be cautious about predicting the effects of profit-sharing. For example, it is possible that it could make the insider–outsider problem even worse if it led the existing insiders to understand better the link between taking on new workers and their remuneration. Also one possible reason for inflation is that it reconciles the inconsistent demands of various groups in society. However, at the moment, wage bargaining is not explicitly about shares. Would moving to a system where workers bargained explicitly about shares of income make a difference? We do not know, but it might.

EMPIRICAL EVIDENCE

The discussion has so far been almost entirely theoretical. Weitzman has argued, though, that Japanese experience provides evidence for the belief that profit-sharing provides a cure for stagflation. It is not easy to assess the validity of statements of this kind. The Japanese may owe their success to other factors: a Weberian, for example, would emphasise the considerable cultural differences. In addition, the Japanese are not immune to stagflation. Among OECD countries, they experienced the sharpest slowing in growth of output after the first oil shock, while inflation reached 20 per cent. A key feature of Weitz-

Table 3.1 Proportion of firms who report a shortage of labour (1976–83)

Country	*Proportion (%)*
France	3.75
Italy	3.21
Japan	2.28
Netherlands	7.05
West Germany	4.71

Sources: Results of the Business Survey carried out among Management in the Community, Commission of the European Communities; *Economic Statistics Annual*, Bank of Japan.

man's arguments is that firms in a share economy should wish to employ more workers at the current pay parameters (in technical jargon, there is excess demand for labour). Yet, using data on the proportion of firms who report a shortage of labour, there is no evidence that Japan is special in this respect. This may be seen in Table 3.1 where we compare Japan with four European countries (for whom comparable data are available) and find that, if anything, Japan had the smallest proportion of firms reporting a shortage of labour over 1976–83. Lest the reader is misled by the fact that official unemployment in Japan is low, it should be emphasised that the statistics seriously understate the extent of the under-utilisation of labour. Each percentage point of unemployment in Japan is associated with a short-fall in output that is five times as great as that experienced in the United Kingdom or United States. This is in part owing to the so-called 'lifetime employment system', with Japanese firms preferring to provide geometry lessons for their idle workers, in contrast to their British counterparts, who fire them. Another important factor in keeping Japanese unemployment figures low is the high proportion of 'discouraged workers'. For example, in 1978, the official unemployment rate in Japan was 2.6 per cent and 6.0 per cent in the United States. However, the estimated numbers of discouraged workers amounted to 8.9 per cent of the labour force in Japan, but only 1.4 per cent in the United States.

Weitzman has us believe that in a share economy changes in money supply (or, more generally, aggregate demand) should not cause output to deviate from its 'full employment' level, and that oil price increases and 'wage push' should not lead to higher price inflation. While we cannot do justice to all the subtleties here (see Wadhwani,

1985), the econometric evidence is not consistent with any of these implications. Indeed it is not even true that import price rises have a smaller effect on domestic price inflation in Japan as compared with other OECD countries. Therefore we do not believe that there is any evidence to suggest that the bonus system in Japan has Weitzman-like effects. This is either because the Japanese bonus system is not a profit-sharing one (in which case the Japanese experience is not relevant), or Weitzman's algebra is flawed. In either case, when all is said and done, we do not feel that we can use the Japanese experience as an argument in favour of introducing profit-sharing.

We have argued earlier that it might be difficult to get a genuine profit-sharing scheme in the United Kingdom. Yet some would argue that it exists in Japan. It is arguable that it is possible there because of certain institutional characteristics that are missing in the United Kingdom. It is likely that the insider–outsider conflict is much less important there. This is partly owing to the fact that firms can take on so-called 'temporary' workers at rates of pay that are considerably lower than that of existing workers. In addition, when lay-offs do occur, they do *not* occur by inverse seniority (as in the United Kingdom or United States) and, therefore, the average union voter is less likely to make irresponsible wage demands. If you add to these the fact that there is a greater degree of trust and closeness between management and workers, the existence of a profit-sharing system becomes easier to understand.

PRACTICAL PROBLEMS

Let us turn to what we think could be an important practical problem with the operation of the system of profit-linked pay. This arises because earnings will be linked to historical cost profits. The accounting profession in the United Kingdom have failed to agree on an appropriate inflation accounting standard, with SSAP16 having now been withdrawn and nothing having been put in its place. Gross trading profits are overstated during times of inflation and firms could find the profit-linked component of pay rising very rapidly, with no genuine improvement in profitability having occurred. When inflation peaked in 1974, British industry experienced a severe liquidity crisis, made much worse by the fact that companies had to pay tax on the (artificial) profits arising from stock appreciation. The government saved the day then by introducing stock relief. But, unless firms can persuade their workers to moderate their demands for higher base pay when the profit-linked component rises artificially during times of inflation, they could face a serious cash flow crisis with important implications for investment and jobs.

A related issue of some importance is the manipulation of the profits figures by the firm. Even under a cosmetic scheme the firm would have an obvious incentive to understate this figure, in the hope that workers will regard it as arising from an unexpected, but genuine, change in business fortune. The scope for 'creative accounting' is almost limitless – the existence of transfer pricing, and the fact that existing accounting standards on things like currency changes or research and development give the firm considerable latitude ensure that. This could lead to increased conflict between the workers and the firm. It has been suggested that this could be reduced if workers' remuneration were tied to dividends. However this might introduce an undesirable distortion in the dividend decision. In addition, since dividends are much smoother than earnings, any advantages of a 'medium-boiled' nature would be partially eroded as workers' remuneration would be less sensitive to unexpected business fluctuations.

It is sometimes argued that an advantage of profit-sharing over incomes policies as an anti-inflation weapon is that it does not create additional micro-economic distortions. However introducing tax incentives in order to encourage profit-sharing will create a myriad of distortions. New firms who cannot persuade their workforce to accept profit-sharing (because of the very high degree of risk) will find that they have to pay more (in before-tax terms) than their competitors because their workers do not benefit from the government's tax advantages. This is hardly consistent with the present British government's official stance of encouraging new firms. Employers in other sectors in the economy which are non-profit-sharing – public corporations, the public sector and private sector firms who, for whatever reason, do not want to share profits – will find themselves confronted with demands for higher pay in order that they may obtain a level of after-tax remuneration that is comparable with their counterparts in profit-sharing firms who do benefit from the government's tax incentives. This will lead to a reduction in employment in these sectors, which will partially offset the gains made in the profit-sharing sector.

It is worth reminding ourselves that tax incentives could be very expensive. Under the proposals initially suggested in the government's 'Green Paper', the cost could have been of the order of £1 billion per year or equivalent to 1p off the basic rate of income tax. If the scheme were not to have Weitzman-like effects (for reasons discussed above) income tax cuts might be preferable. They would be much simpler to implement, would not create distortions between sectors and companies need not worry about having to divulge sensitive information.

We also need to be told in advance how the success of the scheme will be assessed. We have already argued that the number of employees who appear to take it up could be meaningless, since there may be cosmetic schemes. How then does the Treasury propose to assess the effectiveness of the scheme? Indeed, if Professor Weitzman really does believe his algebra, will he tell us when he expects us to achieve full employment or, at least, how much extra employment he hopes to generate? Ideally, we would like Professor Weitzman to play the following Popperian game – he should define the 'success' or 'failure' of the scheme in advance, and tell us that if unemployment remained above a certain number he would regard his theory as having been falsified.

CONCLUSIONS

We have argued that there are circumstances when introducing profit-sharing might not significantly affect the rate of unemployment. Indeed it is possible that the tax incentives would be misused in that there might be cosmetic profit-sharing schemes, with nothing fundamental having changed. Therefore it behoves us to be cautious about predicting the effects of profit-sharing.

Annex: Effects of profit-sharing on remuneration and profits

(a) Effect of profit-sharing scheme if employment and average remuneration remain unchanged

	Before profit-sharing	*With profit-sharing*
1. Number of employees	10	10
2. Minimum weekly wage	£ 200	£ 160 ('base wage')
3. Minimum total wage costs to employer [(1) × (2)]	£2000	£1600
4. Average value-added per employee	£300	£300
5. Total value-added by all employees [(1) × (4)]	£3000	£3000
6. Gross operating profit [(5)−(3)]	£1000	£1400
7. Profit to be distributed to employees to preserve total remuneration [Line (3)]	—	£400
8. Share of profits to go to employees [(7)÷(6)]	—	2/7
9. Profit share per employee [(7)÷(1)]	—	£40
10. Total remuneration per employee [(2)+(9)]	£200	£200

(b) Effect on profit-sharing firm of taking on an extra worker producing an extra weekly value-added of £200

	Before extra worker	*With extra worker*
11. Number of employees	10	11
12. Base (minimum) weekly wage	£160	£160
13. Total base wage costs	£1600	£1760
14. Total value-added by all employees	£3000	£3200
15. Average value-added per employee [(14)÷(11)]	£300	£290.90
16. Gross operating profit [(14)−(13)]	£1400	£1440
17. Profit per employee [(16)÷(11)]	£140	£130.90
18. Profit-share per employee [(2/7)×(17)]	£40	£37.40
19. Remuneration per employee [(12)+(18)]	£200	£197.40
20. Total employee remuneration [(19)×(11)]	£2000	£2171.40
21. Share-holders' profits [(14)−(20)]	£1000	£1028.60

Lines 19 and 21 show that there is a fall in both the average remuneration per worker and the average shareholder's profit per worker but a rise in total shareholders' profits

Notes

1. This is an extended version of a lecture delivered in the House of Commons on 24 June 1986. Sushil Wadhwani is a Research Fellow at the London School of Economics.
2. The effects of profit-sharing on a single company's wages and profits are shown in more detail in the Annex.

4 Profit-Sharing, Motivation and Company Performance[1]

Saul Estrin

This chapter investigates whether profit-sharing might, via incentive effects, be expected to improve company performance. It starts at the theoretical level, where very strong arguments have been put forward linking profit-sharing with improved employee motivation. Critics can however point to perfectly respectable counter-arguments with more pessimistic conclusions. As the issues cannot be completely resolved at the theoretical level, the way forward is to study the empirical evidence.

Drawing on information from Western Europe and the United States, we examine the effects of profit-sharing on workers' attitudes, industrial relations, productivity and profitability. Our findings suggest that profit-sharing does have a mildly beneficial impact on corporate performance, though the benefits from participation in ownership and decision making may be at least as great.

INVOLVING THE WORKERS

Profit-sharing is one of a number of possible ways to involve employees more directly in the workings of their company and of the wider economic system. While the categories shade to some extent one into the other, it is worth bringing out the distinctions at the outset since the motivational impact of each scheme differs. Indeed the lack of precision in this area derives in no small part from the common blurring of the differences between the various forms of employee participation.

Profit-sharing involves linking some proportion of labour remuneration to company profitability; an incentive payment to be paid either in cash or in shares. It is by intention the least participatory of the various schemes on offer, entailing no necessary increase in employee participation in company decisions. Indeed, with Weitzman's cash-based proposal, the broader economic benefits actually hinge on *ruling out* any workers' involvement in employment decisions. Even with share-based schemes, workers' share ownership will only be enhanced to the extent that they do not sell their holdings at the first available opportunity. Even if they do retain the bulk of their allocation, particularly in the early years, they can only hope to influence corporate choices in the same way and to the same extent as any other small private shareholder.

A second category of scheme entails encouraging financial participation by employees in their own companies, for example via employee stock ownership plans or rights issues available only to the workforce. It would be possible to achieve employee share ownership through a share-based profit-sharing scheme, but in principle there are some important differences between the two forms of participation. Firstly, employee stock ownership seeks to link workers' wealth, as well as some proportion of their income, to the success of the firm. The tie to the company is therefore, it is hoped, greater and more long-term, and one might expect increased opportunities for a greater motivational effect. Moreover, far from ruling out employee participation in decision-making, financial participation seems likely to be associated with increased worker involvement in company decisions, either individually as private shareholders or acting collectively as a pressure group on management. To make the point, consider the ultimate limit of each scheme. With profit-sharing, it is merely a situation where workers' incomes are derived entirely from profit. However the logical limit of financial participation is the employee-owned firm, controlled either directly by the workforce or by managers ultimately responsible to them.

The third category is employee participation in decision-making, which can operate without reference to either profit-sharing or share ownership via mechanisms such as collective bargaining, works councils and the election of worker representatives to company boards. This approach to employee participation has found particular favour in West Germany and inspired interest in the United Kingdom during the 1970s, culminating in the Bullock Commission Report. It is useful to distinguish between the motivational effects of 'low-level' participation in decision making, which concerns choices directly affecting workers on the shop floor, and 'high-level' participation, which concerns broader corporate strategies. The former type of participation appears to have an unambiguously positive effect on company performance but the findings for the latter, which has been criticised for giving the workers power without responsibility, are more mixed. However participation in decision making is largely peripheral to the issues discussed here, except in so far as it is associated with workers' participation in finance or in profits.

PUBLIC POLICY

Turning to the public policy aspects of profit-sharing, one can envisage three broad reasons why the authorities might wish to encourage the widespread introduction of workers' participation in profits or in ownership (see also Bradley and Gelb, 1986). In the first place, there are a number of persuasive social, political and ethical arguments in favour of such proposals, linked to one's broader vision of the way that society should develop. Participation, it is argued, increases employee responsibility in the work-place and beyond, strengthens the natural democratic structures and, by allowing workers to share in the success of the business, enhances human dignity. For society as a whole, profit-sharing and wider share ownership are inextricably linked with the redistribution of income and wealth, giving workers a stake in the productive capital of the country. In that sense, the current policy pressures are perhaps analogous to the various attempts in Europe during the eighteenth and nineteenth centuries to distribute land to the peasants in order to harness their energies for the broader well-being of society. These arguments point most directly to encouraging wider share ownership, though they are not of themselves inconsistent with profit-sharing schemes, particularly share-based ones.

To this groundswell of opinion can be added a number of purely economic arguments, and these tend to favour profit-sharing rather than wider share ownership. The ideas have been developed most forcefully by Martin Weitzman, as in Chapter 2, though important contributions have also been made by James Meade (see Meade, 1986). The two key themes have concerned the greater flexibility of wages under profit-sharing and the increase in the aggregate demand for labour associated with a wedge being driven between the average and marginal cost of labour to the firm. The analysis suggests that profit-sharing may offer the government an effective way to reduce unemployment and may also act as a bulwark against future bouts of stagflation. The appropriate limits to Weitzman's claims are still under discussion (see Wadhwani, 1986) but his work has stimulated much of the current British government's policy response.

The third possible reason to support profit-sharing or wider share ownership is the effect that they might have on employee incentives and motivation. If such schemes are widely disseminated, there are grounds to expect an impact on the efficiency, profitability and longer-term economic performance of companies, thereby improving the broader functioning of the microeconomy. However in this case the relative effects of profit-sharing as against employee ownership are not straightforward; one can find arguments in favour of sponsoring both forms of participation. The major aims in the remainder of this chapter are therefore to sort out some of the conceptual issues for economists in this area, and to use evidence from various experiments in the western world to derive conclusions about the most appropriate type of schemes from the motivational point of view. On this basis, we intend to judge the current government's proposals to stimulate profit-sharing.

Despite the considerable current interest in the topic, the idea that workers should be paid in part out of profit or own shares in their company is not new. The first theoretical arguments were in fact developed by the German economist, J. H. von Thunen in 1848, and the implications of profit-sharing and employee share ownership have been explored by economists as diverse as J. S. Mill, Marshall and Samuelson. However, with the notable exception of Jaroslav Vanek's work (see Vanek, 1965), prior to Weitzman's contributions the discussion tended to focus on motivational and managerial questions. The crucial point about this earlier literature is that, except for the broader social and political reasons noted above, which lie outside the ambit of purely economic evaluation, the issue of public intervention was not raised. If employee participation improves company performance, the gains are available for private appropriation without the need for government intervention. Some one-off expenditures might be sensible – to educate industrialists to the advantages of the scheme or temporarily to subsidise its introduction as a counter to initial managerial suspicions. However, if the productivity advantages are really there, the schemes would be self-supporting thereafter. Weitzman on the other hand has isolated a broader public benefit from profit-sharing, the predicted elimination of stagflation, but in the assumed absence of motivational effects can find no reason for firms to introduce or sustain such a remuneration system. His solution is therefore the long-term subsidy by the government of all such schemes to ensure that profit-sharing is maintained throughout the economy. Thus, though both the incentive and the Weitzman-type scenarios can provide a rationale for the widespread introduction of profit-sharing, they differ in their implications for government policy: Weitzman-type arguments point to permanent tax benefits to support such a scheme while motivational arguments favour at best a temporary subsidy.

The motivational arguments concerning increased employee participation in profits and shares have therefore been largely ignored in the recent resurgence of interest in the subject. At this point in the debate, they deserve a more thorough airing, especially in the light of the questions being raised as to the general validity of Weitzman's arguments in the British context. The incentive literature may provide a more durable and convincing case for employee involvement in their companies, though not necessarily via cash-based profit-sharing. These issues are of particular relevance to the current policy debate since, in contrast to Weitzman's macroeconomic analysis, the motivational approach *cannot* provide a justification for long-term government intervention in support of profit-sharing, such as permanent tax concessions. In that sense, these arguments generate conclusions more in line with current policy proposals for a temporary subsidy.

THE PREDICTED EFFECTS OF PROFIT-SHARING ON COMPANY PERFORMANCE

In this section we will briefly survey the effects that economic theorists have suggested profit-sharing and other forms of employee participation could have on various aspects of company performance. The bulk of authors in the area have argued for a positive relationship but the more pessimistic analyses cannot be ignored. Discussion has focussed on the association between various forms of employee participation and productivity, either of labour or of the organisation as a whole. In the empirical section which follows we shall also consider employee satisfaction and corporate profitability, both predicted to be positively associated with enhanced productivity and efficiency.

Employee participation in profits or in ownership may be expected to affect productive efficiency by altering (a) workers' intensity of labour or effort, (b) the productive skills of the labour force and (c) the company's general organisational atmosphere and efficiency. Though there is necessarily some overlap, we shall consider the effects separately.

(a) Workers' Effort

This is normally put forward simply in terms of private financial incentives. Consider an employee on a fixed salary. He or she has no direct economic interest in the quality or intensity of his work and, because of this, firms will have to set up a complex monitoring system of supervisors and foremen to ensure that effort levels and quality standards are maintained. If the same worker is instead paid at least in part out of profit, the level of remuneration will be related, however weakly, to his or her personal efforts. If workers are materially motivated, they are likely to work harder. Moreover, under such a system, an individual's pay depends on the work intensity of fellow employees, making it important to monitor their activities more keenly than hitherto. Apart from reducing monitoring costs, this may lead to a fundamental change in attitudes at the work-place, with positive peer group pressure to increased work intensity replacing the traditional tendency to overlook or support colleagues' shirking.

The greater the proportion of salary paid as a profit-share, the sharper the individual incentives of this sort will be. Similar arguments can be made in support of wider share ownership, since improved effort can increase both equity values and income via dividends. However, the stock market valuation of employee share holdings may be influenced by many factors in addition to individual workers' effort, so financial participation may not be the best way to pick up these private incentive effects. This is therefore a motivational argument in which profit-sharing would seem to dominate share ownership or participation in decision making.

However the incentive argument hinges on the existence of a clear and significant relationship between effort and remuneration via profit-sharing, and this is unlikely in large companies. Indeed, writers in the property rights tradition such as Jensen and Meckling (1979) have suggested that profit-sharing could actually encourage shirking by workers. In contrast to strictly individual incentives, which would link each worker's remuneration to his marginal product, group incentive schemes such as profit-sharing give each worker in a large company only a tiny fraction of any additional benefit due to his own effort, thereby creating an incentive to enjoy the full benefits of shirking or on-the-job leisure. This case is probably overstated since the beneficial impact of individualised incentives may be offset by the losses induced by rivalry and competitive disruption in search of private gain. It all depends on the technology of the plant: mass production versus autonomous work groups; small scale versus large. Profit-sharing does at least provide incentives against competitive behaviour within the firm and in support of positive collusion to raise effort and productivity. In large firms the effectiveness of the scheme will depend on linking pay to group effort at a relatively low level such as the workshop, far below that of the company as a whole. The administrative costs of running profit-sharing of this form in large diversified firms may be high.

(b) The Productive Skills of the Workforce

It is frequently argued that profit-sharing and employee share ownership increase the workers' willingness to remain with a given firm. For example, the improved group awareness and heightened sense of responsibility implied by the new incentive system offers superior conflict resolution, which is likely to reduce labour turnover. This longer average tenure translates itself into higher productivity through its positive effects on workers' firm-specific human capital: the skills and knowledge that workers acquire in association with the particular company in which they are employed. For example, one might expect to observe an increase in the average rate of capacity utilisation as the average level of skill employees have in operating and repairing machinery improves. Similarly one might expect an improvement in the functioning of work groups and the optimal mix of labour types to achieve particular results as familiarity about the strength and weaknesses of specific workers improves. Moreover, many productive skills are acquired with the help of fellow workers, who will be more willing to help others in on-the-job learning when they know that some proportion of the resulting increased profits will accrue to them. Finally, from the firm's perspective, reduced labour turnover should directly reduce total annual employee recruitment and training costs, though not necessarily the average cost per employee per year.

Provided that workers are recompensed for the additional riskiness of their income stream or capital holding, these effects will hold for both profit-sharing and employee share ownership plans. In principle there is little to choose between the two with regard to labour turnover and labour skills, except that, by being more explicitly linked to the long term, equity stakes may provide a greater psychological link between the worker and the company. However it is questionable whether, in and of itself, profit-sharing will promote dramatically reduced labour turnover, particularly in an environment where most firms use a remuneration system of this form. In practice, employee commitment seems most likely to derive from direct involvement in the decisions made by the firm, especially those which affect employees directly at their place of work.

(c) Organisational Efficiency and Atmosphere

Into this category fall the most frequently cited motivational effects. To quote Cable and Fitzroy (1980, p. 166), 'participatory firms – with or without profit-sharing – will produce better outcomes than traditional firms if the *negative* collusion to maximise one party's share . . . can be replaced by *positive* collusion to maximise joint wealth'. The idea is that some form of worker participation – in profits, shares or even decision-making – can alter the nature of the work-place, replacing the traditional employee–manager conflict and worker alienation with co-operation and increased worker responsibility and trust. In this way the 'them and us' attitude which has supposedly bedevilled British industry could be reduced or eliminated, helping company efficiency and profitability to rise.

There are many routes through which improved employee–manager relations could raise company performance. If workers have an increased sense of responsibility, they will be less likely to strike or undertake damaging industrial disputes. Improved employee morale will also show up in lower rates of absenteeism, greater willingness to work together and improved labour flexibility with respect to work practices. If the traditional adversarial relationship between labour and capital is replaced by a more co-operative atmosphere, peer group pressures will be oriented to better work rather than shirking or even sabotage. The costs of monitoring will therefore be reduced. The resulting improvements in communication channels from workers to management can also help to eliminate numerous microeconomic level organisational inefficiencies that workers have no incentive to disclose in a non-co-operative setting, and may in fact promote. This better use of workers' organisational know-how could be coupled with a greater willingness to implement decisions from higher up, in particular with regard to new machinery and technical change. Indeed, rather than resisting technological advance, it is possible that workers will actually generate innovative proposals in their own areas of expertise. The union literature suggests that these 'voice' effects may have a significant impact on company productivity (see Freeman, 1976).

A final strand of argument concerns union power and investment. Employee participation via profits or shares is frequently seen as an alternative to unionisation for the labour force, thereby weakening the union's bargaining power and raising the proportion of the surplus which can be appropriated by owners. A more sophisticated version of the argument highlights the problems innate in the fact that employers must precommit themselves to levels of future capacity via investment, while workers who negotiate annually can wait until the new equipment comes on stream before determining what wages to demand in order to operate it. The fact that employees can, in the future, exploit the inflexibility of capital by increasing their wage demands leads management, now, to under-invest in new equipment. Profit-sharing, and particularly employee share ownership, can break this vicious circle by linking employee remuneration to current and future corporate earnings.

However it is not clear that these benefits will be conferred on all companies which practise employee participation, regardless of the form of that participation. For example, while profit-sharing may engender some sense of identification with the firm, particularly in small companies, the total effect will probably not be large, especially since such arrangements typically minimise the actual involvement of workers in the affairs of the company. One might expect a greater impact from employee stock ownership plans since the link is through wealth as well as income and the possibility exists for some involvement in company decisions. However, once again real changes in attitude in the work-place are likely to be linked with increases in workers' responsibilities and trust in their judgement, which will be most closely associated with participation in decision making. The greatest impact is likely to come when some degree of decision making authority is associated with employee stock ownership, thereby combining workers' responsibility with power over economic choices.

In contrast to the previous arguments, numerous scholars hypothesise that workers' participation could actually have a *negative* impact on productive efficiency. As we have noted, improved efficiency will typically be associated with increased employee identification with the firm, which will entail at the minimum profit-sharing or an ownership stake and at the maximum some involvement in decision making. But participation of this sort is likely to entail less power and discretionary authority for managers. If the managerial input is crucial in determining the company's performance and if managers value power and discretion, greater employee participation will have a negative productivity effect due to shirking by managers. The decrease in management's discretionary authority may be associated with exhaustive information sharing, along the lines of the John Lewis Partnership, and perhaps direct employee involvement in corporate decisions. The necessity to provide information which is easily comprehensible to a large group will be relatively expensive and may slow down decision making. The need to placate employee interests, either of shareholders or pressure groups, will also hinder the decision-making process and may also prevent 'sensible' choices. The cost of achieving a consensus among parties with different objectives and rates of time preference could 'at the extreme' deadlock decision making or lead to inappropriate choices being made.

There are several other reasons to predict that the relationship between various forms of employee participation and company performance could be negative. James Meade (1986) among others has suggested that, far from reducing conflict between management and workers, a profit-sharing scheme could act to increase it. This is because the new remuneration system means that workers are bearing some of the risk from the business without any involvement in the decisions to be taken. Workers may react negatively to the way that profit-sharing confers responsibility without power, particularly when corporate performance is unsatisfactory. Moreover since, under the current arrangements, management has superior information about the levels and sources of profits from the different parts of the business, there is ample scope for dissimulation in the construction of the profit figures upon which the workers' remuneration will be based. These problems, which could lead to serious conflicts over company accounts, will be particularly acute in diversified and multinational corporations. Finally, employee stock ownership plans may cause problems for company investment policies. These schemes typically entail a legal restriction against workers spreading their risks via a balanced asset portfolio, particularly in the early years of the scheme. Workers are therefore inadequately insured against undesirable outcomes, and if they influence the firm's investment policy, they will ensure that risky strategies are avoided. The consequence will be reduced investment and lower productivity compared to a firm owned by fully diversified shareholders.

(d) Summary

In summary, profit-sharing may be associated with improved company performance because of sharpened incentives, longer-term effects on the productivity of labour and improved organisation in the firm. The individual incentive arguments relate directly to profit-sharing but the improvement in productive skills could derive from any scheme which ties workers more closely to their company. Moreover the positive atmospheric or organisational arguments are most convincing when workers are given responsibility for decisions rather than just a share in profits. But this weakness of profit-sharing cuts both ways. For the same reasons the negative effects related to the restriction of managerial authority carry least weight for profit-sharing. The arguments that profit-sharing and other forms of participation could increase conflict and reduce productivity also appear to have some merit, so the overall effects of such schemes remain open to question at a theoretical level. We therefore turn to investigate some of these issues empirically.

THE EFFECTS OF PROFIT-SHARING ON COMPANY PERFORMANCE IN WESTERN EUROPE AND THE UNITED STATES

To the best of my knowledge, the first operational profit-sharing scheme was introduced by the distribution and retail corporation, Sears Roebuck, in 1916. The United States has continued to lead the way in this area, with some 280 000 voluntary profit-sharing schemes covering around seventeen million workers in 1983. Since 1975, tax concessions in the United States have been particularly generous towards employee stock ownership plans (ESOPs), stimulating the development of some 4000 active schemes by 1985 with more than seven million participants. The French in contrast have approached profit-sharing by legislation from the outset, with a law passed in 1967 which required all firms employing more than 100 people to give their employees a share in the companies' development, either via profits or a special investment fund based on capital. It would appear that the effects have been disappointing, largely because the schemes offered few financial advantages to either workers or firms and were strongly opposed by the French trade unions.

As was noted above, German legislation has favoured employee representation via workers' councils and worker directors, culminating in the unique system of co-determination rather than profit-sharing, which remains limited in scope. However a group of around seven hundred firms loosely associated with the AGP, an employers' federation committed to various forms of employee participation, do use a significant number of profit-sharing and employee stock ownership plans. One of the earliest schemes in Britain was developed in 1929 for the John Lewis Partnership, which pays its workers an annual bonus out of profit, in tradeable non-voting and fixed interest shares until 1970 and, since then, by preference of the workforce, in cash. The bonus has reached 20 per cent of average pay during the 1970s and 1980s. ICI's famous profit-sharing scheme began in 1954 and distributes immediately marketable shares to workers. This led the way for other major British companies including Bulmer and the Habitat Mothercare Group. Despite these successful examples, according to the Wider Share Ownership Council, only 2 per cent of British employees benefited from profit-sharing schemes in the late 1970s. However, in recent years, an increasing number of companies are turning to such schemes, a process encouraged by the 1978 and 1980 Finance Acts which empower the Inland Revenue to approve profit-sharing and savings-related share option schemes respectively for certain tax benefits on behalf of the employee and the company. The impact of this legislation has been large; Blanchflower and Oswald (1986) use the Workplace Industrial Relations Survey to estimate that in 1980 some 10 per cent of British workers in private manufacturing and non-manufacturing were eligible to participate in share ownership plans and some 5 per cent of them did so. Almost 40 per cent of those participating did so in schemes which were less than two years old. Around one thousand schemes had been approved by the Inland Revenue under the two Acts by 1986, and in addition there are hundreds of cash and a few share-based profit-sharing schemes under which the employee is liable for income tax on the benefits received.

Our brief survey of the empirical work in this area will commence by considering the effects of profit-sharing on worker and management attitudes and broader industrial relations and economic behaviour. We then go on to consider the effects on indicators of corporate performance: factor productivity and profitability. We conclude by attempting to distinguish between the effects of the differing forms of employee participation.

(a) Evidence on Attitudes, Industrial Relations and Economic Behaviour

Some of the best evidence about the changes in attitudes wrought by profit-sharing and employee share ownership come from West Germany and Britain. Cable and Fitzroy have undertaken a number of studies using a data base for 86 firms in three sectors of West German metal working industries which contain a wide range of quantitative and qualitative variables collected by interview survey methods. Some 48 per cent of firms employ some form of profit-sharing and the data also permit a fairly rigorous evaluation of the 'degree of participation' by workers in company decisions. According to Cable (1986), profit-sharing firms differ from traditional firms in tending to be larger (some 850 employees on average as against 463 for the rest of the sample) and to use more mass production or flow techniques. However, apart from a slightly lower proportion of skilled and male workers in profit-sharing firms, there are no significant differences with respect to labour force structure, training expenditures, the degree of unionisation, or labour turnover among skilled workers. Labour turnover among unskilled workers was, if anything, significantly higher in profit-sharing firms. This is fairly strong evidence against the proposition of output augmentation – relatively few of the attitudinal effects suggested by the theory show up in the West German sample.

The evidence for Britain is more positive. The Wider Share Ownership Council in 1985 reported the results of a questionnaire with 138 respondents, some 50 per cent of them operating profit-sharing schemes and 67 per cent savings-related share option schemes. The results concerning the perceived effectiveness of the schemes are reported in Table 4.1. Some 35 per cent of all respondents with profit-sharing schemes thought that there was some positive effect in each of the areas suggested by the questionnaire. The last two rows of Table 4.1 were not actually answers available in the questionnaire but represent the most common 'write-in' response. It can be seen that profit-sharing and saving-related schemes do appear to have positive though small effects for many respondents in most of the areas mentioned. This is not surprising since the typical amount of profit-sharing is small, around 3 per cent of salaries in the United Kingdom. The most significant effect was through improved employee loyalty or attitudes.

Blanchflower and Oswald (1986) also report the results of the

Table 4.1 Perceived effectiveness of share schemes

	Percentage of respondents with profit-sharing schemes answering		*Percentage of respondents with savings-related schemes answering*	
	Small effect	*Significant effect*	*Small effect*	*Significant effect*
Increased productivity	41	4	23	4
Improved loyalty or attitudes	45	32	40	20
Helped negotiations	36	4	18	2
Facilitated recruitment	35	9	30	5
Reduced staff turnover	36	3	23	5
Increased interest and understanding of company performance	4	7	2	8
Improved communication and feeling of involvement	3	1	1	1

Source: Employee Share Schemes; Copeman Paterson Ltd.

Industrial Participation Association Survey, published in the Income Data Services Study No. 357. The findings suggest that profit-sharing *is* perceived as providing some improvement in workers' attitudes towards the firm, with some 86 per cent of respondents agreeing or strongly agreeing with the suggestion that such schemes are good for the company and the employees; 66 per cent that it makes people take a greater interest in company results; and 65 per cent that it creates a better atmosphere. However typically only a small proportion, less than 10 per cent, 'strongly agree'. Some 47 per cent of respondents agree or strongly agree that profit-sharing strengthens people's loyalty to the firm, but some 34 per cent disagree with the same statement. Moreover the vast majority of respondents, 96 per cent, fail to see profit-sharing as a substitute for an adequate salary in the way that would be necessary for Weitzman-type effects. Even so, while 24 per cent of respondents feel that people are apathetic about profit-sharing, an outright majority of the sample, 51 per cent, disagree or strongly disagree with that statement. The findings from both studies are therefore mildly supportive of the view that, though profit-sharing is fairly small-scale, it is likely to improve company performance somewhat.

Estrin and Wilson (1986) report results from a sample of 52

medium-sized firms in the UK engineering and metal working sectors over the period 1978–82, some 40 per cent of which operate either a profit-sharing or value added cash bonus scheme over the entire period, providing an average 3 per cent of workers' pay. It was found that there are no significant differences between the profit-sharing and traditional firm sub-samples over the period with respect to output, employment, pay and other indicators of company behaviour. However as Table 4.2 below shows, significant differences do emerge with respect to important behavioural variables from the perspective of the theory. Thus there is significant evidence of improved atmosphere in profit-sharing firms; working days lost owing to strikes per employee are some 50 per cent lower while leaving rates and labour turnover levels for both skilled and unskilled workers are significantly reduced. There is also evidence that profit-sharing is acting as a substitute for individualised incentive schemes; the proportion of workers paid via piece rates are much lower in profit-sharing firms. However it would appear that profit-sharing does not act as a substitute for unionisation; in fact the proportion unionised in such firms is on average higher, as is the tendency for these schemes to emerge in companies more prone to unionisation, with a higher proportion of males in the labour force and with multiplant operations. While it is hard to establish causality, these data suggest that profit-sharing may in fact sharpen labour incentives, increase employee tenure and improve the industrial relations atmosphere as predicted by the theory, in which case we should expect to observe significant improvements in efficiency in such firms.

(b) Evidence on Productivity and Performance

Numerous case studies attest the possibilities for improved efficiency and performance in companies which introduce profit-sharing or employee stock ownership plans (see in particular Bradley and Gelb, 1986). However, convincing statistical evidence is still rare and is bedevilled by problems of causality: is profit-sharing merely an indicator of the true causal factor – 'good management' – rather than an independent determinant in its own right?

In his study, Cable (1986) does report average capital and labour productivities in the profit-sharing and non-profit-sharing groups. Both are in fact slightly higher in the profit-sharing group, by some 3 per cent and 10 per cent respectively, but the differences are not statistically significant. In the Estrin–Wilson sample, as can be seen in Table 4.2, there are also no significant differences in labour produc-

Table 4.2 Comparisons of means: profit-sharing and conventional firms in the UK metal working industry, 1982

	Non-Profit-Sharing	*Profit-Sharing*	
Working days lost due to strikes, etc. per employee	13.1	8.4	†
Quit rate	5.6	4.4	*
Percentage operatives paid in piece rates	22.8	16.3	*
Percentage labour force who are male	78.2	82.7	**
Turnover of unskilled workers	4.65	3.83	*
Turnover of skilled workers	4.34	3.51	*
Percentage of labour force unionised	72.0	87.8	*
Number of plants	1.4	1.6	*
Value added per worker	10.2	10.9	
Value added per unit of fixed assets	2.9	3.7	*
Rate of return on capital employed	−1.7	13.7	†

Source: Estrin and Wilson (1986). All value variables in thousands of pounds.
† denotes significant difference at 99% level.
* denotes significant difference at 95% level.
** denotes significant difference at 90% level.

tivity between the two groups of firms (value added per worker or per man hour), though the level is higher on average in the profit-sharing group. However the average productivity of capital (value added per unit of fixed assets) is significantly higher in profit-sharing firms, and by a considerable amount, over 20 per cent.

A technically more sophisticated way to analyse productivity effects is to estimate whether combined factor productivities – the quantity of value added produced by given amounts of capital and labour when factor proportions have been controlled for – are significantly affected by profit-sharing or other forms of employee participation. Studies of this form have been undertaken by Cable and Fitzroy (1980) for Germany, Jones and Svejnar (1985) for Italy and Defourny, Estrin and Jones (1985) for France, the latter two using large enterprise-level data sets primarily comprising worker-owned firms. All three studies report positive significant association between total factor productivity and the degree of participation in profits, equity and decision making, with profit-sharing providing the most consistent source of output enhancement. Thus, though the Cable–Fitzroy study draws heavily on participation indices, it also concludes that profit-sharing exerts a positive effect on company productivity. Jones and Svejnar link value added to factor inputs and numerous other proxies for participation, including the average payment to workers out of profits and average workers' capital stakes in the firm. Profit-sharing emerges as the most significant source of output augmentation, though individual worker ownership levels and the extent of participation also have a positive impact. Defourny, Estrin and Jones report that the typical productivity effect from participation is relatively small, around 5 per cent of output, with profit-sharing the most important source of productivity augmentation. These studies, though admittedly on fairly specialised samples, therefore strongly support the notion that profit-sharing improves corporate efficiency.

(c) Effects on Company Profitability

Findings on the relationship between profit-sharing and profitability are rather less clear-cut, though the broad direction of the evidence is still positive. Blanchflower and Oswald (1986) report on a number of American studies which compare the profitability of firms with and without employee share ownership plans. While the most widely quoted study, by Conte and Tannenbaum (1978) does find that profitability is on average higher in firms with employee ownership plans, the results are not statistically significant and the findings of more recent studies suggest either that there is no effect, or that firms with employee share ownership plans are actually less profitable than their conventional counterparts.

Using the German sample discussed above, Fitzroy and Kraft (1985) find that rate of return on capital is on average 21.8 per cent for firms with profit-sharing but only 14.3 per cent for firms without it. They use econometric methods to test for the effects of profit-sharing on profitability when other factors have been controlled for and with an explicit attempt to model the channels of reverse causality. Their findings strongly support a positive significant relationship between profitability and profit-sharing. The Estrin–Wilson study also finds statistically significant differences between average rates of return on capital in profit-sharing and non-profit-sharing firms. As can be seen from Table 4.2, while the average rate of return on capital is negative for the latter group in 1982, it averages 13 per cent in profit-sharing firms. While the actual levels of profitability vary considerably from year to year, the profit-sharing group maintains a statistically significant positive gap in every year between 1978 and 1982 except 1980.

Finally, Richardson and Nejad (1985) attempt to analyse the

relationship between financial participation by employees and profitability by comparing the share price performance of profit-sharing and non-profit-sharing firms between 1978 and 1982. If profit-sharing raises profitability, this should be reflected in the rate of change of the share price. They report that, over the period, the average annual share price change for a sample of companies with employee ownership schemes is 21 per cent, while for those without such schemes it is 16 per cent. These differences are statistically significant at the 10 per cent level. Though as always it is hard to infer causality from tests of this sort, these studies fail to refute the existence of a positive association between profit-sharing and company profitability.

(d) The Relative Impact of Different Forms of Participation

While the evidence is not overwhelming, the data quoted provide a *prima facie* case in favour of a positive relationship between various forms of workers' participation and corporate performance. We conclude this section with a brief and speculative discussion of whether one can identify differences in the scale of productivity enhancement according to the form of employee participation.

It should be noted at the outset that, despite the clear-cut conceptual distinctions between the different forms of employee participation, they cannot always be separated out convincingly in practice. Moreover many of the studies cited stress that the various forms of participation interact with each other to increase productivity. For example, Cable and Fitzroy view profit-sharing as likely to be more effective in the context of relatively more participative firms, while Jones and Svejnar highlight the interrelationships between profit-sharing and employee ownership.

If we commence by comparing profit-sharing in cash or in shares, using the Workplace Industrial Relations Survey, Blanchflower and Oswald (1986) investigate the impact of share-based schemes on investment and employment. Using data for 1980 which include schemes passed under the 1978 Finance Act, they find no significant differences in the United Kingdom between profit-sharing and non-profit-sharing firms with respect to either area of decision making. Though it is early to draw final conclusions, their study suggests that, if profit-sharing is to have an impact, it will be via cash rather than share-based schemes.

A few studies have compared the relative effects of different forms of participation from the perspective of the organisational behaviour literature. For example, Rosenberg and Rosenstein (1980) investigate the effects of workers' participation in a unionised foundry between 1969 and 1975, using an index of participative activity including factors such as the frequency of consultative meetings, the relevance of the topics discussed and the number of interchanges. They conclude that increases in productivity are significantly related to increases in participative activity, the association being much more important than that for a group bonus plan tied to productivity. They argue that profit-sharing might therefore not be an effective way to enhance productivity.

A number of important studies have been carried out by the Canadian, Professor Richard Long, as to the relative impact of employee share ownership and involvement in decision-making on workers' attitudes and organisational performance. On the basis of questionnaires sent to workers and managers in a medium-size regional trucking company, he concludes that share ownership and participation in decision-making do significantly increase workers' involvement, motivation and satisfaction, the ownership effects coming through despite a fairly small average investment. After comparing the separate impacts of the two, he concludes: 'Although share ownership does, in and of itself, appear to have beneficial effects on certain job attitudes, employee participation in decision-making appears generally to have stronger effects. Since it cannot be assumed that employees' share ownership will automatically lead to this increased participation, conscious efforts to develop effective employee participation need to be made' (Long, 1978 p. 761).

Finally, using the West German data set, Cable (1986) directly compares the effects of participation with the effects of profit-sharing on various dimensions of company behaviour. The data set is twice partitioned into two groups, the first according to whether or not firms operate profit-sharing schemes and the second using responses by workers and managers about their involvement in various company decisions from job design to investment to divide the sample into 'high' and 'low' participation groups. There is weak evidence that high profit-sharing and high participation go together, but profit-sharing is not necessarily associated with higher employee share ownership. Cable finds that on average participative firms are relatively smaller, spend more on training and apprentices and employ significantly more skilled workers. Though profit-sharing firms are more likely to use mass production techniques, participative firms tend to organise around smaller, more independent work groups and their control spans are therefore shorter. Unlike profit-sharing firms, on average, the participative group have significantly lower labour turnover, particularly for less skilled workers, but both sorts of firm display average or below average levels of unionisation. Finally, as for the profit-sharing group, participative firms have higher average levels of capital and labour productivity than their more traditional counterparts, significantly so with respect to capital.

Overall, Cable's findings suggest that company performance will be improved in certain ways by both profit-sharing and employee involvement in decision making. However some of the most important elements highlighted by economic theory, including labour turnover rates, work patterns and the organisational and industrial relations atmosphere, are affected more by employee participation in decision making than by profit-sharing. As Cable concludes 'profit-sharing . . . appears to be more a matter of substituting group for individual incentives in certain categories of traditional production'.

CONCLUSIONS

Despite the pessimistic predictions of some analysts, the fragments of evidence so far accumulated suggest that increased employee participation in profits, in shares or in decision making, is often associated with improved industrial relations, organisational efficiency, factor productivity and profitability. There is no magic formula involved and counter-examples exist, but in several different countries the average effects appear to be small, but positive and significant.

These findings have broader implications than just for the efficiency of individual firms; they suggest that employee participation could increase employment. If average labour productivity is greater in firms operating such schemes, the search for maximal levels of profit will induce more employment provided wages are not increased disproportionately. This is because, if a given labour force has a higher average and marginal product with profit-sharing, it is profitable to increase employment to drive marginal product down to the going wage rate. This proposition is supported by the Estrin–Wilson study, which finds labour demand for a given wage to be some 13 per cent higher in profit-sharing firms, the bulk of the difference probably deriving from productivity enhancement.

Our findings indicate two possible deficiencies with the current British government's proposals to foster profit-sharing via tax benefits. In the first place, it is not clear that the greatest impact on productivity and profits derives from profit-sharing, as distinct from employee share ownership or participation, particularly in 'low level' decisions. The interrelationships in this area are not yet well understood, but the evidence suggests that profit-sharing works primarily as a specific sort of group incentive scheme, the impact of which will be blunted in large or diversified organisations, while the effects of employee share ownership and participation may be rather more deep-rooted. In the light of the interactive effects between the different forms noted in several studies, and given the primitive state of our knowledge in this area, it seems wise for government policy to foster experiments across a broad range of employee participation schemes rather than concentrate efforts on one particular approach, profit-sharing.

Moreover the findings relate to a rather lower level of profit-sharing than has been discussed in some quarters and than is implied by the Weitzman scheme, typically less than 10 per cent of workers' incomes. The positive incentive effects may be offset by workers' reaction to the increased riskiness of their income stream if, as was suggested in earlier government proposals, say 25 per cent of incomes are derived from profit-sharing, although recent government initiatives seem to be aimed initially at rather lower levels than this.

Finally, as we have noted, unlike the situation with Professor Weitzman's scheme, motivational arguments provide no case for permanent public subsidy of profit-sharing. Employee participation can lower the cost of monitoring workers, raise productivity and increase profits, all phenomena which would be gladly welcomed by many companies. Since employee participation is typically in the interests of the people who introduce it, there is no inherent reason for government involvement, except perhaps to provide publicity and information. More realistically, there is likely to be managerial inertia and the introduction of such schemes may generate significant short-term costs, a major counter-incentive for many firms. This implies that the government should provide temporary subsidies to firms during the introduction of profit-sharing and other forms of employee participation, but that these should be withdrawn when the schemes are operating successfully.

Note

1. This is an extended version of a lecture delivered in the House of Commons on 24 June 1986. Saul Estrin is a Research Fellow at the London School of Economics.

5 Collective Bargaining, Economic Management and Employment[1]

David Basnett

INTRODUCTION

Perhaps it seems a novel thought that 'collective bargaining' and 'employment' are concepts worthy of consideration together. Often a very crude and unthinking assumption is made that the former is the enemy of the latter. Yet the value of the Employment Institute lies in providing a framework in which all of us who share the basic view that the economy can be managed to provide fuller employment, can assess the contribution our own organisations can make.

Amongst practitioners of collective bargaining, there is an enormous frustration with the prevalence of the view that bargaining is a *problem* to be contained or suppressed. We seem to be caught between two very inadequate schools of thought. One holds that trade unions – and trade unionists – must be weakened in order that free market forces can operate without impediment. Flexibility, in other words, must rule supreme. The other holds that the economy's problems can only be put right by extensive state intervention of a sort which does not welcome the contribution which trade unions can make. This view elevates state power to a level which promises greatly – but which has little respect for the *independent* role of unions and their members.

The approach of the present government has been to suppress collective bargaining using the crudest kind of twin-track approach. One track has been a legislative assault on trade union rights and organisation, designed to narrow the scope and agenda of lawful trade unionism. The second track has been an economic policy which, by the severity of the recession it created, drastically reduced the level of bargaining activity. A major theme in what follows is that it is the very survival of collective bargaining under this unprecedented pressure that is the remarkable phenomenon of the 1980s.

Neither the government nor supporters of a more interventionist approach by the state (including a mix of crude pay limits and bureaucratic state planning) has appreciated that collective bargaining is something which trade unionists have built up as the instrument of *solving* problems. So the second theme of this chapter is that the extension of collective bargaining is an important route to planning and managing the economy.

We need to consider how to combine two central vital requirements. First, how to rebuild and give back confidence to structures of collective bargaining. This will be an essential component of the process of widening democracy throughout our society after a series of attacks on freedom and democratic involvement. Second, how to carry this process through in a way that contributes directly to national economic goals.

My intention is to help in the preparation of this task. It is a different route from the more mechanistic prescriptions of monetarists on the one hand and those of macroeconomists with a distrust of pay bargaining on the other. It is, however, a route which is more attuned to the real pressures and priorities which we face.

To bring this argument out I shall examine the present state of collective bargaining and some of its complexities, and explore the implications for public policy. I shall go on to discuss how far the policies already drawn up by the TUC, and agreed between the TUC and the Labour Party, match up to these implications, and the areas where further talking is needed. A particular issue to be addressed is the part that can be played by a Fair Wages Strategy, the need for which was stressed in the 1985 TUC–Labour Party Liaison Committee document, *A New Partnership. A New Britain*.

So far as wages and salaries are concerned my central argument is this. The management of the economy to provide higher employment puts a responsibility on the major economic institutions to ensure that the factors under their control do not move in an aberrant way. If wage pressures were to lead to destabilising price movements, or had no regard to productivity trends, the result would be unsettling for an agreed strategy for jobs. That is the argument for unions taking account of wider factors in wage movements.

Experience in the past has shown, however, that any approach to incomes policies which is designed simply to put the lid on collective bargaining is doomed to failure. A policy for collective bargaining which contributes some stability to wage costs without undermining its own survival as an essential social process, seems to me to require the following:

(a) a foundation of fairness in terms of who gets what, and how they get it;
(b) a strategy which relates the policy to discussion of the constraints and opportunities in the economy year by year;
(c) a visible pay-off for those who make sacrifices. This could be higher employment in some areas. But given the difficulty of matching up contribution and pay-back there should be a general widening of involvement in economic decisions;
(d) some sort of 'insurance policy', providing an allowance for contingencies, fall-backs and good old-fashioned mistakes.

These are thoughts which I try to pursue in what follows. There are gaps. There are – I have no doubt – weak points in the argument; and there are some declarations of faith. But I am not ashamed of putting it forward, warts and all, because this is a crucial area in which we need to feel our way forward and not be afraid to have genuine debate. And that should go for the employers too.

For the trade unions a key purpose of the debate must be to establish that an extension of collective bargaining can make an effective contribution to democratic economic management and planning. But an overriding objective must also be to set out the principles of behaviour in the first year of an expansionist government.

COLLECTIVE BARGAINING TODAY

The Government's Attack on Bargaining

The assault on trade unionism and collective bargaining has been central to the government's programme. It has been an attack carried out across a broad front. The deliberate and explicit use of mass unemployment as an instrument of social and economic policy has of course been a major ingredient.

It is worth stressing the importance of this by recalling the near-universal view prior to 1979 that breaking the postwar consensus against mass unemployment would for evermore be politically unacceptable. What happened in practice was that the rapid increase in unemployment in the early 1980s led to fear and insecurity with a corresponding lowering of expectations and bargaining activity.

At the same time privatisation and contracting-out of public service functions was conceived and carried through in large part as an industrial relations policy. The aim was to break up and undermine trade union structures in areas whose growth had been crucial to the trade union movement's fortunes in the previous two decades. Closely linked to this was the aggressive use of the government's own position as employer – unilaterally tearing up the pay research agreement in the civil service, creating the conditions for the 1980 strike in the steel industry and later disputes in the NHS and mining and so on.

It is the direct legislative changes introduced by the government, however, that constitute the other central feature of their attack. The main elements of those changes can be summarised in the following way. First, by greatly narrowing the definition of a 'trade dispute' the scope of lawful trade union activity was sharply restricted. In effect, in a period in which employers were organising and operating in increasingly sophisticated and integrated ways, trade unions were debarred from mobilising an effective response which, say, involved solidarity action.

Second, very heavy penalties were designed for any union action which strayed beyond these boundaries and quite explicit encouragement was given to a more litigious pattern of industrial relations behaviour. Third, a whole series of measures amounting to state interference in the internal workings of independent organisations was implemented. The fact that these measures were advanced in terms of accountability and democracy should not obscure the primary motivation: to wrap unions up in a series of resource-wasting and time-consuming diversions at the expense of their organising and negotiating functions.

Just as important – though less remarked upon – has been the removal of legislative support for collective bargaining. The removal of the Fair Wages Resolution ended a measure which since the last century had given some basic protection to those working on contracts for central government and local authorities. In much the same way Schedule 11 of the Employment Protection Act – scrapped in 1980 – had provided a valuable procedure for ensuring that the terms of collective agreements could be properly applied. Now we have the attack on the Wages Councils and the direct encouragement of second-class employment.

The underlying theme of this legislative project has been not just to minimise the area of joint discussion and agreement but also to promote a particular model for trade unionism. This model has been made quite explicit in a series of statements, especially the notorious 'Blue Paper' on Employment (Department of Employment, 1985). In it, collective organisation and negotiation is limited to the place of work and to the 'bread and butter' issues that affect people there. Any further role beyond these confines is seen on the one hand as 'political' and therefore unacceptable (a difficult proposition to maintain now in the wake of the avalanche of YES votes in the political fund ballots) or on the other hand as economically distorting and an obstacle to flexibility in the labour market.

There are a number of comments which can be made about this model. One is that it is based upon a fallacy or myth. The fact is that many issues that affect workers at the work-place cannot be solved at that level because they stem from decisions taken elsewhere: that is the central argument for extending collective bargaining. A health and safety problem in a particular plant, or a dispute over bonus earnings, may well be bound up with a corporate decision to introduce a new work system or technological process.

If such issues are to be resolved through negotiation and agreement – and it is very important that they should be – it is essential that trade union structures and collective bargaining are extended to corporate level. Even this may be insufficient. To get to grips adequately with some of the really big industrial problems which we face, a response is required beyond the level of the firm, at the strategic level of the sector. This was indeed one of the most important and innovative features of the Industrial Strategy of the 1970s. In effect the message was that the extension of collective bargaining into decisions at sector level was the route to agreed decisions on industrial policy. It was also seen as the way to make more sense of issues affecting individual companies and plants. I would argue that not enough resources or effort were put into this aspect of the industrial strategy. But there were some signal successes: the Wool Textiles Scheme for example. This was in essence a rationalisation scheme set up for a sector with over-capacity; but it brought the unions into the heart of it by requiring their agreement on a company-by-company basis.

What is indisputable is that it was exactly this innovative trend in collective bargaining and strategic industrial policy that the present government brought to a sudden end. Trade union involvement in the instruments of industrial strategy and finally the strategy itself were effectively terminated within the first year or so of their taking office. Thereafter the disappearance of any coherence in industrial policy went hand in hand with the precipitate collapse of manufacturing industry.

Employers' Attitudes

I have spent some time talking exclusively of government attitudes and actions because the attack on collective bargaining owes much more to the rhetoric of Tory dogma and myths than to any analysis of the real world. The attitudes and behaviour of employers have on the other hand been more complex. There have, it is true, been some quite spectacular instances of wild *macho management*. These have constituted more or less a fringe, however, and have tended to be in the public sector. The instances are ones with which we are all very familiar.

At the other extreme is a core of traditionally progressive employers who have continued to maintain decent standards of industrial relations behaviour. These are the ones who acted on the real lessons of the 1930s: that apparent gains in managerial power made during recessions can carry with them great costs in terms of grievances and resentment in future years.

Between these two extremes there has been a considerable mix of experience. There have been attempts in some sectors to decentralise bargaining, either on a regional or a divisional basis. There have also been instances of fairly major overhauls of payment systems. It would be hard to describe this as a unified or concerted strategic push on the part of employers. The *ad hoc*, the hand-to-mouth and the quick fix have predominated.

Certainly, however, there have been plenty of instances of employers trying to by-pass or undermine existing industry-wide structures. This has been a fairly constant feature across a range of sectors although it has varied in intensity. In some cases quality circles have been deliberately used to set up structures which compete with negotiating structures. Briefing groups, newsletters and other forms of management 'communications' have been used in order to weaken the flows of information between union members and representatives and strengthen an employer's ability unilaterally to set the agenda. In yet other instances employers have used consultation – setting up or reviving joint consultative committees – as a pre-emptive tactic:

trying to ensure that certain issues do not become collectively bargained but stay instead within channels over which management exercises more control. This was perhaps best summed up by a personnel manager who was quoted in a TUC survey as saying, 'We have a policy of workers' involvement; but we want it to stop short of actual involvement'.

The Survival of Bargaining

This then is a picture of bargaining coming under attack. It is an attack marked on the one side by legislative measures which directly confront trade unions and reduce the scope of bargaining and on the other side by employer attempts to side-step or by-pass union-based negotiating structures.

So in the face of this pressure it is the survival of collective bargaining that is such a striking feature of the 1980s. Compare the dire predictions with what has actually happened. Far from being marginalised or made to appear irrelevant, trade unions and collective bargaining have emerged in robust shape as the process which actually delivers the goods. This can be seen by looking at three measures: the presence of trade unions in the economy; the extent to which active bargaining is taking place; and the scope of that bargaining.

As far as the first of these is concerned the figures speak for themselves. There has been a sharp drop in absolute trade union membership, from a peak of 12 million in 1979 to just under 10 million by 1986. But this is almost solely a function of the terrible drop in employment caused by government policies. The density of union membership – the proportion of employees in employment who belong to unions – has not dropped nearly as sharply. It has moved from just over 50 per cent to around 45 per cent in six years. Of course this is not to strike a complacent note or to ignore the very important shifts in the employment structure which pose new challenges to unions. But it is to stress that, after the worst recorded slump and a string of hostile laws, unions – far from being beaten back to the fringes – continue to represent more or less half of the labour force.

On the second aspect, the activity rate of bargaining, some recent evidence shows that the number of shop stewards has declined less rapidly than jobs in their plants, leading to an increase in their proportionate position. The evidence also shows a high level of activity and influence on the part of shop stewards, across the range of industries.

The third aspect, the scope of the bargaining agenda, is touched upon by evidence stressing the importance which many employers attach to continuity in their relationships with unions. The evidence highlights the fact that, in a period marked by major decisions on structural change, employers have by and large chosen to pursue these by negotiated solutions. This observation has to be qualified, of course, in respect of those instances where employers have chosen to use structural change as an excuse to confront and attack trade unions.

It has also to be acknowledged that the balance of power within the negotiating relationship has swung towards employers. But the inescapable fact is that experience in the real world is utterly removed from the 'union-free' fantasies of the Conservative Party's ideologues. Indeed the few instances in which thorough-going attempts have been made to drive unions out – and at present we need look no further than Wapping – stand out very much as exceptions. Events at Wapping have shown that under this government's laws an unscrupulous employer can tear up agreements and leave workers without any comeback. They have also shown, however, the huge costs entailed in doing so, and they have suggested that that cost is unacceptable.

Where there has been a genuine search for solutions to problems it has been change through agreement, not the Norman Tebbit guide to practical living, that has shown the way to lasting benefits.

The Bargaining Agenda

If the structures of collective bargaining emerged as unexpected survivors in the early 1980s, the agenda of issues with which it has had to deal has certainly evolved. Beneath the surface a huge increase is taking place in the complexity of the structure and content of the bargaining system.

In this section I want to illustrate some of these complexities. In doing so I hope to generate a debate where at present silence reigns. My argument is that many parts of the complex of issues stem from this government's policy. They are content to try simply to squeeze the lid down on this particular pot: it will be their bequest to a future government that actually wants to tackle unemployment. My fear is that before even analysing these pressures such a government will decide that it too has to squeeze a lid down (albeit a different form of lid) on the bargaining system. But this is running ahead of my argument. Let us first have a look at some of the pressures and complexities.

The operative level of bargaining. Here there are conflicting pressures at work, especially in manufacturing. There is the pull towards corporate level bargaining on issues such as pensions and training. On the other side is the push – often opportunistic – towards decentralising decisions on pay towards local bargaining. The extent to which this has occurred is patchy and some companies have zigzagged through a confusing set of changes.

The overall effect of these pressures has been to complicate the structure of bargaining in this important respect: it is now less clear at what level the critical decisions are taken which have knock-on effects elsewhere. More than ever before the various levels of bargaining are all important. All must be involved in any concerted attack on economic problems and it would be a mistake to try and override any one of these. One important relevant finding which has emerged is the extent to which many firms in the private sector have succeeded in isolating their internal labour markets from external pressures – including the pressure of government pronouncements on pay levels or norms.

Pay Anomalies. There has been a colossal build-up of pay anomalies, grievances and pressures during the period of neglect of the last seven years. Space permits only illustrations of this:

(a) Public service pay has fallen by between 15 and 20 per cent below its 1979 comparable level.
(b) The relative pay of women, having moved upwards in the wake of the Sex Discrimination Act, has fallen back again. The current series of equal value cases is showing how badly most pay structures need reforming in order to eliminate systematic discrimination.
(c) District comparisons, a vital contribution to the 'glue' of the pay system, lost statutory support when the government abolished Schedule 11 of the Employment Protection Act. Since then long-established pay relationships have become hopelessly distorted.
(d) Skill differentials, the impact on which of the Social Contract was singled out for attack by the Tories at the time, are in a mess.

Figure 5.1 Winners and losers

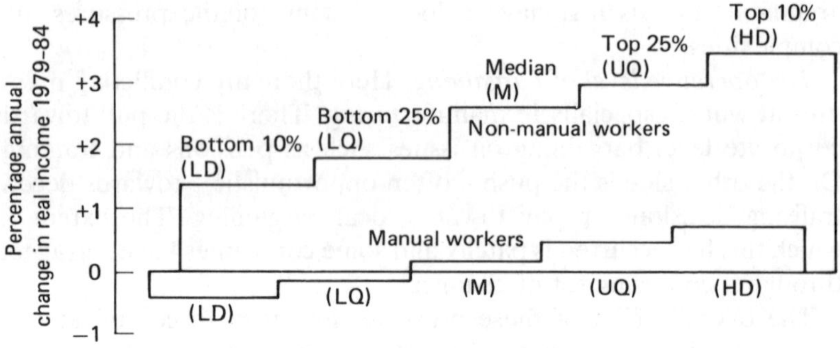

Note: Diagram shows annual percentage changes in real earnings, 1979 to 1984, for those on the respective quantile points. The top line is non-manual workers; bottom line is manual workers.
Source: New Earnings Survey.

> Engineering craftsmen such as toolmakers and fitters, for example, have on average received no increase in real pay since 1979. This is aggravated by the general cutback in training during the recession leading to the absurdity of skill shortages in some areas while four million are unemployed.

Low Pay. Under this government the low pay problem has developed to the point where in Britain in 1986 over a million workers earned less than £100 a week. The poverty which this represents cannot be allowed to continue.

Growth of Inequality of Income. Figure 5.1 merits reflection. It is reproduced from the 1985 TUC Economic Review. This picture is drawn from nationwide information (the New Earnings Survey). It reflects the power of systematic inequality cutting right across the structure of individual collective agreements.

Employment patterns. The labour market has changed substantially since 1979. There is scope for debate about how many of these changes are permanent or cyclical, but the extent of them is not in question. The combination of recession, sectoral restructuring and changes from technology has left its mark. Amongst the most noticeable effects are the large rise in part-time employment of women in service sectors (but not manufacturing), the overall decline in full-time employment – especially for men – and significant changes in skill categories.

Implications for Public Policy

When these developments are considered together it is clear that they present a series of new and complex issues. These issues face both negotiators and those involved in drawing up and implementing public policy, especially concerning employment. Again my approach has to be illustrative but let me set out some examples of these issues. My purpose is not to attempt definitive answers to them. Instead it is to stress the extent of the complexity and the hopeless inadequacy of simplistic responses based on single norms or rules.

There are three obvious examples of such issues. The first concerns *poverty*. What is the most effective mixture of action on pay rates and improvements in targets to attack poverty? The contours of the poverty map have shifted over recent years. There is a major problem of poverty wages across some whole sectors – textiles, catering, distribution, for example – and occupations which must be tackled through the structure of earnings. Another major factor in poverty derives from the circumstances of parts of the population. Old age, unemployment and family responsibilities are major contributors. Action beyond wage bargaining will be required to make significant improvements on this: action in particular to improve benefits – child benefit, supplementary benefit and pensions. Above all there is the fact that poverty in Britain today is largely reflected in women's living standards. Action is therefore required on the systematic discrimination (often built into long-established pay structures) and the limited opportunities for economic fairness which face women.

The second example concerns *relative earnings*. There is a widespread acceptance in the trade union movement, and beyond, that the principle of fair comparison should be available for use in the public services. The present government's abolition of the Comparability Commission, their scrapping of the Fair Wages Resolution and their unilateral breaching of the pay review arrangement in the civil service are seen as major contributors to the huge backlog of pay anomalies throughout the public services.

Just to say that we believe in comparability, however, is not enough. A string of issues then arises. For example, there is no point in instituting a procedure which compares low-paid workers in the public sector with low-paid workers outside as the basis for pay determination. Our commitment to ending poverty wages points more to the sort of system used by the Pay Research Unit for the civil service before its abolition. One merit of the system was that it excluded comparisons with clearly exploited sections of workers. We should certainly be guided by the fact that it would be disastrous to establish a new system of comparability for the predominantly female public service areas of employment which simply reflects and reinforces the sex bias that prevails in the most backward areas of the private sector.

There are other issues, beyond the tension between comparability and giving priority to action on low pay. How many comparability bodies do we need? One overall commission or individual procedures for the different branches of the public services? What would the relationship be to the local authorities and their secretariat, LACSAB? These issues are not insoluble but they do require some detailed – and fairly urgent – attention.

The third example is of an issue linked in with the tendency towards a dual labour market. There is legitimate debate about the extent and nature of this tendency. What is not in doubt however is the pressure from employers towards *skills that are specific to the firm* rather than belonging to an occupational trade. This is a key feature of the internal labour market where firms poach skilled workers from other companies and then contribute only training which is of direct benefit to them. The problem that this causes against a background of cuts in public support for training is that it does not do enough to protect and advance cross-company vocational skills. Yet we do have significant shortfalls in key areas such as computer-skilled trades, electronics engineering, and some construction skills. Our bargaining strategies and pay structures will have to grapple effectively with these issues.

THE NEW PARTNERSHIP

So far the themes of this chapter have been twofold: the survival of the structures of collective bargaining and the complexity of many of the issues with which it has to deal. A lot of this thinking is implicit in the lines of policy which have emerged from discussion between the TUC and the Labour Party in recent years. In particular the statement produced in 1985 by the TUC–Labour Party Liaison Committee, *A New Partnership. A New Britain*, is built on this analysis.

A Fair Wages Strategy

In two central ways collective bargaining and its extension is at the heart of policy development. The first is the notion of a Fair Wages Strategy. The passage of the joint statement which dwelt on such a strategy is set out below:

> The next Labour Government will thus need a strategy for fair wages. This will entail restoring provisions scrapped by the present Government, such as Schedule 11 and the Fair Wages Resolution, and building on the 'equal value' amendment to the Equal Pay Act. In the light of the Government's attack on Wages Councils, we are considering the whole scope of statutory support and whether it can be developed in a more comprehensive way than before. In particular, we must end low pay and reduce insecurity, especially for public sector workers, by establishing agreed comparability mechanisms. Negotiators could use these mechanisms when required to prevent incomes from getting out of line and to ensure a proper rate for the job.

The significance of this passage is that the concept of 'fair' is seen to apply to the procedures by which pay is determined as well as the actual level of pay which results. It envisages extensive rights to comparability and to arbitration and it involves the whole gamut of statutory support needed to end low pay and reduce insecurity of employment. As far as unions are concerned it reflects very much the push to develop a more coherent approach to the value of people's jobs – one which does not substitute for bargaining and organisation but assists trade unions to overcome problems arising from the weakness of some groups.

A National Minimum Wage

Also bound up very closely with this is the question of a *statutory* national minimum wage – a policy which in the past has divided opinion among trade unionists but support for which has grown substantially in recent years. That support is still by no means unanimous, however, and the TUC's position (in spring 1986) is that there should be an examination of the minimum wage issue, including joint discussions with the Labour Party.

The striking factor is that the emerging shape of this examination is very much concerned with the type of issues I have been discussing. Examples are: In what form should Wages Councils be re-established? How should their scope and coverage be determined?

How can we distinguish between unfair differentials (such as those based on sex discrimination) which may be squeezed, and differentials which are seen as fair because they reflect legitimate notions of skill and responsibility? How should we deal with the consequences in particular sectors where the short-term impact is likely to be large?

Industrial Relations and Industrial Democracy

The debate about the national minimum wage and its contribution to an overall Fair Wages Strategy is guided by the need to underpin and support – and not undermine – collective bargaining. Interestingly this is increasingly the attitude behind the discussions on industrial relations legislation. There is a widely emerging consensus that the positive framework of law which we seek to put in place of the present government's legislation should not be discussed in terms of the legal status, powers and immunities of trade unions so much as the rights and abilities of individuals and workers collectively to organise and act and be treated decently as employees collectively.

In other words, the extension of collective bargaining and of industrial democracy should be at the heart of our proposals. This in turn means that policies on workers' rights and trade union organisation should be seen as an integral part of the approach to economic strategy. The reason is that the focus is put on the question of what we want the law to do, what functions to support and what positive outlets for trade unions to facilitate.

In fact this takes us directly into areas in which, behind the scenes, a lot of thinking has been done in recent years. Extending the scope of bargaining into new areas of decision making is not simply a question of national level contacts between trade unions, employers and government – important though that level can be on occasions. Rather it is a question of building on the experience of local economic initiatives, enterprise boards and product and efficiency bargaining to provide a systematic and creative trade union input at all levels of decision making.

The statutory underpinning which this requires has two angles. The first is to provide a series of new rights in the areas of information, disclosure, consultation and representation. These could be fitted together in the way that best builds on the circumstances of the particular bargaining unit. The second is to link industrial planning decisions and assistance by the government with agreed business plans between companies and their trade union representatives. In this way planning itself would become a spur to industrial democracy, giving working people new responsibilities in areas such as investment, new technology and all the wider areas from which they are presently shut out.

When a government tries to put an end to unemployment and sets out to work in concert with the trade unions our aim will be to find agreed answers to these issues and at the same time to widen the democratic involvement of workers and their unions. Whatever else that entails, it will not mean a quiet life. It will require a substantial increase in bargaining activity at all levels. It is vital to recognise this point and to reject any approach which seeks solutions in a further suppression of collective bargaining.

COLLECTIVE BARGAINING AND ECONOMIC MANAGEMENT

Building on Strength

So far I have been concerned to stress the value of collective bargaining as an instrument of democratic advance and of problem solving. I have also aired some of the complexities and pressures which have built up in recent years. The theme of this section is that these complexities should be seen as a source of strength, not of embarrassment. They are after all a measure of our standing as practitioners in the real world rather than as abstract theoreticians. They also indicate that collective bargaining should be directed towards curbing the excesses of market forces so that the market system can deliver for labour.

If we can accept that proposition then I hope that we can move on to a further one. That is that it is vital to avoid treating some areas as taboo or policy 'no go' areas. Traditional concepts of 'free' collective bargaining are not robust enough to carry all the weight of our policy aspirations. The danger is – as this decade has demonstrated – that this will simply lead to unions being constrained within a ghetto called 'free' collective bargaining and further and further removed from an ability to meet our members' priorities.

In fact I have long believed that the opposition expressed within unions to interference with 'free' collective bargaining is more a rejection of traditional style incomes policies than a declaration of faith in the justice and efficiency of untrammelled collective bargaining. There is no sharp line which divides the sphere of collective bargaining from that of other instruments of policy, nor should we try and draw one. *But that in turn means that collective bargaining cannot proceed as if it were untouched or uninformed by developments in other spheres of activity.*

There is an imperative towards talking about the linkages and the consequences of actions on one plane for another one. The consequence of not talking about the full range of policy issues in this way may be that we find ourselves without contingency plans. Indeed the result may well be worse. If we failed to address the full agenda we could lurch from a period of turning a blind eye to certain problem areas to one of crisis management and panic action. Under such circumstances the lesson from my experience is that there is a terrible danger of panic action, leading to solutions that are more third rate than second best, but to which we then have to devote all our available political energy.

So a thorough debate is important. It must involve all the principal actors and it must aim to produce clear and widely understood objectives. It should be a debate which contributes to a process of economic management which allows for the planning of contingencies, for fall-backs and for the inevitability of the unexpected! It is in such a context that I, and many others, have stated that this would entail an understanding that, if all aspects of national economic management are on the agenda, then so will wage determination be on the agenda.

Agreeing on the Problem

In this section I want to move on from the general proposition about the need for negotiating change at the national level. My intention is to address the specific issue of the movement of costs in the economy. Inflation is a prime example of the type of subject we should not make a taboo. There is a fear of inflation and, in some quarters, there is an even bigger fear of talking about inflation. My direct and bitter experience is that if we run scared of inflation we will at some stage run into a crisis and find ourselves with very few options. At that point the likelihood is that we will be bounced into a course of action that will be neither popular nor, in the medium to long term, tenable.

In trying, carefully, to initiate a debate on this issue, it is first necessary to dispose of those propositions with which I do not agree. The first of these is that fiscal expansion – action to defeat unemployment – will feed straight into inflation. This view is held by a variety of groups and individuals and is expressed with varying degrees of emphasis. At heart it is a view that the structure of the economy is now such that any increase in GDP will 'split' more towards monetary movement (that is, prices) than towards real output and therefore jobs.

While acknowledging the extent to which industry's capital stock has been diminished by the recession, I regard this argument as pessimistic to the point of fatalism. With unemployment at a 'true' level of anything up to four million and considerable unused capacity in industry there is plenty of scope for expansion without stoking up a dramatic inflationary surge. This would be even more the case if an expansionary policy gave priority to infrastructure investment on the one hand and public services on the other. In both cases unused resources can be matched directly to unmet needs so there would be direct production and employment effects.

A second proposition which I think should be discounted is that the United Kingdom is particularly prone to inflation. The notion that wage inflation in particular is somehow a 'British disease' goes quite deep into national mythology. That may or may not be true. But if there *is* something distinctive about inflation and the United Kingdom it is probably the openness, through the trading and financial systems, to internationally generated price movements rather than to any internal inflationary pressures.

This has been argued recently by Wilfred Beckerman, who has demonstrated the importance of international commodity prices for UK inflation. Indeed he infers that the recent reduction in UK inflation has very little to do with domestic policy but derives mostly from the 'softness' of international price movements. I would not push the argument so far. It remains intuitively plausible to me that if you engineer the sharpest ever slump in industrial output in the United Kingdom one of the consequences will be a slow-down in price rises.

There is a final proposition which, in its simple form, I wish to dispute as the basis for a proper analysis of inflation. This holds that there is something inherently inflationary in the collective bargaining system; that rapid and generalised wage inflation will rear its ugly head the moment that the brakes are released. Now it is clearly wrong to assert that there is no connection between fiscal policy and inflation. Equally it is misguided to believe that what happens to wages has no bearing on the course of prices. But it is also wrong –

and a disastrous basis for policy making – to think that there is 'a' unique and straightforward wages problem.

The whole thrust of my argument has been about the enormous variations in the circumstances and experiences of particular bargaining groups. The pressures that have built up are complex and differentiated, not homogeneous. It would therefore be a critical mistake to base policy on the expectation of a generalised and uniform wage cost pressure. This is not, of course, to dispute the undoubted linkages which exist between various parts of the bargaining system. The implications of that are discussed later.

Having spent some time clearing the ground of propositions about inflation and wages with which I disagree, let me now spell out the one with which I agree. It was well put by Lord McCarthy in his recent Fabian pamphlet *Freedom at Work* (McCarthy, 1985). The argument concerns a government which is trying to expand the economy and the key phrase is: 'What it [the government] should seek to avoid is a general escalation of earnings, which gathers growing force as employment expands until it endangers the Government's plans for the economy'.

The emphasis here is on the dangers of disturbance, uncertainty and disorder. This is surely the right emphasis and the correct basis from which to proceed. The worry of people concerning the prospects of an expansionary government is twofold. The first fear is that 'go' will shudder into 'stop' with a messy and politically damaging interlude. The second and connected fear is that a backlog of competing claims on real resources will, in the absence of any framework for regulating them, express themselves in disorder and escalation. In both cases the worry is – if you will excuse the trade union jargon – at least as much about procedure as about the substantive outcome.

How Does the Policy Match Up?

Now the interesting point is that when the problem is defined in these terms it can be seen that existing TUC policies – particularly those contained in the New Partnership statement – do measure up to a considerable extent. In particular they do go a long way to providing the framework within which changes, realignments and the correction of anomalies can take place without creating a damaging sense of overall instability.

Let me spell this out in terms of some of the key pressure points. The first is the *public services*. There is a widespread acknowledgement of the systematic discrimination that millions of workers, including some of the very lowest paid, have experienced since 1980. This was highlighted by the recent iniquitous decision to reserve the use of comparability mechanisms almost exclusively for the top paid public servants.

There is a public commitment in joint TUC–Labour Party statements that comparability will be available to negotiators in the public services as appropriate. This is matched by an understanding in the public services that anomalies that have developed over seven years cannot be put right within seven days. Awards will have to be phased in, and ground caught up by degree. That, I believe, can be accepted so long as the guarantee of systematic and purposeful movement towards righting this particular wrong is a firm one.

Rather the same considerations apply in the case of *low pay*. Again there is a widespread acceptance that there is a legitimate case for this being a priority area for action. The fear that such action will simply jack up the whole wages structure is reflected in policy in two ways. The first is acknowledgement that many aspects of low pay need to be tackled within the bargaining group – or indeed by widening the bargaining group. The current agreement for local authority manual workers shows exactly how progress can be made through a combination of eliminating the bottom grades and carrying out a thorough-going joint job evaluation.

The second way is the growing realisation that any across-the-board minimum wage would have to be accompanied by measures to deal with the economic circumstances of specific sectors; that it too would need to be phased in; and that it would apply overwhelmingly to women workers. A key fact on this last point is that in the wake of the Equal Pay Act differentials between men and women *were* changed significantly.

As far as the *private sector* is concerned our policy commitments emphasise the need for machinery that allows for orderly adjustment. Measures equivalent to the Fair Wages Resolution and Schedule 11 of the Employment Protection Act, together with the possible extension of rights to arbitration, would go a long way towards providing a framework for settling anomalies.

Above all there is the greater acceptance that it is impossible to address all aspects of living standards purely through the wage packet. Our members and their families are more and more concerned with the social wage aspects of their standard of living. Housing, transport, education, social services and, for far too many, social security are very important aspects of their lives. They look upon trade unions as one of the mechanisms whereby they seek to improve these aspects of the quality of life. Sometimes they recognise the trade-off between the individual wage and the social wage and are prepared to weigh one with another. They may certainly have a recognition of the advantages of this if they have an involvement in the process of drawing up priorities. In any event workers certainly expect their unions to have some influence on the social wage as broadly defined.

A PROGRAMME FOR THE FIRST YEAR

The message from the previous section is that the main components of a framework for orderly bargaining can already be found in the various policy statements and commitments which the unions have made. Some may be tempted to leave it at that and proceed as if the problem had been settled. That temptation must, however, be resisted, for a major difficulty is that many of these elements will take time to bring fully into operation. This point applies also to other components – such as a form of Price Commission, perhaps encompassing the area of the Monopolies and Mergers Commission and capable of making judgements on efficiency, organisation, structure and prices.

For a government that is committed to doing something about unemployment time is going to be a commodity in very short supply. Jobs must be the priority and a new government must not be faced with a fight on all fronts simultaneously. There is no doubt that an expansionist government – even one trying to work in concert with other economies – will come under pressure, especially within foreign exchange markets, and will be scrutinised very closely indeed. This places a premium on drawing up a clear programme for the first year of an expansionist government. Something in the order of £2–3 billion will have to be committed to investment in the infrastructure as a first step to a proper programme of economic reconstruction. Equally it is obvious that current expenditure of some £1–2 billion will need to be committed to public services and to manpower and employment programmes.

Support of such elements in a first-year programme could be found across quite a wide spectrum of opinion. There are other elements, however, which might cause some to have cold feet, but which I regard as essential. Foremost among these is the phased introduction, along an agreed timetable, of the various elements of our Fair Wages Strategy. Some of these would take time – Parliamentary time. The introduction of a replacement for the Fair Wages Resolution and for Schedule 11, as well as improvements to the Equal Pay Legislation, will all require legislative time.

By that stage we will also be in a position to judge how much legislative intervention will be introduced to tackle low pay. Some is inevitable. The current onslaught on Wages Councils requires redress, and the TUC and Labour Party are cohering around proposals for a statutory National Minimum Wage. This too will require phasing in; as will any industry-specific subsidies to alleviate the impact in sectors where low productivity and poverty wages go together.

In other words, I can outline a first-year programme in which there are two clear and strong features: on the one hand, a strong and steady fiscal boost; on the other hand, deliberate progress towards constructing a system for fair rewards at work.

'A Year for Britain'

Under these circumstances the trade union movement would have to – and be able to – say something concrete about the actual pace and level of wage settlements. It would be collective suicide to undermine a government which was taking action to restore jobs and bring back equity in the determination of living standards, and which was under pressure as a result. At this stage I certainly part company with those who decry the movement's ability to take such a stance. Let me explain why.

In effect we would be saying that, while progress was being marked off against a series of milestones on fair wages and employment growth, we would make sure that the negotiations taking place in that wage round refrained from producing accelerating and destabilising deals. Such an approach – in effect giving a 'Year for Britain' – is not unprecedented. Nor is it pie-in-the-sky. It is directly in line with the frustrated feelings of many trade union negotiators who, without any shred of justice, have been accused of in some way 'causing unemployment' but who have been offered no outlet for integrating their own activities with the pursuit of wider priorities.

What would this entail? In the trade union movement we have already put forward the idea of a National Economic Summit. This would be an opportunity to bring together representatives of all the major economic groupings. Not only would it discuss economic prospects and priorities. Out of it would be bound to emerge some general understanding of what broad target for overall wage growth is consistent with other targets. This could be as generalised as a matrix of economic relationships; a round table discussion on broadly defined options.

It could readily become something more sharply focussed, however. The significance of 'targets' or 'understandings', especially when they are shared by employers and trade unions, should not be underplayed. After all, one of the prominent features of recent years has been the stubborn persistence of a 'going rate' of pay settlements across a wide range of industrial sectors. The effective range of percentage deals has in fact been quite narrow. This is something that has caused great offence to monetarist-inclined ministers and the more ideologically, as opposed to practically, disposed of employers' spokesmen.

What it shows is how far the institutions and practices of collective bargaining can act as a force for stability, *if they are part of an integrated national agreement*. In effect collective bargaining has delivered pay rises of, on average, about two to three per cent above the rate of inflation fairly consistently. Even though the dispersion around the average has become wider the general trend is remarkable in its consistency and should be seen as something to build upon.

A Target for Wages Growth

The conclusion I would draw from this is that it would be quite possible to discuss and agree a target for wage growth which could find quite ready expression in wage bargaining. Certain conditions would, of course, have to be met. In particular it would need to be clear:

(a) that the target(s) is agreed and endorsed in a tripartite setting;
(b) that it is not drawn so rigidly as to make itself irrelevant;
(c) that it is clearly accompanied by immediate action and clear targets to bring down unemployment;
(d) that above all it is seen as a device for phasing in the durable instruments of a Fair Wages Strategy that would provide a long-term framework for orderly collective bargaining at all levels.

Going from the abstract to the particular, I am outlining the following sort of arrangement. Let us postulate that a government comes to a tripartite Economic Summit and declares its intention of putting the defeat of unemployment at the top of the nation's agenda. It also acknowledges that collective bargaining must be supported by a Fair Wages Strategy in order to make considerations of equity central to the determination of living standards. Under these circumstances why should the representatives of the trade union movement not respond along these lines: 'Wage negotiations have been producing outcomes roughly in the order of inflation plus two or three per cent. To reduce the pressure on an expansionist government, let us move to a position in which outcomes reflect the rate of inflation plus one per cent; or even just the rate of inflation.'

This would inevitably entail aspects of rough justice. But they would be less pronounced in so far as progress was really made on fair wages, ensuring that the average figure actually reflected a generally-shared movement in living standards. Such equity would certainly dampen down any pressures to evade such a policy.

The Role of Employers' Organisations

This is a timely point to underline that I have included in my outline of events a clear role for employers' organisations. This is important. The implication is that employers should bring to the table their concern over unit labour costs, profitability and so on.

The other side of that coin is that they should recognise that there will be challenges to them. They will have to recognise that two things are demanded of them. First, to order their own demands into a set of priorities which match up to the coherence that I am arguing that trade unions can achieve. Second, to act with the unity and purposefulness which I am outlining for the trade unions. I think that it is only fair to suggest that for the employers this should be the price of their presence at the summit table.

CONCLUSION

If this broad approach and its more detailed implications can be accepted then the pressure of a first year of expansion could be handled. It will – I am convinced of this – require monthly meetings between the TUC Economic Committee and Government Ministers. It will also require the monthly meetings at the NEDC – or whatever planning mechanism succeeds it – to be more than an exchange of hostile platitudes. These meetings will have to have a much more open agenda so that both the CBI and the TUC can come to trust the forum as one where problems can be aired and solved.

The central theme of my remarks has been that economic decline and industrial relations failure have gone hand in hand with a breakdown in communications between those who at national level can help to put things right. I am trusting that the other side of that coin will be that an expansionist economic policy will go together with putting a premium on dialogue rather than surly silence.

I hope this is so. And I am sure that we cannot afford to wait until after the next election before trying out one another's plans. My challenge to employers is also a request: that they realise that the magnitude of the problems facing us means that we must start talking *now*. I think that before the next government comes into office there should be some broad agreement between the TUC and the CBI on the direction in which we should go. If we have that, then I think we have a fighting chance of putting our collective resources to good use.

Note

1. This is an extended version of a lecture delivered on 10 March 1986 in the House of Commons. Lord Basnett was General Secretary of the General, Municipal, Boilermakers and Allied Trades Union until December 1985, Chairman of the TUC Economic Committee until April 1986 and a Council Member of the Employment Institute.

6 An Incomes Policy to Help the Unemployed

Richard Layard and Stephen Nickell[1]

THE FOURTEEN POINTS

Our argument has fourteen points:

1. More demand would without doubt generate more jobs.
2. It would also generate more inflation, assuming no incomes policy.
3. Inflation is mainly caused by wage increases.
4. Therefore, to get more jobs without increasing inflation, we must find a new method of restraining wage increases.
5. The aim of such wage restraint is not to reduce real wages, but to control inflation.
6. It must, if possible, be based on agreement between the TUC, CBI and government.
7. There must also be some method of making any centrally-determined policy bite at the level of the individual bargaining unit.
8. The policy will be doomed if it attempts to impose an absolute limit on the growth of pay, for this prevents decentralised changes in relativities, and, once the limit is broken, the policy collapses.
9. It follows that we need (i) a 'reference level' for the growth of average hourly earnings in every firm and (ii) a financial penalty for firms exceeding that level. If the firm exceeds the reference level, it should pay a heavy fine proportional to its excess wage bill.
10. Such a counter-inflation tax is administratively straightforward and can be collected jointly with PAYE income tax.
11. The policy should not discourage profit-sharing nor productivity agreements. This can be ensured by not counting against the permitted growth of workers' incomes any genuine growth in profits paid to workers.

12. In the public sector, we need a single public sector pay information board, and a presumption that pay in public services will grow at a comparable rate to that in comparator groups.
13. We should restrain dividends as well as pay. We should therefore subject dividends to the same reference level, using the same tax mechanism to discourage excessive distributions.
14. Those who reject these suggestions should feel obliged to suggest some better way of generating more jobs without increasing inflation.

DEMAND AND JOBS

Our first two propositions are absolutely fundamental. For incomes policy is a hassle, and one would only mention the whole business if it could deliver us literally millions of jobs. So our first need is to establish that extra demand can create millions of jobs. The second is to show that, without incomes policy, such an expansion would lead to rising inflation.

If anyone doubts the effect of demand on jobs, one has only to look at the record of the 1930s. Unemployment peaked in 1932 at about 17 per cent (see Figure 6.1). Over the next five years it fell to under 9 per cent, and before war broke out it was down to 5 per cent. During the war it fell further to 1 per cent. Such falls ran far beyond what even the most optimistic people had imagined possible in the early 1930s. The more common opinion then, as now, was that unemployment existed because:

(a) people did not want to work (due to benefits), or
(b) the unemployed were unsuited to any work that could be provided, or
(c) increased mechanisation meant that enough jobs could never be created.

Such 'structuralist' opinions were endorsed by many of the most respected economists of the day (Casson, 1983); to read their utterances gives one a frisson of *déja vu.* And yet what happened? Demand blew and unemployment was scattered. One can argue about the details of why demand rose.[2] From 1935 there is little doubt about the role of spending on rearmament, and in the earlier phase there is little doubt about the role of housebuilding, stimulated by

Figure 6.1 Unemployment and inflation in the 1930s

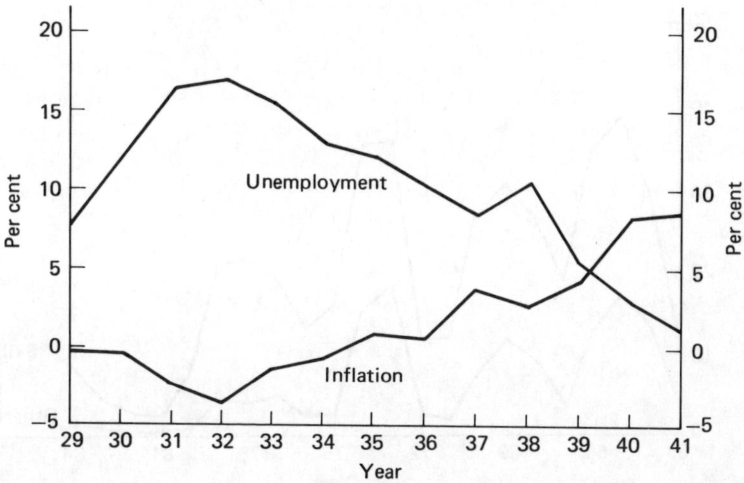

Note: *Unemployment* a percentage of civilian labour force. *Prices* are GDP deflator.
Source: Feinstein, C. H. (1975) *National Income, Expenditure and Output of the UK 1855–1965*.

cuts in interest rates (Worswick, 1984 and Middleton, 1981). But the basic point is that, once the demand arose, the people went back to work:

(a) It turned out that people did want to work if enough attractive jobs were around.
(b) The unemployed turned out to be much more skilful than anybody had imagined – many of them served with distinction in the war.
(c) It turned out that the machines could be made to produce much more if the demand was there – since spare labour was available to work them.

This does not mean that the structuralists were totally wrong, for, as we shall see, unemployment was cut at the cost of higher inflation. As our own work (Layard and Nickell, 1987) shows, structural issues are still with us and pose major obstacles to reducing unemployment without increasing inflation. But that is a second issue. The first point is that extra demand could provide many more jobs.

Figure 6.2 Shortage of skilled and other labour

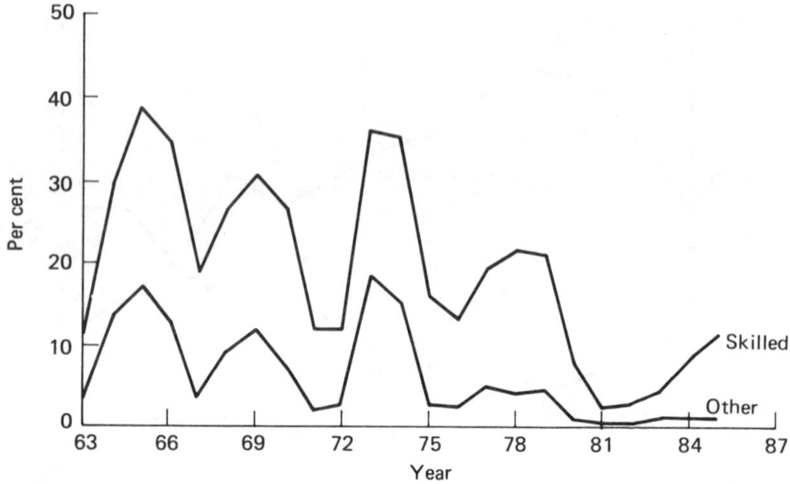

Note: Percentage of firms expecting output to be limited by shortages of (a) skilled and (b) other labour.
Source: CBI *Industrial Trends Survey*.

Moreover our structural problems are often grossly exaggerated. We do not have a major shortage of skilled labour. On the contrary, in the early stages of this cycle fewer employers reported skilled labour shortages than in any previous cycle – see Figure 6.2. There are severe shortages in a few sectors, but the general position is one of exceptional slack. The answer is more demand.

JOBS AND INFLATION

But, if this is true, why does not the government just get on with it? The answer, of course, is the fear of increasing inflation. That this is a risk emerges clearly from the record of the late 1930s (see Figure 6.1). It is confirmed by our own studies of the postwar period. These show a clear relationship between the level of unemployment and the rate of change in inflation. If unemployment were to be reduced permanently below say 2 300 000 on current (1986) definitions of unemployment, inflation could be rising permanently (unless we have an incomes policy). This is the depressing feature of the situation. We cannot just choose to have lower unemployment and higher, *but stable*, inflation. The problem would be permanently rising inflation. That is unacceptable.

Moreover things are in fact worse than the figures quoted imply. For the effect of the high recent unemployment has been to produce a legacy of long-term unemployed who are demoralised and unattractive to employers. Thus if we attempted to reduce *general* and genuine unemployment by more than say 300 000 in one year we should be likely to find inflation rising. Things would not be so bad if, instead of *general* reflation, we followed the line of the House of Commons Employment Committee (1986) and aimed the reflation directly at the long-term unemployed. But even so without an incomes policy we should be very lucky if we could get unemployment down quickly (and substantially) without pushing up inflation.

PRICE INFLATION AND WAGE INFLATION

Our focus in controlling inflation has to be on wages. For wage increases are the primary source of price inflation. As soon as one says this, somebody points to episodes when the two have diverged. This mainly happens when import prices run ahead of (or behind) wages. Divergences of this kind can arise from two sources.[3] First, there can be changes in world commodity (or oil) prices relative to the general world price level. For example commodity prices have recently fallen, with the effect that our retail prices have risen much less than our wages. However major episodes of this kind are fairly infrequent and if they happen we have to accept them. It is no good complaining about sources of inflation which arise from events outside our control. The other way in which import prices can rise faster or slower than wages is through changes in the real exchange rate (meaning the exchange rate adjusted for our prices relative to world prices). Such changes can happen over a few years but they eventually get unwound.[4]

Thus changes in relative import prices can alter the relation of prices to wages but such changes cannot go on indefinitely. The same is true of indirect taxes and employers NICs which cannot go on changing indefinitely. The only thing which can go on indefinitely is changes in money wages. Thus changes in money wages are the main source of continually changing prices. If we ignore relative import prices and taxes the fundamental determinant of prices is unit labour costs. Now

Figure 6.3 Rate of growth of hourly earnings of male manual workers

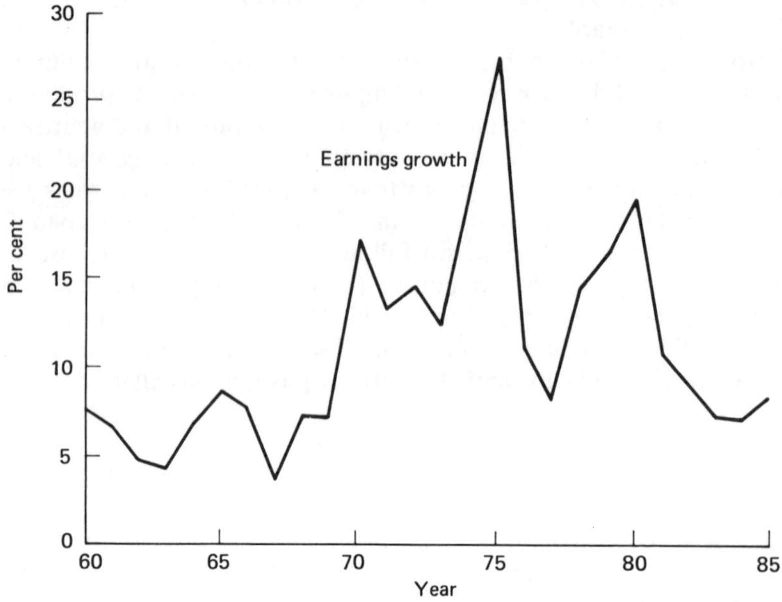

$$\text{Unit labour cost} = \frac{\text{Wage per worker}}{\text{Product per worker}}$$

Thus, for given productivity growth, wage inflation is the prime determinant of price inflation.

THE CASE FOR INTERVENTION

So how does wage inflation change, and why did wage inflation remain so stubbornly at around 7½ per cent for four years despite the very high level of unemployment (see Figure 6.3)?[5] Let us start with some basics. The prices which firms set, adjusted to exclude the effects of import prices, are determined as a mark-up *M* on unit labour costs. (The mark-up in public sector enterprises is an administered element.) So

$$\text{Price} = (1+\text{M})\ \text{Unit labour cost} = \frac{(1+\text{M})\ \text{Wage}}{\text{Productivity}}$$

Figure 6.4 The labour market

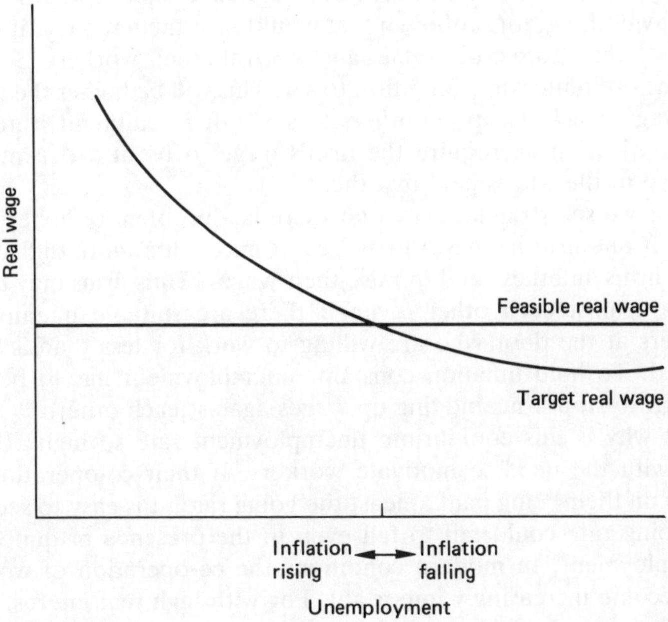

This determines the real wage, since real wages are money wages relative to prices.

$$\text{Real Wage} = \frac{\text{Wage}}{\text{Price}} = \frac{\text{Productivity}}{1+\text{M}}$$

Let us call the real wage as determined by pricing the 'feasible real wage'. This is charted as a horizontal line in Figure 6.4.[6] So the real wage is basically determined by the way prices are set. But there is also the target real wage which is what wage-setters aim at when setting wages. This is affected by the unemployment situation and is lower when unemployment is higher. If inflation is stable, unemployment must be just high enough to make the target equal to what is feasible. If the target goes above this, inflation will start increasing – the extra inflation is a way of bringing the target and feasible wages temporarily into line.

The question therefore is: Why does it take so much unemployment to bring the target real wage into line with what is feasible? This answer depends on the relative role of firms and unions in wage setting. Let us start with firms. Firms, if free to choose wages, would not pay nothing, for, although that would save them money, it would not help them to recruit, retain and motivate their workers. So there is some optimum wage for a firm to set. This will be higher the higher the wage which it expects others to set. For recruitment, retention and motivation all require the firm's wage to be at a decent level relative to the wages paid by others.

Thus we see straight away that there is a problem of 'externality' here. If one firm increases its wages, it makes life more difficult for other firms and they tend to raise their wages. Thus firms may bid up wages against each other, even if there are suitable unemployed workers at the door who are willing to work for less than is being offered. To hold inflation constant, unemployment has to be high enough to stop firms bidding up wages against each other.

But why is this equilibrium unemployment rate so high? Let us start with the need to motivate workers. If their co-operation depends on their being paid at least the going rate, it is easy to see how the going rate could fail to fall even in the presence of quite high unemployment. In modern conditions the co-operation of workers has become increasingly important. For with high real interest rates firms have cut back their stocks and thus need to be able to match production much more closely to sales.[7] Thus co-operation and the absence of argy-bargy at the work-place are now of paramount importance. Similarly, turning to recruitment and retention, firms are undoubtedly aware that a proportion of the unemployed are not willing to work in existing jobs at prevailing wages. In consequence, high unemployment is less effective than it would otherwise be at preventing the bidding up of wages. For all these reasons it takes a lot of unemployment to stop firms bidding up wages against each other.

The resulting unemployment level is in no sense optimal. For an 'externality' is involved: when one firm raises its pay, it induces other firms to do the same. Where an externality exists, there is always a case for government intervention. This can take the form of regulation, which is often clumsy, or of financial incentives to induce the participants to take into account the public interest as well as their own. In this case, for any given level of money spending, there is a public interest in low money wages and prices, because this will generate more jobs and more output. Since firms will tend to bid up wages above the optimum, the government has to act in order to promote the interest of all (including the collectivity of firms) in having a lower price level.[8] Of course if the CBI could do the job on its own, as Willie Brown (1985) has proposed, that would be fine. But it is very questionable whether the CBI could exert that degree of authority over its members.

In addition there is the crucial issue of the role of unions. On average, unions play a bigger role in the public than the private sector. Some would argue that unions are now having little influence on private sector pay.[9] This is to overstate the position. Clearly high unemployment has reduced union wage demands below what they would otherwise have been. But the union presence is there, and union wages have not fallen relative to non-union wages (Layard and Nickell, 1986). In fact it is hard to distinguish clearly between cases where firms pay more 'voluntarily' to avoid industrial hassle and those where they are 'forced' to pay more through collective bargaining.

So to sharpen the issue let us focus briefly on how wages are determined in cases where the union is the dominant influence on wages. The union will not seek an infinite wage because this would lead to job loss for its members. But in choosing wages there is no obvious reason why it should take into account the interest which the unemployed have in being employed. Unemployment will have some influence on wage demands, through its influence on union strength and on the alternatives open to union members. But it will take too much unemployment to exert the necessary restraint. So once again there is an externality. Unions tend to bid up wages over the prevailing level unless unemployment is at a very high level. Once again there is a case for government intervention.

THE AIM IS NOT TO LOWER REAL WAGES

We need to be very clear about exactly what is the aim of the intervention. It is *not* to reduce real wages. For as we have seen real wages are basically determined by the way in which firms mark prices up on wages. So if wages are lower, prices would be lower too. The Chancellor has done a dreadful disservice to the cause of wage restraint by saying that its basic aim is to reduce real wages. In fact the Treasury's own paper on 'The Relationship between Employment and Wages' (January 1985) showed that if nominal wages were held down, any incipient fall in real wages could be offset by lower tax rates made possible by higher employment. The basic point is that, even if additional employment did require some small rise in producer prices relative to wages, this effect could easily be offset by using the higher tax receipts generated by extra output to cut either income tax rates or VAT.

So what, to repeat, is the aim of wage restraint? It is to reduce the level of unemployment needed to stop employers and unions from trying to set wages above the going rate. How is this to be done?

THE ROLE OF CONSENSUS

It is unlikely to be successful unless it has the backing of what Europeans call the 'social partners', especially the TUC, CBI and government. The evidence in Bean *et al.* (1986) favours the view, put forward by Bruno and Sachs (1985), that what they call 'corporatist' economies are better able to weather economic shocks than are economies that are non-corporatist. An economy is considered more corporatist the more of the following arrangements apply: employers co-ordinate their actions, national trade unions can instruct their branches, and bargaining is at the national level. Thus the most corporate economies are (in order) Austria, West Germany, Netherlands, Norway, Sweden, Denmark and Finland. It is notorious how much better than average these countries have done (except for the Netherlands) in withstanding the shocks of the last fifteen years. And it seems likely that this is because the national interest has been more effectively reflected in wage-setting behaviour.

The United States is of course an exception to this story and one can plausibly argue that there are two forms of organisation either of which works reasonably well (Metcalf and Nickell, 1985):

(a) Strong unions and well-organised employers, bargaining nationally, or
(b) Weak unions and unorganised employers.
What does not work well is the middle way:
(c) Strong unions, bargaining locally with unorganised employers.

Thus there are two ways we could go, towards the United States or towards corporatism. The government has been pushing us towards the United States, but the effects of its trade union laws on wage behaviour have hardly been sensational. In practice we have to accept our history. We are not a frontier society. We have a strong labour movement that will one day be again represented in government. The only direction to move is in the direction of corporatism.

So what is needed is an annual economic assessment (or call it what you will) preceding the Budget. This would first review the level of productivity growth. From that it would work out what level of wage growth would be consistent with a stable growth of unit labour costs and hence of prices. Over the immediate future (with our high existing unemployment) it would be a mistake to go for zero inflation – the cost in jobs would be too high. The aim should rather be to lock in the existing underlying rate of growth of the GDP deflator.[10] So suppose we want unit labour costs to rise at x per cent, which might have been 3–4 per cent in recent years. We need to lock in wage growth at x per cent plus the rate of productivity growth (say 2 per cent, to be conservative). But it is important to be clear what wages we are talking about here. We are *not* talking about settlement wages or basic rates. We are talking about the total of earnings per productive unit of work – that is, in practice, about hourly earnings.

How can we keep the growth of hourly earnings from increasing above $(x+2)$ per cent? First, we have to have a reference level for what is generally acceptable. Because average earnings will tend to rise faster than the reference level, this has to be substantially lower than $(x+2)$. A safe level would be $(x-1)$, proposed by David Basnett (chapter 5). If this could not be achieved through negotiation and x could, the government might decide in favour of x.

TRANSMITTING THE CONSENSUS TO THE BARGAINING TABLE

Having reached this agreement, the next question is, how can we make it affect what actually gets paid? If we were Austrian or Swedish with strong centralised unions and employers' organisations, these institutions might ensure that the agreed pay was delivered. But Britain is a much bigger country. Even if we work to develop the power of our corporate institutions, it will take decades before they are able to make their members deliver year after year.

In extreme cases, of course, they can do it now. From 1975–7 the incomes policy was a TUC triumph. It reduced wage inflation by 20 per cent (from 28 to 8) with no further increase in unemployment, whereas Margaret Thatcher, faced with a similar crisis, rejected incomes policy and used an extra two million unemployed to achieve a smaller reduction in inflation.

NO ABSOLUTE PAY LIMIT

But the problem with the 1975–9 type of incomes policy was that it imposed absolute limits on the growth of pay. The limit was laid down centrally, and, when it was broken, the policy was considered to have collapsed and the government lost face. We clearly cannot, for long, have absolute limits on the growth of pay. For such limits mean the end of free collective bargaining – the outcome is already predetermined. Neither employers nor unions want that. Employers want to be able to use pay to recruit, retain and motivate. Unions want to be able to fight for their members' interests, as they see them.

So we cannot have an old-style incomes policy, except briefly in a crisis of exploding inflation (which fortunately we are not yet in). On the other hand, an unregulated free-for-all works dreadfully against the public interest, as we explained earlier. So how do we bring the national economic assessment to bear on the outcome of individual bargains, freely arrived at? Only one plausible way has been suggested and that is a financial incentive.

A FINANCIAL INCENTIVE

For reasons of political acceptability the incentive would have to be on employers. Given their ultimate responsibility for pay, this is not inappropriate. Thus suppose that the reference level of pay was 4 per cent. Any firm whose hourly earnings rose less than that would be untouched. But if hourly earnings rose more than that, by say 6 per cent, the firm would have to pay a stiff tax on the whole excess wage bill – in this case on 2 per cent of its wage bill (or to be precise on two 106ths of it). The appropriate rate of tax would be, say, one hundred per cent.

So whenever the employer conceded £1 more than the reference level, it would cost him £2: £1 given to the worker and £1 to the Inland Revenue. This would certainly make him think twice about paying over the going rate. Equally if a union forced him to pay it, the risk of job loss would be much greater, and this should make the unions pause to think twice.[11]

What would in fact be likely to happen? The majority of bargains would probably be struck at the reference level. They would also be fairly tightly defined, so as to minimise drift above the level. However some firms would undoubtedly wish to pay more. They might be trying to expand their workforce, in which case a rise of relative pay would be an efficient way of attracting workers. Or they might be wanting to upgrade their workforce faster than the national average, and this again would entail a rise in average pay. Or they might wish to make a productivity deal with their workers, whereby an inefficient manning practice was bought out by a rise in pay. All such firms would choose to pay more than the reference level. So there would be a spread of earnings growth across firms. Few would pay as much as $x+10$. But $x+4$ might be quite common, with the majority nearer to $x+1$. The overall average would probably be between $x+2$ and $x+3$.

That will do well enough. For remember the context. The context is that we are able to provide perhaps a million jobs that we could not otherwise provide. If we did that in the normal way we could not hope to lock in the inflation rate. With this device we can. Individual employers and unions will of course complain about interference. But their wishes are in fact inconsistent. On the one hand, they want a more buoyant economy, and on the other they do not want the (minimal) interference needed to make it possible.

NOT AN ADMINISTRATIVE NIGHTMARE

How much interference would in fact be involved? Would it be an administrative nightmare? Not at all. The tax could be collected simply, at the same time as PAYE. The definition of earnings would be the same as for PAYE, so the Inland Revenue already have the basic details of the tax base. The firm would simply compute its average hourly earnings (averaged over all its employees), compare this with the reference level and send in a cheque to the Revenue. This would be done quarterly, by comparing earnings with those in the same quarter one year earlier. There would be no scrutiny of individual settlements, nor of the pay of any particular individual. At present the audit of the whole of PAYE and NI at the firms' end requires under 500 inspectors. So there is no reason why the audit of the counter-inflation tax should require more than 100 or so more inspectors.

This assumes that the tax would be confined to firms with over 100 workers. This would mean that under 20 000 companies would be involved, compared with nearly a million pay-points for PAYE. This would save greatly on administrative cost both to the Revenue and to firms. Most of the firms affected have computerised payrolls, which include the hours for which they have paid their hourly paid workers.[12] Moreover, in large firms cheating is less likely, both because firms value their reputations and because a manager who cheated would be less likely to gain personally from the firm's cheating. To stop firms trying to avoid tax by setting up new firms to employ their more skilled workers, the tax would have to apply to the 'group' as a whole (That is, to any company *and* its subsidiaries).[13] But it would in practice be computed at each 'PAYE pay-point'. Genuinely new enterprises would be excluded. But there might be problems connected with changes in the ownership of existing enterprises. These can be handled provided it is understood that, wherever there has been continuous economic activity, that activity is deemed to have a past.

There are doubtless many ways in which firms will try to evade the tax. But this is true of all taxes. People tend to assume that the taxes we already have are securely founded, while any new ones are insecure in the extreme. But, when one looks into it, it seems that a counter-inflation tax could be quite straightforward. It would be much less of a bureaucratic nightmare than a prolonged old-style incomes policy, with a Relativities Board and all of that.

A GATEWAY FOR PROFIT-SHARING AND PRODUCTIVITY DEALS

As we have seen, go-ahead firms would be likely to end up paying more tax than others. They already do of course. But we want our arrangements to cause the minimum possible distortion in the economy. We cannot avoid introducing *any* new distortions, and in a second-best world it is inevitable that any desirable change will have *some* undesirable side-effects. But we do want to minimise them.

There are two big problems with the scheme as we have outlined it so far. First, it discourages productivity deals to buy out bad manning practices. Second, it discourages profit-sharing. For suppose all labour earnings (including profit-share payments) are included within the ambit of the tax. Then if a firm has a profit-sharing scheme and does well, it will be penalised, owing to the higher labour earnings. Fortunately we can deal with both these problems by a single device. We should exempt from the tax all increases in profit-share payments to workers which result from genuine increases in profits. By this method we encourage the use of profit-sharing as a method of rewarding improved productivity (thus avoiding the perils of the productivity deal in which pay is increased but productivity is not delivered).

Nothing but good could come from this proposal. However it should be contrasted with an apparently similar proposal from which no good would come. This is the proposal that *all* profit-share payments to workers should be exempt from the inflation tax. This would be disastrous. For consider a firm that paid £100 a week last year and would (in the absence of the tax) pay £110 this year. We now introduce the inflation tax with a 4 per cent reference level and full exemption for all profit-share payments. The firm simply relabels the £110 as:

£104 – Wage
£6 – Profit-share payments

Firms often know enough about their profits a year ahead to be able to hit on the right percentage of profit (say *y* per cent) such that *y* per cent of profits turns out to give £6 per worker.

However in this example the increase in profit-share payments does not result from a genuine increase in profits. Profits have, it is true, increased but this is because something that would otherwise be wages has been relabelled profits, and at the same time the workers' share of profits has been increased from zero to *y* per cent. Shareholders' profits have not changed. Thus a genuine increase in profits means an increase in shareholders' profits. If, before the year begins, the firm agrees to pay workers a fraction α of shareholders' profits (That is, $\alpha/(1+\alpha)$ of total profits), then the earnings growth for purposes of the inflation tax should be computed as:

$$\frac{\text{Earnings this year} - \alpha\ \text{Change in shareholders' profits}}{\text{Earnings last year}}$$

This assumes no change in man-hours. The general formula is given in the Annex, which also gives a numerical example to show more fully how the proposal would work.[14] The basic point is that it *is* possible to make a tax-based incomes policy compatible with the encouragement of profit-sharing and productivity.

Before leaving the subject of profit-sharing there is one other point to be made. In Chapter 2, Martin Weitzman argued that profit-sharing *as such* can reduce the level of unemployment consistent with stable inflation, in which case an incomes policy might be unnecessary. But, as Sushil Wadhwani points out in Chapter 3, for profit-sharing to have a major effect of this kind at least two assumptions must be satisfied. First, under the new arrangement unions must have no more influence over employment than they do now (despite the fact that extra employment would appear to reduce income per worker). Second, the wage and profit-share formula must not be used as a cover for guaranteeing workers the same income as before (given that for a year ahead it is not too difficult to forecast profits).

These are big requirements. The most likely way in which profit-sharing might help the underlying employment situation is this. At any one time some firms' prospects are improving and others worsening. Profit-sharing may do little or nothing to help employment in the prosperous firms, but it should reduce the decline in employment in those that suffer difficulty. This would have some favourable effect on aggregate employment, but the effect might not be large.

In our view the main arguments for profit-sharing are quite different from Weitzman's and overwhelmingly strong. These are that it would provide an incentive to productivity and promote a co-operative spirit in industry. They are old arguments but quite sufficient. To expect profit-sharing to cure stagflation as well is too much.

THE PUBLIC SECTOR

The arrangements we have proposed so far would apply to the private sector and public enterprises. This is where the heart of the stagflation problem lies, for two reasons. First (and most obvious), that is where prices are formed. But prices are based on wages, and there is therefore the second issue of the mutual interaction of public and private sector wages. Public service wage settlements get much media attention because they involve large numbers of workers *and* they involve the government. The impression is often given that they set the lead for wage inflation. But in fact the position is otherwise (See Zabalza and Kong, 1983). Public service wages have little effect on private sector wages, which are basically determined by the cost of living and unemployment (plus other labour market influences). However private sector wages do set the pattern for public service wages, because in the long run public service wages do follow on, as the principle of comparability suggests.

The problem is that comparability operates in such an erratic way. Thus, though there is no marked trend in the relation between public and private sector pay (Layard, 1984), the relativity lurches around, causing general aggravation. It is highly desirable to stop this. The existence of a reference level for pay would clearly help. The basic principle of comparability has to be that public sector groups get the same percentage rise as their comparator groups in the private sector. We shall never sort out at exactly what *level* public sector pay should be, compared with the private sector. But fairness should be satisfied (and recruitment and retention achieved) if public sector pay grows at the same rate as the private sector pay of roughly comparable groups.

For this purpose a comprehensive and publicly-responsible public pay information board is needed, covering the whole public sector (and comparable private sector groups). Next, there has to be a presumptive rule which governs the conduct of public pay bargaining. The reference level is central here. There would be a presumption that public service workers get the reference level *plus* a catch-up equal to the difference between last year's private sector pay growth and last year's reference level. (This formula could be modified to allow extra increases for government employees whose occupation was in shortage or whose comparator group had grown faster than the private sector average. Any extra payments of this type would of course be deducted when calculating the overall public sector catch-up). In this way average pay in government and the private sector would grow in line.[15]

In the nationalised industries the tax might have an additional effect through the incentive which it provided to employers to resist wage increases (just as in the private sector). This incentive would obviously not hold if it was known that the industry's external financing limit, which the government imposes, would be increased to pay the tax: and doubtless this would sometimes occur. Thus it may be that the tax would have little direct effect on miners' pay. But it would profoundly affect all public pay (even that of miners) through its effect on private sector prices and wages.

DIVIDEND RESTRAINT

Finally, there is the question of non-labour incomes. We cannot appear to be controlling only one type of income, even though (broadly speaking) slower inflation would lead to an equal slowdown in the money value of profits. The most obvious step is to limit the growth of dividends. We should therefore apply the same reference level to the dividend per share as to the wage per worker. Any increases above this level would be subject to the same rate of tax.

This device would not, it is true, control the whole of capital income. If a firm distributed less of its profit, it would retain more, and this would tend to be reflected in a capital gain in the share price. But at the level of the whole economy, a generally lower level of inflation than otherwise would be associated with lower growth of money dividends and lower money capital gains. If we focus on the actual distributions from the company sector, this should be enough to convince the public of our even-handedness. If not, we should step up the capital gains tax, which we should do anyway.

OTHER POLICIES

To conclude, we ought to consider what other policies might be desirable. The first and most obvious is price control. Some might argue that, if we want to control price inflation, we should not bother about wages at all but should rather control prices. But there are major problems with direct controls on prices. First, it is very difficult to measure prices when the quality of the product can be changed and when new products are constantly coming into existence. These problems are much less severe with different qualities of labour. Second, the prices of different goods grow (and should grow) at very different rates, whereas the wages of different types of worker grow (and should grow) at fairly similar rates. Because of differences in productivity growth, we expect the price of electronic calculators to fall, and the price of haircuts to rise in line with wages. One could not contemplate any policy that treated all price increases on the same lines. So prices policy means allowing firms to charge prices which give them a reasonable profit margin on top of the cost of wages and raw materials.

But what is 'reasonable'? In the late 1970s the rule was the margin prevailing in the best three of the last five years. Even with such a procedure there is endless room for argument over the measurement of profit, depending on the treatment of capital cost. Price control is thus bound to involve a major bureaucratic apparatus. If it is effective, control on margins may in many cases discourage investment. But it will equally often be ineffective. Many firms would argue that under it they push up their prices faster than they otherwise would, in order to establish a nice high base in case the next bureaucrat next year is tougher than this year's bureaucrat. So any attempt to control prices is either likely to be inefficient or ineffective. However political considerations may make it inevitable, and it would be far better to have a wages and prices policy than to have neither.

Another issue is whether the wages policy should not be scaled to allow more rapid growth in the incomes of the low-paid. The idea here is that a major argument for incomes policy is that it enables you to kill two birds with one stone – to control inflation *and* to alter the structure of pay to help those who are worst off. But unfortunately one stone aimed at two birds often misses both. The inclusion of the flat rate element in the policy of 1975–6 set up tensions which helped to destroy incomes policy later in the 1970s. And income was redistributed very little (Ashenfelter and Layard, 1983). We do need a radical redistribution of income. But the connection between family poverty and low pay is not particularly close (Layard, Piachaud and Stewart, 1978). So it is much better to deal with poverty through benefits and taxes in the Budget than through wages policy.[16]

Coming back to the inflation issue, a whole host of other proposals have of course been made.[17] But they all fall down on grounds of either efficacy, practicability or acceptability. It is not easy to find proposals which satisfy all these criteria. What we are suggesting would control inflation, is administratively feasible, and has support from a wide range of opinion. (See, for example, Davies, 1986 and Brittan, 1986.) It also has some clearly undesirable side-effects. If anyone can suggest how to avoid these difficulties and yet deal with the central problem, we should be delighted. But it does not help to find fault, without suggesting an effective alternative. To give up on incomes policy is to wash one's hands of the unemployed.

Annex

The counter-inflation tax modified so as not to discourage profit-sharing

We want to modify the inflation tax in such a way that, if workers increase their efficiency and firms use profit-sharing as a way of rewarding them, the firms are not penalised. In other words we want a *gateway. This suggests that we should exempt from the inflation tax all increases in profit-share payments which result from genuine increases in profits.*

This apart, we must expect that firms will in general treat profit-share payments as a part of labour cost and will set prices as a mark-up on labour cost. If labour cost stays the same but more of it is profit-share payments, we cannot count on prices being lower. We cannot therefore exempt from the inflation tax all profit-share payments, but only the increases in profit-share payments resulting from an increase in genuine profit. If we exempted all profit-share payments, a limit on wage rises might well have no effect at all in limiting labour costs.

For example suppose the reference level for wages was 5 per cent. Consider the firm in Table 6.1 (assumed typical of the economy). If there were no reference level for wages, it would raise wages by 10

Table 6.1 Exempting profit-shares from the inflation tax

		Next year		
	This year	*No tax*	*Tax (but profit-share exempt)*	*Tax (profit-share not exempt)*
		(A)	*(B)*	*(C)*
Price	1	1.05	1.05	1
Per worker:				
Output	150	157	157	157
Revenue	150	165	165	157
Shareholders' profit	50	55	55	52
Wage	100	110	105	100
Workers' profit*	—	—	5	5

*9 per cent of shareholders' profit.

per cent and prices by 5 per cent (given 5 per cent productivity growth). This is shown in Column A. With a wage norm of 5 per cent, backed by a penal tax, it will accept the norm, as in Column B. Since it can still raise prices by 5 per cent, this gives it more profit than it would otherwise have had (not due to efficiency but to the lower wage). It can thus afford to pay out an additional £5 per worker in profit-share and still have the same profit it would otherwise have had left over for its shareholders. If the profit-share is exempt from the inflation tax, this is what will happen.

It is simply *wrong* to say that a wage limit with no limit to profit-share payment affects prices 'because only profitable firms can afford to pay the profit-share'. If there is general price inertia, *the wage limit automatically increases the potential profits out of which the profit share is paid*. So any firm can pay its workers in total renumeration exactly the same as it would otherwise have done.

The only way to stop this is to include all labour costs in the tax. This is illustrated in Column C. We assume that profit-sharing gets established due to the Chancellor's financial inducements but total labour costs are contained at 5 per cent due to the tax. We now get prices stable. For the economy in general we can only have an effect on inflation if we have a reference level for wages which includes most of labour costs.

But now consider an exceptional firm where productivity grows much more than the general level (owing to, say, a productivity deal). We want this firm to be able to share the proceeds of the exceptional productivity growth with its members. Say this growth is 20 per cent (as compared with 5 per cent for the economy as a whole) and that as before the norm on labour costs is 5 per cent. We must now exempt from the inflation tax any increase in worker-income due to the increase in shareholders' profit. In this example we assume that, aware of the impending profits surge, workers have negotiated a 20 per cent profit share linked to a small wage cut. The result is an increase in shareholders' profit per worker of £21 (That is, £71–£50). The inflation tax norm now applies to all workers' renumeration *excluding that due to the rise in shareholders' profits*. Thus we take the increase in total renumeration (£9) and deduct from it the increase due to the increase in profit (evaluated at the current profit-share percentage). This exemption is thus 20 per cent of the £21 increase in shareholders' profit – £4. Thus the growth in non-exempt renumeration (£5 = £(9–4)) falls within the inflation tax limits. Although the

Table 6.2 A gateway for profit-share schemes

	This year	*Next year* *As C but no tax on share of profit growth*
Price	1	1
Per worker		
Output	150	180
Revenue	150	180
Shareholders' profit	50	71
Wage	100	95
Workers' profit*	—	14

*20 per cent of shareholders' profit.

workers' incomes have gone up by 9 per cent, the 5 per cent norm has not been breached. Nor have prices risen, despite the 9 per cent increase in worker incomes (see Table 6.2).

In terms of mathematical formulation the inflation tax is thus equal to

$$t[W_1+\lambda_1\pi_1-\lambda_1(\pi_1-\pi_0)-(W_0+\lambda_0\pi_0)\frac{H_1}{H_0}(1+n)] =$$

$$t[W_1+\lambda_1\pi_0-(W_0+\lambda_0\pi_0)\frac{H_1}{H_0}(1+n)]$$

where t is the tax rate, λ is the ratio of workers' profits to shareholders' profits, and π is total shareholders' profits. W is total wagebill, H is total manhours, and n is the reference level. Subscript 0 means last year and 1 this year. Given this approach, firms engaged in wage negotiations already know in advance the effect of profit-share payments on their tax-base: it contributes $\lambda_1\pi_0$ – this year's profit-share percentage times last year's profits.

The reason that the profit share has to be defined in terms of shareholders' profits is that, if workers are paid less in wages and more in profits, this automatically raises profits as normally measured. But this element of the rise in profits is spurious, unless it is accompanied by a rise in shareholders' profits.

Thus we *can* integrate profit-sharing and the inflation tax. Once a given profit-share percentage has been in existence at the same level for two years, then we simply exempt all increases in profit-share payments from the inflation tax. It is only increased payments resulting from an increased profit-share percentage which we cannot afford to exempt from the inflation tax.

How would we administer the exemption? The best approach would be to charge the inflation tax on full PAYE earnings and then let firms apply for refunds. For this purpose we would need a standard definition of shareholders' profit which should be as defined for Corporation Tax (before adjustment for capital allowances). The profit-share agreement would of course have to be registered before the beginning of the period for which refunds were claimed.

Notes

1. Richard Layard is Professor of Economics at the London School of Economics and Head of the Centre for Labour Economics. He is Chairman of the Council of the Employment Institute. Stephen Nickell is Professor of Economics at the University of Oxford and Director of the Institute of Economics and Statistics. He is a Council member of the Employment Institute. The first version of this text was published in October 1986.
2. The discussion of whether the recovery was spontaneous or otherwise is not important to our argument. There are also considerable philosophical difficulties in defining what point is at issue in that debate (for example, whether the money supply or interest rate is to be considered exogenous).
3. The basic equation is:

$$P = \alpha W + (1 - \alpha) \frac{P_1}{E}$$

therefore

$$\frac{W}{P} = \frac{1}{\alpha} - \frac{1 - \alpha}{} \frac{P_1/P^*}{EP/,P^*},$$

where W is wage. P domestic price, P_1 world price of our imports, E the price of our currency, P^* the world price level.
4. The real exchange rate rose from 1977 to early 1981 and then fell. To balance the current account as oil output falls and unemployment falls, the real exchange rate will have to fall still further. At that point retail prices will inevitably rise faster than unit labour costs, and real consumption wages will fall permanently relative to what they would otherwise have been.
5. For fuller discussions of the answer see Layard (1986) and Layard and Nickell (1987).
6. In fact there is some evidence (Layard and Nickell, 1987) that the mark-up falls as unemployment rises. So the line for the feasible real wage in Figure 6.4 slopes up to the right, and real wages are determined

by price-*and* wage-setting behaviour. But the feasible wage line is flatter than the target wage line.

7. We are grateful to John Cahill of the CBI for this point.
8. It is slightly artificial to take the level of money spending as given. For a more rigorous analysis entirely in real terms see Jackman and Layard (1986a and 1986b).
9. See for example the survey conducted for the Institute of Directors and published in its Bi-Monthly survey of Business Opinion, August 1985.
10. Some people we respect have at times advocated a wage freeze, with the aim of eliminating inflation. We doubt the wisdom of this. It would be very likely to destabilise the situation and build up pressure for a later resumption of inflation. The one virtue of the present situation is that the underlying rate of inflation has been so stable (at around 4 per cent) for so long (since 1983).
11. For a much more rigorous analysis of how the tax would affect outcomes see Jackman and Layard (1986a and 1986b).
12. Other workers would be counted as 35 hours (full-time) or 20 (part-time).
13. Defined, say, as any company in which it had a 75 per cent stake or more.
14. The Annex is taken from C. Huhne, R. Jackman and R. Layard, 'Arrangements to encourage profit-sharing and to contain inflation', mimeo, February 1986, which, as far as we know, is the original source of the proposals discussed in this section.
15. This is only so if inflation is stable. Rising inflation would hurt public sector workers whilst falling inflation would help them.
16. The main criticism of incomes policy in Brittan and Lilley (1977) is that it must necessarily get mixed up with redistribution. But this cannot be inevitable, and was not even the case after 1976.
17. The most carefully worked out is that by Meade (1982). This and many others are reviewed in Chapter 9 of Layard (1982), which also discusses the pros and cons of a counter-inflation tax in a lot more detail.

7 Regional Policy and the North–South Divide

Harvey Armstrong and Jim Taylor[1]

INTRODUCTION

Since the 1920s, successive British governments have grappled with the problem which has become known as the north–south divide. Job opportunities have been consistently worse in many northern parts of Britain than in the south and this has led to successive attempts to create more jobs in areas of high unemployment. Britain is still faced, however, with severe regional problems. Regional differences in unemployment, for example, have been worse in the 1980s than at any time since the Great Depression in the 1930s.

Opponents of British regional policy argue that it has been a failure: it is an expensive luxury which should be abolished at the earliest opportunity. Supporters of regional policy argue exactly the opposite: it has not succeeded because it has been far too weak. This chapter takes the second of these two views. It argues that regional policy *can* be an effective instrument for creating jobs but that the government will need to play a far more active role if regional policy is to succeed. Policy makers will have to be willing to commit substantially more money to regional development policies if regional policy is to become an effective method of creating jobs in areas of high unemployment. Equally important is the need for a fresh approach which goes far beyond previous attempts to create more jobs in depressed areas. Most important of all is the need for a regional policy which is capable of halting and if possible reversing the increasing concentration of jobs and people in the South-East. The broad outline of a new approach to regional policy is suggested.

Our first task is to examine the severity of Britain's regional problem. Attention is deliberately focussed on regional differences in job opportunities since these play a critical role in determining living standards. How substantial are the existing regional differences in job opportunities? To what extent have they changed in the 1980s? Why have market forces failed to eliminate these regional differences in job opportunities? Having examined these issues, we then turn to regional policy itself – its past performance, its recent decline and our proposals for its future.

We should make it clear at the outset that we have deliberately excluded any discussion of regional policy in Northern Ireland. This is because Northern Ireland has had its own special brand of regional policy and requires separate treatment.

THE REGIONAL IMPLICATIONS OF THE 1979–81 RECESSION

For over thirty years following the end of the Second World War, employment prospects for those already in the labour force and for those about to join it were generally regarded with optimism. The hopes and aspirations of the 1950s, 1960s and 1970s very quickly turned to despair in the 1980s as firms cut back on their labour requirements in the face of the worst recession since the 1930s. Unemployment climbed from under 6 per cent in 1979 to over 12 per cent three years later. Since unemployment had averaged 1.7 per cent in the 1950s, 2.0 per cent in the 1960s and 4.3 per cent in the 1970s, unemployment rates exceeding 12 per cent in the 1980s came as a severe shock.

This plunge of the economy into the most severe slump since the 1930s left many scars on Britain's industrial landscape, the two most significant being the rapid decline of the manufacturing sector and the concentration of job losses in certain regions. Since the collapse of manufacturing employment had considerable influence on the regional distribution of job losses, it will be useful to begin by briefly describing recent employment trends in the manufacturing sector.

Employment in manufacturing fell from an all-time peak of 8.6 million employees in 1966 to 5.1 million in 1986. More significantly, about 60 per cent of this loss of manufacturing jobs occurred between 1979 and 1986. This sharp decline in the fortunes of the manufacturing sector had substantially different effects in different regions. Employment in manufacturing fell far more severely, for example, in Scotland, Wales and the regions of northern England than in East Anglia, the East Midlands and the South West (see Table 7.1). Since 1979, the northern regions of the United Kingdom have lost around one-third of their manufacturing jobs. The adverse effects of the collapse of manufacturing are best illustrated, however, by job losses

Table 7.1 Percentage change in employment by region and by broad sector, 1965–86

	Manufacturing as a % of total employment			*Percentage change in employees in employment*					
				Manufacturing		*Non-manufacturing*		*Total*	
Region	*1965*	*1979*	*1986*	*1965–79*	*1979–86*	*1965–79*	*1979–86*	*1965–79*	*1979–86*
East Anglia	28.3	29.3	26.4	+24.0	−2.4	+17.0	+13.1	+19.0	+8.5
South-East	32.0	25.0	19.0	−21.5	−25.4	+10.3	+6.2	+0.1	−1.7
South-West	29.0	27.5	23.8	+4.7	−14.8	+12.6	+3.2	+10.3	−1.8
East Midlands	42.7	39.0	32.8	−1.6	−18.0	+13.7	+7.5	+7.2	−2.4
West Midlands	50.8	44.0	34.8	−17.6	−28.6	+9.6	+4.9	−4.2	−9.8
Scotland	34.3	28.7	21.8	−16.6	−31.8	+8.0	+1.5	−0.4	−10.2
Yorks/Humberside	41.5	35.2	25.9	−18.1	−35.0	+7.7	+1.1	−3.0	−11.6
North	36.1	32.9	25.1	−10.7	−34.1	+3.5	−3.7	−1.7	−13.7
North-West	44.0	36.3	28.0	−22.6	−34.7	+7.3	−4.5	−5.9	−15.5
Wales	30.3	30.5	23.5	0.0	−35.9	+0.4	−8.6	+0.3	−16.9

Note: June data used for calculating percentage change in employment.

Sources: *Employment Gazette*, January 1981 and February 1987; *Regional Trends*.

Table 7.2 Changes in employment in Liverpool by broad sector, 1978–84

Sector	*Employment* 1978	1984	*% change* Liverpool	UK
Manufacturing	87 550	47 455	–45.8	–24.2
Other production industries	13 970	10 660	–23.7	–12.4
Blue collar service industries	108 070	87 500	–19.0	4.8
White collar service industries	85 755	85 000	–0.9	5.1
Total	295 345	230 615	–21.9	–3.7

Sources: *Financial Times*, 28 November 1986, page IV; *Economic Trends*.

in particular areas such as Liverpool. Between 1978 and 1984, Liverpool lost nearly one half of its manufacturing jobs (see Table 7.2). Almost two-thirds of the jobs lost in Liverpool during this period were due *directly* to the decline in manufacturing.

The fragile economies of the north find it much harder to ride the storms of national recessions than those in the south with the result that the scars of the 1979–81 recession are far deeper and will be more difficult to remove than those suffered by the south. That the north has suffered greater blows than the south is evident from the sudden and very sharp increase in regional differences in unemployment rates during the early 1980s (see Figure 7.1). Whilst unemployment in the Northern region increased by 8.5 percentage points (from 10.4 to 18.9 per cent) between 1980 and 1985, unemployment increased in the South East by 5.7 percentage points (from 4.2 to 9.9 per cent). Regional differences in unemployment rates therefore indicate that, whilst the chances of getting a job worsened in all regions during 1980–5, the deterioration has been more severe in the north than in the south.

The economic weakness of the north relative to the south is further illustrated by the greater severity of long-term unemployment in the northern regions. On average, those unemployed in the north were unemployed for a longer period than was the case in the south (see Table 7.3). These regional differences in the severity of long-term unemployment have important implications for regional policy since the long-term unemployed are likely to be more difficult to re-employ than those unemployed for only a short time. This is partly because the skill gap between those in work and those out of work widens as the length of time spent out of work increases. Those in work are able to update their skills as new products and new processes are invented. The skills of the unemployed therefore become increasingly

Figure 7.1 Regional unemployment differences: GB regions, 1974–87

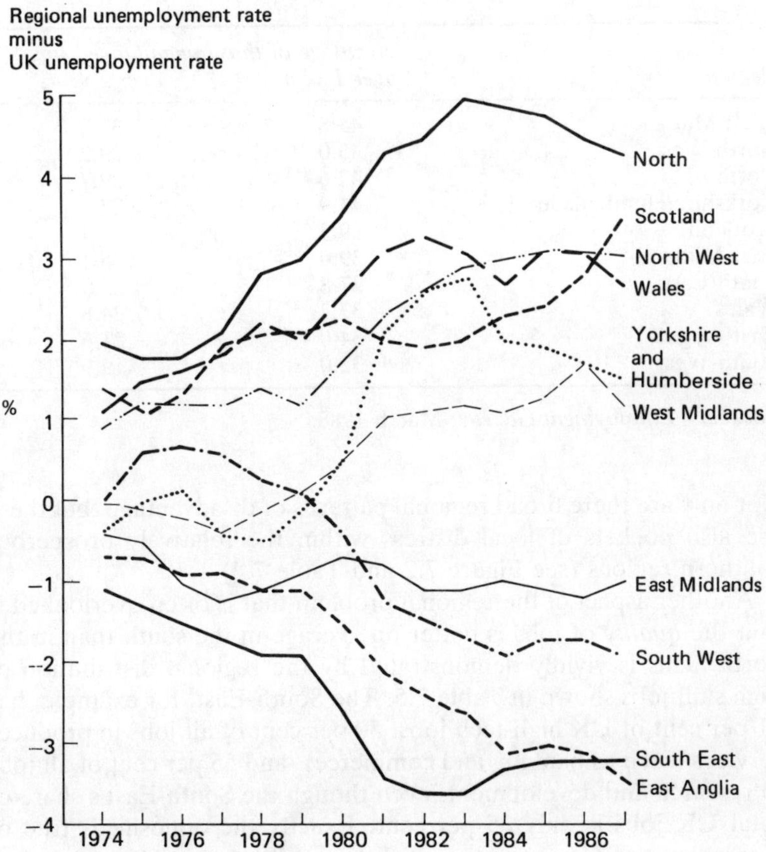

Source: *Employment Gazettes*.

less useful as the time spent out of work lengthens. The morale of people who are unemployed for long periods may also be seriously damaged and this makes the long-term unemployed less attractive to employers (see Chapter 9).

The very high rates of unemployment experienced in the 1980s in the northern regions should not blind us to the fact that unemployment black spots now exist in all parts of Britain. Even the South-East was hit hard by the 1979–81 recession with unemployment rates rising to well over 10 per cent in some counties (such as East Sussex, Kent and Essex). The unemployment problem is clearly complex.

Table 7.3 The problem of long-term unemployment in the regions of Great Britain, 1988

Region	*Percentage of those unemployed for:* *over 1 year*	*over 2 years*
West Midlands	45.8	31.8
North-West	43.0	29.2
North	42.6	29.7
Yorkshire/Humberside	41.9	27.8
Scotland	39.3	25.4
East Midlands	39.0	25.1
South East	37.8	23.5
Wales	37.7	24.8
East Anglia	34.0	21.6
South-West	32.0	19.9

Source: *Employment Gazette*, March 1988.

Not only are there broad regional patterns of disadvantage, but there are also pockets of local distress within the relatively prosperous southern regions (see Figure 7.2 and Table 7.4).

Another aspect of the regional problem that is often overlooked is that the *quality* of jobs is better on average in the south than in the north. This is vividly demonstrated by the regional distribution of high skill jobs shown in Table 7.5. The South-East, for example, has 41 per cent of UK high-tech jobs, 50 per cent of all jobs in producer services (such as banking and commerce), and 55 per cent of all jobs in research and development, even though the South-East's share of total UK jobs is only 35 per cent. Exactly the opposite is true of Yorkshire and Humberside, which has well below its 'fair share' of jobs in these high skill industries.

More evidence of the north–south divide is provided by the migration of people into and out of regions (Brant, 1984). People of working age tend to move out of areas where jobs are scarce and into areas where jobs are plentiful. It is not therefore surprising to find large numbers of young adults moving into areas such as Greater London and out of areas such as Merseyside. The strong pull of the south for young, highly-skilled workers is vividly reflected by the regional distribution of UK graduates. The south attracts far more than its 'fair share' of graduates compared to other parts of the country (see Table 7.6). This is further evidence of virtuous circle

Figure 7.2 Unemployment rates in GB travel-to-work areas, February 1988

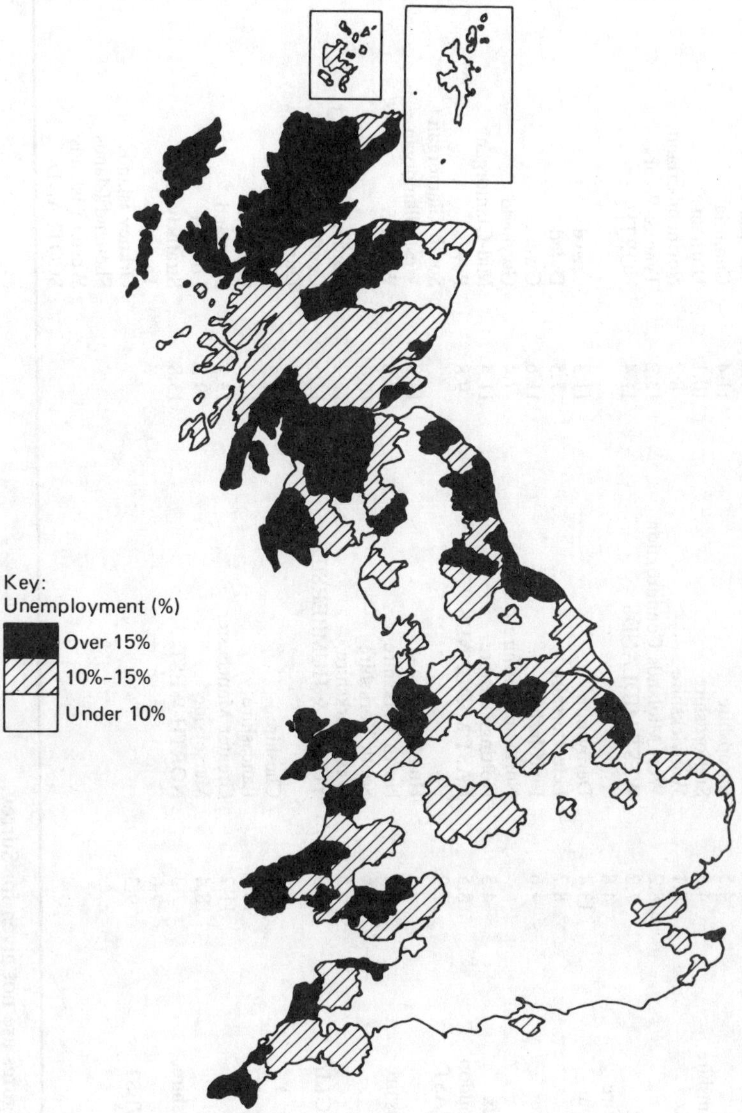

Source: *Employment Gazette*, April 1988.

Table 7.4 Unemployment rates in the counties and regions of Great Britain, February 1988

Bedfordshire	7.2	Hereford and Worcester	9.4	Cleveland	19.0
Berkshire	4.5	Shropshire	11.4	Cumbria	9.6
Buckinghamshire	4.8	Staffordshire	10.1	Durham	15.7
East Sussex	8.1	Warwickshire	8.7	Northumberland	14.0
Essex	8.2	West Midlands Connurbation	13.2	Tyne & Wear	16.3
Hampshire	7.2	WEST MIDLANDS	11.4	NORTH	15.1
Hertfordshire	4.8				
Isle of Wight	13.4	Derbyshire	11.3	Clwyd	14.1
Kent	8.7	Leicestershire	7.5	Dyfed	16.3
Oxfordshire	4.6	Lincolnshire	11.6	Gwent	14.3
Surrey		Northamptonshire	7.4	Gwynedd	17.7
West Sussex	4.3	Nottinghamshire	11.4	Mid-Glamorgan	16.5
Greater London	8.5	EAST MIDLANDS	9.8	Powys	10.8
SOUTH-EAST	7.2			South Glamorgan	11.7
		Humberside	14.0	West Glamorgan	15.2
Cambridgeshire	6.1	North Yorkshire	8.8	WALES	14.3
Norfolk	9.6	South Yorkshire	16.4		
Suffolk	6.5	West Yorkshire	11.2	Borders	9.1
EAST ANGLIA	7.3	YORKS & HUMBERSIDE	12.5	Central	15.9
				Dumfries & Galloway	13.2
Avon	8.7	Cheshire	11.3	Fife	15.4
Cornwall	16.6	Lancashire	12.2	Grampian	9.1
Devon	11.7	Greater Manchester	13.1	Highland	15.8
Dorset	8.4	Merseyside	19.3	Lothian	12.1
Gloucestershire	7.3	NORTH-WEST	13.8	Strathclyde	17.7
Wiltshire	7.0			Tayside	13.9
SOUTH WEST	9.3			Orkney Islands	13.4
				Shetland Islands	7.5
				Western Islands	21.9
				SCOTLAND	14.6

Note: Figures are not given for Surrey.

Source: *Employment Gazette*, March 1988.

Table 7.5 Some indicators of job quality in British regions

	Percentage of total GB employees in each sector (1984)			
Region	*High-tech manufacturing*[a]	*Producer services*[b]	*Research and development*	*All industries*
South-East	41.1	49.6	55.0	34.6
East Anglia	3.0	2.8	7.2	3.4
South-West	9.3	7.0	7.7	7.4
East Midlands	5.7	4.3	4.7	7.0
West Midlands	10.8	7.6	4.3	9.4
Yorkshire/Humberside	3.2	5.8	2.2	8.5
North-West	11.8	9.2	7.0	11.0
North	3.8	3.5	3.0	5.1
Wales	3.7	2.8	1.7	4.3
Scotland	7.7	7.4	7.2	9.1
Great Britain	100	100	100	100

Notes:
[a] Includes office machinery, data-processing equipment, electrical and electronic engineering, aerospace equipment, instrument engineering.
[b] Includes banking, finance, insurance, business services.

Source: *Employment Gazette*, January 1987.

Table 7.6 Regional distribution of graduates in the United Kingdom

Region	*% of total 1980 graduates working in region in 1986*	*% of total GB employees 1984*	*Column 1 divided by column 2*
South	50.3	42.1	1.19
East Anglia	4.8	3.4	1.41
Midlands	13.1	16.4	0.80
North	19.0	24.6	0.77
Wales	3.7	4.3	0.86
Scotland	9.1	9.1	1.00
GB	100	100	1.00

Note:
1. The data refer to graduates of UK universities, polytechnics and colleges who graduated in 1980 and who were in full-time employment in 1986.
2. The regions are as follows: South = South-East and South-West; Midlands = West Midlands and East Midlands; North = Northern region, North-West, and Yorshire and Humberside.

Source: *National Survey of 1980 Graduates and Diplomates*, Department of Employment, London; *Employment Gazette*, January 1987.

effects operating in the south whilst vicious circle effects occur in the north.

MARKET FORCES AND REGIONAL DIFFERENCES IN UNEMPLOYMENT

According to the theory of demand and supply, regional differences in unemployment should be automatically eliminated by market forces. The ability of market forces to reduce regional unemployment differences, however, has been the subject of fierce debate. Those with faith in the market economy argue that regional unemployment differences are a direct result of market imperfections and that the regional problem would solve itself if these market imperfections were removed. 'Removing market imperfections' really means three things:

(i) making wages more responsive to local unemployment levels (That is, allowing wages to fall in areas of high unemployment relative to low unemployment areas);
(ii) improving the incentive for unemployed workers to move from areas of high unemployment to areas of low unemployment;
(iii) making it easier for firms to move out of high-wage areas and into regions where labour costs are lower.

The market economy approach argues that regional unemployment differences would automatically be eliminated if these three steps were taken. The fall in wages in areas of high unemployment would lead to an increase in the demand for labour. Unemployed workers would move from areas where jobs are scarce to areas where jobs are plentiful. Finally, firms would move from high wage areas to low wage areas.

This kind of thinking indicates an over-optimistic view of the way in which labour markets operate. In the real world, wages very rarely fall even in areas which have very high levels of unemployment. In addition, some economists argue that the existence of generous unemployment benefit means that there is no incentive for low-skill workers to take low-paid jobs.

The downward 'stickiness' of wages has led some economists to propose that the government should take a more active approach to making wages more competitive (that is, lower!) in areas of high unemployment. The main proposals are as follows:

(i) Unemployment benefit should be reduced in order to encourage the unemployed to take low-paid jobs.
(ii) National wage bargaining should be discouraged and wages should be determined locally, taking local unemployment levels into account.
(iii) The wages of those working in the public sector should be cut in areas of high unemployment in order to set an example to employers in the private sector (Brittan, 1986). The government would also be more inclined to transfer its own expenditure to such areas if wages were lower.

Whether any of these policies would reduce regional differences in unemployment is doubtful. Cutting unemployment benefit, for example, would certainly provide an added incentive for the unemployed to take on low-paid jobs. But past experience suggests that the cuts would have to be severe if unemployment is to be substantially reduced. Unemployment benefit fell considerably (in relation to average weekly earnings) during the early 1980s at the same time that unemployment was rising to its highest postwar level. It should also be remembered that cutting unemployment benefit still further (compared to average weekly earnings) would reduce the living standards of a large number of people who are already below the poverty line.

The policy of cutting wages of public sector workers in areas of high unemployment is unlikely to have much effect on regional unemployment differences. The short-run effects of such a policy may well be harmful to high unemployment areas since a reduction in wages will reduce the amount which these workers spend within their own locality. This in turn will cause further jobs to be lost, at least in the short run. There is certainly no guarantee that this reduction in local expenditure would be offset by an increase in employment which might (or might not) result from lower labour costs. Private sector employers, for example, may not follow the wage level set by the public sector since they may fear that wage cuts will reduce the morale of their workers, which in turn will reduce productivity. The end result of wage cutting in the depressed areas is that such areas would be low-wage and low-skilled. Such a cure would be as bad as the original problem. It is surely better to aim for a solution which

Table 7.7 Migration into and out of GB regions 1985–6

Region	*In-migration (in thousands)*	*Out-migration (in thousands)*	*Balance of inward and outward migration (per thousand population)*
East Anglia	68	43	+10.2
South-West	129	95	+ 7.6
East-Midlands	51	47	+ 3.8
Wales	95	80	+ 1.4
South-East	246	252	− 0.3
Yorkshire/ Humberside	74	85	− 2.2
Scotland	43	55	− 2.3
North	42	50	− 2.6
North-West	82	102	− 3.1

Note: The information in this table refers to migration to and from the rest of GB (i.e. excluding Northern Ireland and the rest of the world). Moves within regions are also excluded.

Source: OPCS Monitor MN 87/2, *Recorded Internal Population Movements in the UK, Mid-1985 to Mid-1986*, London, 1987, table 1.

leaves regions with a high-wage, high-skill workforce, where the high wages are justified by the high productivity of the local workforce.

Neither would it be wise to rely on migration as a way of reducing regional unemployment differences. The migration of people between regions is only a very small proportion of the total population of each region and is far too small to reduce regional unemployment differences significantly. Indeed, nearly as many people move *into* high unemployment regions as move out (see Table 7.7).

There are three main reasons for being pessimistic about regional policy based upon encouraging more migration. Firstly, past experience indicates that the unemployed are far less likely to migrate than those who already have a job since the unemployed do not have the necessary funds to finance such a move. Lack of finance is a major stumbling block for many potential migrants.

Secondly, there seems little prospect that the government itself could do much to increase the flow of migrants from the north to the south other than reducing house prices by making more building land available. Financial inducements to migrants, for example, have existed continuously in Britain since 1928 but their effect has been minimal. It has recently been suggested, however, that migration

Table 7.8 House prices and house price inflation in GB regions, 1987–8

Region	*Average house price (1988)*	*% increase 1987–8*
Greater London	80 300	27.7
South-East	74 100	26.0
East Anglia	58 900	39.3
East Midlands	40 100	18.0
West Midlands	41 500	22.1
Yorkshire/Humberside	30 700	9.1
North-West	34 800	10.8
North	31 000	7.0
Scotland	36 500	5.2
Wales	33 900	10.6
UK	50 700	17.3

Source: Halifax Building Society.

from the north to the south would increase considerably if council houses were made available to those willing to move (McCormick, 1987). This proposal would involve more council houses being built in the south (financed by central government) and making a greater proportion of the existing stock of council houses available to those moving into the south from high unemployment areas in the north. A further proposal is that the costs of migration should be made tax-deductible.

Making more council houses available to people willing to move from the north to the south would not necessarily have a substantial effect on migration. It should not be forgotten that many unemployed workers actually own their own homes and it is unlikely that they would be willing to move from their own home in the north to a council house in the south, even if this was regarded as a temporary measure. The north–south price differential for houses is now a substantial deterrent to north–south migration (see Table 7.8). If we also recognise that people are often unwilling to move from north to south for personal and family reasons, it seems most unlikely that the council house proposal would stand much chance of reducing regional unemployment differences.

The third reason to be pessimistic about a regional policy based on encouraging more migration from north to south is that outward migration from areas of high unemployment could have serious detrimental effects on the economic health of these communities.

Migration tends to be selective. The people most likely to move out of high unemployment areas are the most highly skilled and most ambitious workers who already have a job. Such people often wish to improve their career prospects by moving to another area. The self-selecting character of migration inevitably harms the long-term economic prospects of high unemployment areas, which are left with a poorer quality workforce when the most productive and most enterprising people move out.

The drain from the north of the most highly skilled and most enterprising workers is a serious matter. When coupled with the reluctance of southern businesses to grasp the opportunities provided by lower labour costs, cheaper land and low cost premises in the north, we must be pessimistic about the ability of market forces to have any significant effect on regional unemployment differences. Even if wages were more flexible downwards and even if people were less reluctant to move out of high unemployment areas, this would not solve Britain's regional problem. Indeed, the policies which have been suggested to make the labour market more efficient may make the regional problem worse. The migration of high quality labour from north to south not only damages the growth prospects of the north, it simultaneously strengthens the south.

It is precisely because market forces cannot be relied upon to reduce regional differences in job opportunities that successive British governments have decided that it is necessary to have a regional policy. Even the present Government, with its strong commitment to the market economy, has recognised the need for government intervention if the north–south divide is to be controlled.

THE CASE FOR REGIONAL POLICY

Regional policy began life in the late 1920s when grants were offered to unemployed miners to induce them to move to areas where jobs were more readily available. Further policies were introduced in the 1930s (such as the designation of Special Areas in 1934) when the collapse of shipbuilding, iron and steel, textiles and coalmining caused unemployment to rise to catastrophically high levels in those areas heavily dependent upon these staple industries.

The motive behind the creation and early development of regional policy was therefore the reduction of unemployment in areas where it was exceptionally high. The same motive lies behind regional policy in the 1980s. This is vividly demonstrated by the Government's view (our italics):

> Now we are moving into a situation where an attempt is being made to make the policy much more cost effective in terms of *a single guiding objective, that objective being to reduce regional disparities in employment opportunities* on a stable long-term basis. (House of Commons Paper 378, 1984, p. 22)

A variety of arguments have been used to justify creating jobs in depressed areas in order to reduce regional unemployment differences. First, regional policy can be justified on grounds of *equity*. The sense of unfairness and injustice has been the main driving force behind regional policy throughout its sixty year history. The desire to see a fairer distribution of income and employment opportunities between the regions of the United Kingdom remains a powerful argument in favour of a strong and effective regional policy.

Secondly, regional policy has been defended on *social* and *political* grounds since regional unemployment differences contribute to social and political problems. The close correlation between social problems and living standards, for example, means that the areas of highest unemployment are likely to suffer from the highest crime rates and the poorest health. Social problems are made worse by the geographical concentration of unemployment (for example, in the major connurbations) because of the adverse effect that such concentration has on motivation. Once it gathers momentum, the downward spiral of economic decline becomes increasingly difficult to reverse.

Thirdly, a number of *economic* arguments can be advanced in favour of regional policy, the most obvious being that high unemployment represents an inexcusable waste of the nation's resources. A reduction in unemployment through the creation of more jobs would yield substantial output gains for the entire nation. We could *all* be better off.

The economic case for regional policy is further strengthened by the fact that the national recovery since 1985 now appears to be running into production bottlenecks. This is because of a shortage of productive capacity in many parts of the manufacturing sector, particularly in consumer goods industries. The Confederation of British Industry's capacity utilisation index (Figure 7.3) shows a higher reading at the beginning of 1988 than in the unprecedented boom

Figure 7.3 The CBI index of capacity utilisation

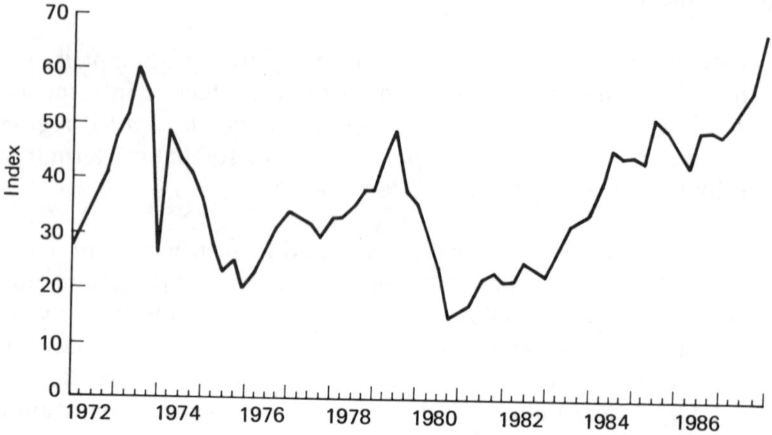

Note: This index of capacity utilisation is the percentage of respondents who said that they were not working below 'a satisfactory full rate of operation'. The responses are weighted by the employment level in each industrial sector.
Source: *Quarterly Industrial Trends Surveys*, Confederation of British Industry.

year of 1973. The damaging effects of the 1979–81 recession on the manufacturing sector and the slow recovery of manufacturing investment since 1981 have left Britain with a severely reduced stock of industrial plant.

The very low unemployment rates now being experienced in many parts of the South East (for example 2.7 per cent in Crawley, 3.3 per cent in Winchester and Basingstoke, and 3.5 per cent in Tunbridge Wells in early 1988) provide further evidence that inflationary pressures are not very far below the surface. One symptom may be the much higher rate of increase in house prices in the south than in the north during 1987–8 (see Table 7.8).

A national expansion geared to using the unemployed labour of the high unemployment regions would help to reduce the adverse inflationary effects that are now occurring as a result of the continuation of strong national growth. It is difficult to see how an annual growth rate of 4 per cent can be sustained without this leading to inflationary problems. Regional policy should therefore be seen as an essential ingredient of a strategy of national economic expansion.

Regional policy has also been justified on the grounds that it helps to prevent unnecessary and potentially harmful population movements. Social overhead capital (schools, hospitals, houses and so on) already exists in the north and additional public investment is needed for every additional person living in the south. The case for regional policy is now very strong. Not only is there a serious waste of resources in the north due to the high levels of unemployment, there is also increasing pressure on land and the cost of premises in the south. This not only threatens the London greenbelt but is also fuelling the inflationary pressures which are beginning to arise in the labour markets of the south. Stimulating the economic revival of the north would help to relieve this pressure on the South-East, thus helping to solve two problems at the same time.

Some economists have argued that a better way to deal with the labour shortages and inflationary pressures in the south would be to release more land for housebuilding so that house prices will stop rising so quickly. This would make migration from north to south more attractive, therefore reducing labour shortages in the south while at the same time reducing unemployment in the north. Once again, however, we run up against the problem of 'cumulative causation'. Faster growth in the south causes a further widening of the north–south divide as migrants transfer their demands for goods and services from north to south; and the opposite occurs in the north as the out-migration leads to further decline.

The choice therefore seems to be between giving in to market forces, which are leading to an ever-increasing concentration of people and jobs in the south, and attempting to make the north economically stronger through more effective job creation schemes. Regional policy aims to do the latter.

TRADITIONAL REGIONAL POLICY AND ITS EFFECTIVENESS

Although regional policy existed in a weak form before the Second World War, it did not gather a head of steam until after the publication of the famous 1944 White Paper on *Employment Policy* which committed postwar governments to a policy of full employment. The vast increase in government control over the national economy during the Second World War led to the belief that the government possessed the power to keep unemployment well below the levels of pre-war years. Since regional differences in unemployment had been a major feature of the 1930s depression, one of the central aims of the full employment policy was to create jobs in problem regions. The belief that this policy could succeed was reinforced by the virtual disappearance of regional differences in unemployment during the war. The demobilisation of nearly five million people from the armed services at the end of the war inevitably led to rising unemployment and to the consequent re-emergence of regional unemployment differences. These differences were small, however, compared to the 1930s.

A variety of regional policy *instruments* was brought into being during the early postwar years. Many policy instruments such as loans to firms, government-built factories, industrial estates, land reclamation and financial help to migrants, were policies already tried in the 1930s. Expenditure on these policies was, however, increased after the Second World War. Other policy instruments were entirely new, the most significant of these being the strict control imposed on the location of new manufacturing plants. Firms wishing to build new plant in non-assisted areas (especially the South-East and the West Midlands) had to obtain an Industrial Development Certificate from the Board of Trade. Many firms were denied permission to expand in the South-East and West Midlands and some of these chose to relocate in the assisted areas of Scotland, Wales, Northern Ireland, the North and parts of the North-West. Although location controls were not enforced with the same enthusiasm by all governments, they did nevertheless prove to be an effective method of diverting industry to the assisted areas. The controls were especially effective during the immediate postwar years and again in the 1960s and early 1970s. They were suspended in 1981 and subsequently abolished.

From the early 1960s, regional policy was gradually reinforced. Tax incentives were introduced and these were followed by larger grants to firms locating their new plant and equipment in designated assisted areas. In addition to these investment grants, a labour subsidy (the Regional Employment Premium) was introduced in 1967. The aim was to encourage manufacturing firms to increase their employment levels in the assisted areas as well as to invest in new plant and equipment.

Traditional regional policy began to fall apart in the mid-1970s. Labour subsidies were the first policy instrument to be abandoned.

Serious doubts about the effectiveness of labour subsidies were reinforced by opposition to such long-term help for firms from Britain's EEC partners. The Regional Employment Premium was opposed by the EEC because grants of this type were regarded as giving British producers an unfair advantage in the European Community market. They also tend to protect out-dated and declining industries, making it more difficult for newer industries to attract scarce investment funds. The withdrawal of labour subsidies was followed by the ending of controls on the location of manufacturing industry.

A more serious threat to traditional regional policy came from the long-term decline of the manufacturing sector. The ability of manufacturing industry to create new jobs had been in decline since the late 1960s. This was reinforced in the late 1970s as Britain's manufacturers found it increasingly difficult to compete in world markets. This was partly due to the sharp increase in the value of the pound following the discovery and production of North Sea oil. The de-industrialisation of Britain received a further jolt during 1979–81 when a combination of a deflationary fiscal policy and a very restrictive monetary policy led to a dramatic reduction in manufacturing output and employment. Plant closures led to mass redundancies as manufacturing capacity was prematurely scrapped. This rapid decline of manufacturing put the finishing touches to undermining traditional regional policy.

The rise and fall of regional policy in the United Kingdom is best illustrated by government expenditure figures. Expenditure on regional policy rose dramatically in the mid-1960s reaching a peak in 1969 and again in 1975. The downward trend since the mid-1970s is the clearest possible signal that regional policy now has very low priority (see Figure 7.4). As regional unemployment differences have widened, policy makers have become increasingly disillusioned with traditional regional policy.

The disillusionment with regional policy stems largely from the fact that the sudden increase in regional unemployment differences in the 1980s suggests that regional policy has failed – and failed miserably. In our view, this conclusion is contradicted by the facts and must be firmly rejected. Assessing the effectiveness of regional policy is not an easy matter. It is certainly not possible to assess regional policy simply by referring to regional differences in unemployment. Research indicates that regional policy helped considerably during the 1960s and 1970s. Economists at the University of Cambridge, for

Figure 7.4 Regional policy expenditure in Great Britain 1972/3–1986/7 at constant 1980 prices

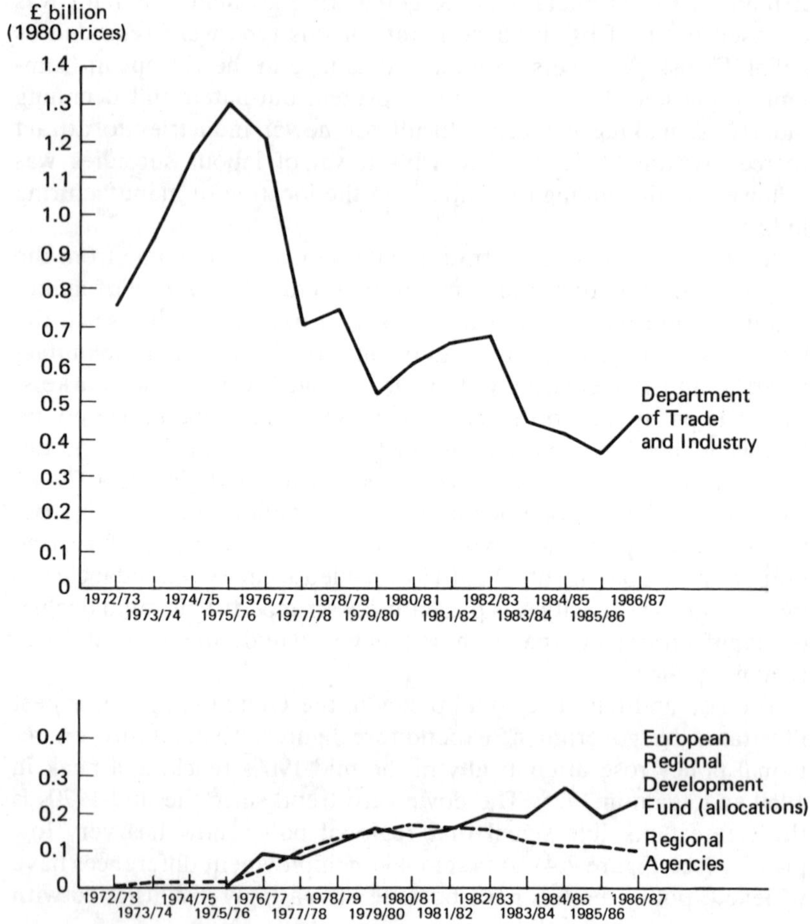

Sources and Explanations: See note 2 on page 171.

example, suggest that regional policy led to the creation of 784 000 jobs in the assisted areas during the period 1960–81. Over 600 000 of these jobs were estimated to be still in existence in 1981. (Moore, Rhodes and Tyler, 1986).

It has been estimated that about 27 per cent of the jobs created by regional policy were in firms which moved into the assisted areas from other regions. The remainder were created by firms already

Table 7.9 The movement of manufacturing establishments into and out of GB regions 1945–81

Region	*Outflow*	*Inflow*	*Net moves*
South-East	1842	195	−1647
East Anglia	72	426	354
East Midlands	274	335	61
South-West	107	423	316
West Midlands	430	96	−334
Yorks/Humberside	255	261	6
North-West	318	336	18
North	55	420	365
Wales	40	626	586
Scotland	64	367	303

Note: These data refer to the establishments which survived up to the date of enumeration.

Sources: Department of Trade and Industry; *Regional Trends*; Howard R. S. (1968) *The Movement of Manufacturing Industry in the United Kingdom 1945–65*, (London: HMSO).

located in the assisted areas. Just how many of these jobs were entirely new and how many were at the expense of jobs lost in non-assisted areas such as the South-East and West Midlands is unknown. As far as the effectiveness of particular regional policy instruments is concerned, there is considerable evidence that location controls and investment subsidies both had a substantial impact on job creation. Equally important, however, is the fact that these policy instruments helped to protect and renew the industrial base of the assisted areas for over two decades. There can be little doubt that the assisted areas would be in a far worse state at the present time if there had not been a regional policy during the 1960s and 1970s.

Further evidence that regional policy had the desired effect of steering industry and jobs to the assisted areas is provided by data on the movement of industry between regions. A summary picture of the movement of manufacturing establishments between the regions of Great Britain is given in Table 7.9, which shows that the three main assisted area regions (Scotland, Wales and the Northern region) had a substantially larger inflow than outflow of manufacturing industry during 1945–81. As far as these three regions are concerned, regional policy undoubtedly had the desired effect on the geographical movement of industry. Further scrutiny of the inter-regional movement of industry data reveals that it was not only the assisted areas which benefited from regional policy. East Anglia had the second largest number of inward moves of manufacturing establishments even though it was not an assisted area. The main reason for this large inflow into East Anglia was that many firms which were prevented from expanding in the South-East (because of industrial location controls) moved to East Anglia instead (Twomey and Taylor, 1985). A similar explanation holds for the South-West (see Table 7.10).

The movement of manufacturing industry between regions therefore suggests that regional policy was successful in diverting new manufacturing plant from low unemployment regions to high unemployment regions. In addition, controls on the location of industry in the South-East contributed to the considerable spill-over of new plants into East Anglia and the South-West. It is also interesting to note that the West Midlands was a major supplier of manufacturing establishments to other regions during the 1960s and early 1970s. The decline of manufacturing in the past decade has put this situation into reverse: the West Midlands is now designated as an assisted area itself!

Regional policy has therefore resulted in a considerable number of extra jobs being created in assisted areas. Regional unemployment differences and out-migration from high unemployment regions would both have been greater if regional policy had not existed. But have taxpayers got value for money out of regional policy expenditure? According to the White Paper on *Regional Industrial Development* (Dept. of Trade and Industry, 1983), the cost per job created by regional policy was around £35 000 during the 1960s and 1970s (at 1984 prices). Whether this is good value for money depends very much on how long the jobs actually last and whether they can be created more cheaply in other ways. On both counts regional policy seems to have performed quite well. In addition, we need to know how many of the jobs created in assisted areas were simply diverted from non-assisted areas.

Cost-per-job calculations should not, however, be taken at face value since they are based on the *gross* exchequer costs whereas it is the *net* costs which should be relevant from the Treasury's point of view. Each additional job created means higher tax revenue and lower expenditure on unemployment benefits. Until the costs per job created are accurately calculated, it will not be possible to say whether regional policy has given value for money. What little

Table 7.10 The interregional flows of manufacturing establishments, 1945–81

Origin / Destination	South-East	East Anglia	East Midlands	South-West	West Midlands	Yorks/Humberside	North-West	North	Wales	Scotland
South-East	–	379	181	320	36	89	168	192	282	193
East Anglia	19	–	7	1	2	8	7	8	10	10
East Midlands	27	19	–	16	17	68	26	38	38	25
South-West	25	3	6	–	9	2	9	5	36	12
West Midlands	36	6	42	51	–	17	64	28	142	44
Yorks/Humberside	24	4	64	6	4	–	38	80	11	24
North-West	30	6	22	20	17	45	–	44	93	41
North	11	3	7	1	1	11	9	–	2	10
Wales	13	3	1	3	5	4	5	4	–	3
Scotland	9	3	4	4	2	7	6	20	9	–

Sources: Department of Trade and Industry; *Regional Trends*; Howard, R. S. (1968) *The Movement of Manufacturing Industry in the United Kingdom 1945–65* (London: HMSO).

research has been done on this problem suggests that the *net* costs to the Treasury of regional assistance are extremely small.

CRITICISMS OF TRADITIONAL REGIONAL POLICY

Traditional regional policy came increasingly under attack during the late 1970s with the result that several fundamental changes have been made since 1979. The most significant of these changes were incorporated into the 1984 and 1988 reforms to regional policy. Before discussing these in detail, it will be useful to set out the major criticisms levelled against traditional regional policy so that an assessment can be made of the extent to which the 1984 and 1988 reforms represent an adequate response.

The criticisms of traditional regional policy centred mainly on the Regional Development Grant (RDG). This was an investment subsidy paid only to *manufacturing* firms investing in new buildings and in plant and equipment in the assisted areas. The main criticisms levelled against the RDG were as follows:

1. Regional assistance to industry has not been cost-effective. The automatic nature of the RDG has meant that some investment subsidies were paid to firms which would have invested in assisted areas even if the RDG had not been available. The most quoted example of this is the payment of subsidies to oil firms investing in Shetland as a result of North Sea oil. Paying grants to highly profitable firms which have no alternative but to locate in assisted areas is a waste of scarce public funds.
2. The logic of subsidising capital investment in high unemployment areas has been questioned. These subsidies encourage firms to invest in labour-saving technology. This may even lead to job losses by encouraging firms to switch from labour-intensive to capital-intensive techniques of production.
3. Regional investment grants have been mainly limited to firms in the manufacturing sector (see Table 7.11) in spite of the fact that it is the service sector which has been the main source of new jobs (see Figure 7.5). Regional aid was restricted mainly to manufacturing since it was originally intended that new manufacturing jobs should be created in order to replace those being shed by the older staple industries. An additional advantage of concentrating regional aid on manufacturing activities was that a strong manufac-

Table 7.11 Regional subsidies: distribution between the main industrial sectors, 1972/3–1986/7

Sector	*% of total expenditure on Regional Development Grant (old scheme)*
Mining and quarrying	2.1
Manufacturing	94.9
Construction	2.0
Services	0.0
Other	1.0
Total	100

Sector	*% of total expenditure in each sector* *Regional Development Grant (revised scheme)*	*Regional Selective Assistance*
Agriculture, forestry, fishing	0.0	0.1
Energy and water	0.1	0.2
Minerals and chemicals	8.0	13.8
Manufacturing	74.2	84.7
Construction	0.0	0.3
Services	11.7	1.0
Other	6.0	0.0
Total	100	100

Note: The Regional Development Grant scheme was introduced in 1972 and was revised in 1984. Payments under the revised RDG scheme date only from November 1984. Certain services became eligible for the RDG in 1984. The RDG was abolished in 1988.

Source: *Annual Reports of the Industrial Development Act 1982.*

turing sector was believed to be essential for Britain's economic future. A competitive manufacturing sector exporting the major part of its output would help the balance of payments and allow the economy to grow more quickly. These arguments began to weaken during the 1970s as the export potential of Britain's service industries became more apparent. It is extremely unlikely, however, that service sector export earnings could fully compensate for the loss of manufacturing exports.

4. Traditional regional policy was heavily biased towards encouraging firms in the non-assisted areas to move into assisted areas. Insufficient attention has been paid to stimulating the assisted areas to grow 'from within' by encouraging existing firms in the

Figure 7.5 Changes in manufacturing and service sector employment in Great Britain, 1971–87

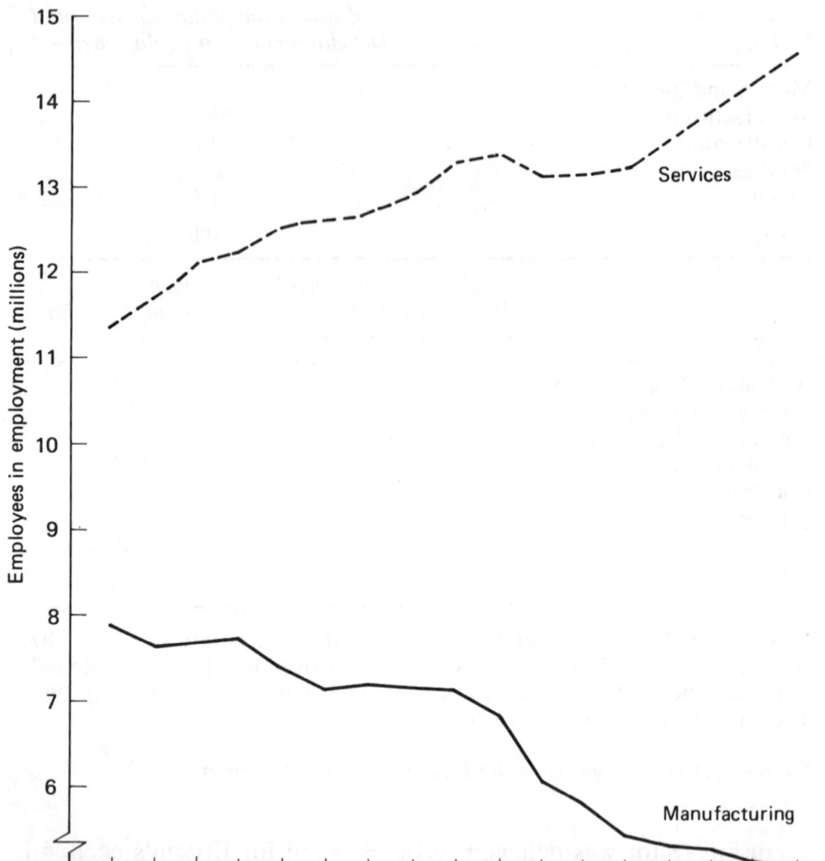

Notes: Figures refer to June of each year.
Source: *Employment Gazette*, Historical Supplement 1 February 1987; *Employment Gazette*, April 1988.

assisted areas to expand and by encouraging new firms to be created.

5. Traditional regional policy relied heavily upon transferring low-skill blue-collar jobs to the assisted areas. Functions such as Research and Development and marketing have not moved north with the result that many of the key activities and key jobs have remained in the South-East.

A more general criticism levelled against traditional regional policy is that the areas eligible for regional assistance have been too broadly defined. In 1979, for example, the assisted areas had over 40 per cent of the working population living within their borders. This resulted in regional policy expenditure being spread very thinly across the assisted areas.

Not all of these criticisms of traditional regional policy stand up to close scrutiny. The argument that grants to firms expanding in high unemployment areas should favour labour-intensive production activities can be challenged on four main counts. First, investment subsidies have the distinct advantage that they help to raise a region's competitiveness by stimulating the use and development of new technology. Encouraging firms to become more labour-intensive is a step backwards and may be a short-sighted policy as far as the future economic development of the assisted areas is concerned. Secondly, subsidising capital-intensive activities may create considerable employment in industries which supply inputs (including service inputs) to capital-intensive firms. The *indirect* employment effects of capital subsidies need to be taken into account, not just the *direct* employment effects. Thirdly, by reducing a firm's production costs, capital subsidies will stimulate firms to expand their output, thereby creating more jobs. Fourthly, most modern fast-growing industries are capital-intensive and not labour-intensive.

Another aspect of traditional regional policy which has been severely criticised is the use of controls on the location of industry. If location controls discourage firms from expanding or if they encourage firms to find an alternative location overseas, this will have harmful effects on output and jobs. On the other hand, research has shown that location controls were extremely effective in diverting firms to designated assisted areas and it would be wrong to dismiss the possibility that they may once again become an effective policy instrument. Increasing shortages of land and labour in the South-East make location controls (or better still taxes on industrial development) a more attractive policy option.

THE 1979–88 REFORMS TO REGIONAL POLICY

The government responded to the criticisms levelled against traditional regional policy in three stages. The first major package of reforms came during 1979–83 under the guidance of Sir Keith Joseph. The main measures were:

1. the abolition of controls on the location of industry;
2. the re-drawing of the assisted areas map to reduce the areas eligible for assistance to a 'hard core' of depressed areas where unemployment was at its highest;
3. a planned cut in regional policy expenditure.

By 1984, the government was ready for its second and more far-reaching reforms to regional policy. The main changes are summarised in Table 7.12 (see also Armstrong, 1986). The government's response to the criticism that regional assistance to industry had not been cost-effective was dramatic. The fundamental aim of the 1984 reforms, brought in by Mr Norman Tebbit, was to cut regional policy expenditure from £700 million in 1983/4 to £400 million by 1987/8. Since this proposed cut in regional policy expenditure followed a period when expenditure had already been declining sharply, these expenditure cuts can be described as no less than draconian.

The main changes to regional policy in the 1984 reforms can be divided into two parts. On the negative side, these reforms abolished the Special Development Areas thereby reducing the maximum grant payable under the Regional Development Grant scheme from 22 per cent to 15 per cent. In addition, Mr Tebbit reduced the areas eligible for full Development Area assistance, but expanded Intermediate Areas by including large parts of the West Midlands. On the positive side, certain service sector industries became eligible for regional aid. These included business and commercial services which served national and international markets. The list of industries eligible for Regional Development Grants was therefore considerably extended. This was a welcome change to regional policy since services are likely to remain the main source of employment growth in the foreseeable future. In addition, a maximum grant per job was placed on Regional Development Grants since the Government wanted to eliminate grants being paid to highly capital-intensive projects. The central aim of the 1984 reforms was to get 'better value for the taxpayer's money' by making certain that regional grants created jobs rather than simply reducing the cost of investment in new and replacement machinery.

The primary motive behind the 1984 reforms was to make regional policy more efficient. But it is difficult not to draw the conclusion that the planned cutback of expenditure reflected a deeply pessimistic attitude towards the benefits accruing from regional policy. This was confirmed in 1988 by the most recent set of regional policy reforms introduced by Lord Young. These are summarised in Table 7.13.

Table 7.12 Summary of the 1984 reforms to regional policy

Regional Development Grant (RDG)	(i)	Certain service industries made eligible for RDGs alongside manufacturing industries e.g. banking, finance, insurance, business services, industrial research and development.
	(ii)	Maximum grant reduced from 22% to 15%.
	(iii)	Cost-per-job limit of £10 000 imposed on RDGs. Firms with under 200 workers exempt from this limit on projects up to £0.5 million.
	(iv)	A grant of £3000 for each new job created available in Development Areas as an alternative to the RDG. Firms receive whichever grant is the more favourable to them.
	(v)	Replacement or modernisation projects not eligible for assistance unless they lead to job creation.
Regional Selective Assistance (RSA)	(i)	Expenditure on RSA to be increased relative to expenditure on RDGs. Switch in emphasis from automatic to selective grants, designed to make regional policy expenditure more cost-effective.
	(ii)	RSA to be used to protect existing jobs as well as creating new jobs.
Policy towards small firms and innovation		New methods of encouraging the growth of small firms and the creation of new firms in assisted areas to be explored. Similar schemes for encouraging technological innovation to be examined.
Designation of assisted areas		Substantial changes to delineation of assisted areas. Special Development Areas abolished and many Development Areas converted into Intermediate Areas (not eligible for RDGs). Parts of West Midlands designated as Intermediate Area for first time.
Expenditure on regional policy by Department of Trade & Industry		Substantial reduction in regional policy expenditure planned for 1985/6–1987/8. Cuts of up to £300 million (from almost £700 million in 1983/4).

Source: Department of Trade and Industry, *Press Notice 681*, 28 November 1984.

Lord Young's changes to regional policy extended the two earlier reforms in several ways. The first and more surprising reform was the abolition of the Regional Development Grant, which has been the linchpin of regional policy in the United Kingdom since 1972. From

Table 7.13 Summary of the 1988 reforms to regional policy

1. Regional Development Grant abolished. Savings in expenditure to be transferred (at least initially) to other regional assistance schemes.
2. Small firms under 25 employees:
   (i) eligible for 15% investment grant up to a maximum of £15 000;
   (ii) eligible for an innovation grant of 50% up to a maximum of £25 000 to support new products and new methods of production.
3. Firms with under 500 employees:
   – will qualify for grants to meet the cost of employing management consultants under the Business Development Initiative Scheme; two-thirds of the cost to be met by the government (compared to one-half in non-assisted areas).
4. Regional Selective Assistance:
   – more money to be made available to offset the reduced expenditure on Regional Development Grants. Only projects that would not otherwise go ahead to be supported.

Source: *DTI–The Department for Enterprise*, Cmnd 278, HMSO, 1988.

now on, all regional grants will be made at the *discretion* of government officials rather than being available to firms *automatically*. The funds that would otherwise have been spent on the Regional Development Grant may now be transferred to the Regional Selective Assistance scheme. To receive selective assistance, however, firms will have to convince government officials that they would only go ahead with their investment plans if government grants were made available.

The boost to selective assistance is being supported by policies aimed at creating new firms and helping small businesses in the assisted areas to expand. Small firms with under 25 employees now qualify for investment grants of up to 15 per cent and grants of up to 50 per cent to cover the cost of introducing new methods of production and new products. Small and medium-sized firms with under 500 employees qualify for grants to meet the cost of management consultants (up to two-thirds of the cost in assisted areas compared to half the cost elsewhere). The introduction of financial aid directed specifically at giving extra help to small and medium-sized firms in assisted areas is long overdue.

Although some of the 1988 reforms, such as the extra help for small and medium-sized firms, are to be welcomed, the new policy contains several serious flaws. First, the abolition of the Regional

Development Grant now makes it more difficult for firms to plan their future investment since they will not know how much financial assistance they can obtain until their negotiations with government bureaucrats have been completed. The overriding advantage of the Regional Development Grant was that firms knew in advance exactly to what they were entitled. The switch to discretionary grants (under the Regional Selective Assistance Scheme) will involve extensive haggling with civil servants over the size of the grant. The regional offices of the Department of Trade and Industry are to be expanded in order to cope with the greater workload which the abolition of the Regional Development Grant will create.

Secondly, the frequent revisions to regional policy during the 1980s are themselves undermining its effectiveness. Are we to assume that the 1984 reforms to regional policy were a failure? Has there been any serious assessment of the 1984 reforms by the government? Major reforms have become a frequent feature of regional policy since 1979. So many changes over such a short period inevitably lead to uncertainty and confusion.

Thirdly, the government has said that 'the changes [to regional policy] do not reduce the planned level of spending on industrial measures'. This suggests that expenditure on regional policy will not be allowed to fall any further. But this commitment to maintaining expenditure does not guarantee that the *real* value of regional policy expenditure (that is allowing for inflation) will be maintained. Moreover, this guarantee of level funding for regional policy is only for three years.

There is much more to regional policy, however, than simply setting expenditure targets. Indeed, there is much more to regional policy than that part of it run from Whitehall. The next section discusses the increasingly important role played by organisations other than central government. These include local authorities, regional development agencies and the EEC.

INDUSTRIAL DEVELOPMENT POLICY: LOCAL AUTHORITIES, REGIONAL DEVELOPMENT AGENCIES AND THE EEC

The reforms to regional policy in the 1980s have taken place against a background of fundamental change in the ways in which depressed areas receive assistance. Firms in depressed areas (or wishing to move to a depressed area) are now faced with an ever-growing number of agencies and organisations offering all kinds of assistance. These include: the Department of Trade and Industry, the Scottish and Welsh Offices, English Estates, the Scottish and Welsh Development Agencies, the Highlands and Islands Development Board, Mid-Wales Development, the Development Commission in rural areas and numerous organisations associated with the European Community. To these must be added an enormous number of local organisations. The local authorities – both county councils and district councils – are actively involved in assisting industry, particularly those authorities located in depressed regions. Many councils have independent enterprise agencies and boards with wide powers (but often very little financial support) to help local firms. In addition, business clubs and enterprise trusts have been springing up in many depressed areas. All these organisations have the same basic objective: to create jobs in areas of high unemployment.

The near-monopoly which Whitehall used to have over regional assistance to industry is gradually being broken. Control has been shifting both upwards and downwards: upwards to the EEC and downwards to local authorities and regional level organisations. The boundaries between regional policy, urban policy, economic development in rural areas, and local authority development initiatives have become increasingly blurred.

Some indication of the shift of control away from Whitehall can be obtained by comparing the expenditure on regional policy by the Department of Trade and Industry with that of the European Regional Development Fund and the various regional agencies in Scotland and Wales. Figure 7.4 demonstrated that the central government is now only one of several participants in regional policy. If the field is widened to include other spending bodies – the local authorities, the urban development corporations, and the rural area agencies – the erosion of central government control is even more striking (see Table 7.14).

The shift in the control of regional spending should not, however, be exaggerated. Whitehall exerts considerable influence over both the total amount of spending on regional policy and the allocation of funds between projects and between geographical areas. The Scottish and Welsh Development Agencies, for example, rely heavily on the central government for finance. Similarly, the allocation of the European Regional Development Fund's expenditure *between projects* is

Table 7.14 Expenditure on 'spatial' industrial policy in Great Britain, 1983–4

		£ million
(a)	*European Economic Community*	
	European Regional Development Fund	46
	European Investment Bank (loans)	92
	European Coal and Steel Community (Conversion Loans)	52
(b)	*Central Government*	
	Department of Trade and Industry	
	Regional Development Grants	439
	Regional Selective Assistance	82
	Department of the Environment	
	Urban Programme (industrial projects)	54
	Enterprise Zones	40
(c)	*Regional Organisations*	
	English Estates	41
	Development Commission (industrial)	22
	Scottish Development Agency	85
	Welsh Development Agency	44
	Highlands and Islands Development Board	27
	Mid-Wales Development	7
(d)	*Local government*	
	County Councils	120
	District Councils	321

Sources and Explanations: see note 3 on page 173.

determined largely by Whitehall. The influence of Whitehall on industrial development expenditure by local authorities is less direct but none the less substantial since the amount that local authorities can spend on economic development is limited by their revenue base. This revenue base is determined by how much local authorities are allowed to raise locally to finance economic development and how much the government is willing to provide from central funds. The influence of Whitehall on industrial assistance is therefore still very strong.

Yet in spite of the fact that Whitehall ultimately holds the purse strings, the development of regional policy in recent years has been significantly influenced by the greater participation of local authorities, regional development agencies and the EEC. Their contribution to the development of depressed regions needs to be recognised since their involvement will probably increase in future years.

Local authorities and industrial development

Local authorities in many parts of Britain responded to the sharp increase in unemployment in the early 1980s by creating their own economic development initiatives. These included the clearing of derelict land to provide space for new business premises, building small workshops for sale and for rent, and setting up industrial development bureaux to provide advice to small businesses, especially those just starting up or expanding their existing operations. In addition, funds have been created to provide loans and small grants to help firms to expand. Local development policies are sometimes conducted through the creation of an Enterprise Board or Agency, which in some cases have become more directly involved in local development through buying shares in small and medium-sized firms.

Although the initiative shown by local authorities in attempting to create jobs in their own localities must be welcomed, this trend towards greater involvement by local authorities in assisting private industry has its danger. One is that the cost of providing new jobs may be increased as a result of local authorities bidding against each other when offering financial assistance to firms. If firms respond to local authority grants and loans by 'shopping around' for the best bargain, local authorities may have to increase the size of the grants and loans on offer. The problem is made worse because local authorities vary in wealth and the poorer authorities may not be capable of competing with the richer authorities. Moreover, the existence of competitive bidding means that some of the new jobs attracted by local authorities are simply diverted from other local authority areas. In addition, expenditure on economic development by local authorities is sometimes funded by cutting back on other spending programmes (such as housing), causing job losses elsewhere in the local area. The effects of local authority initiatives therefore need to be carefully monitored. If it is discovered that local authority development initiatives begin to operate to the detriment of the poorer authorities, it will be necessary for the central government to take steps to prevent this.

Regional Development Agencies

The second significant change in industrial assistance to depressed areas has been the steady extension of the activities of the Scottish and Welsh Development Agencies. Set up in 1976, these agencies have used their wide-ranging powers to become actively involved in new ways of assisting industry. Their functions include acquiring and developing land for the construction of business premises, improving the environment, and constructing development programmes for particular areas. Another more general function of the Scottish and Welsh Development Agencies is to promote the advantage of locating in these two areas to mobile firms such as multinational companies. They also provide financial assistance to private companies.

One of the major advantages of the Scottish and Welsh Development Agencies is that they are able to take an active part in the development of their own regions. They help to co-ordinate the activities of a wide range of organisations (such as local authorities, housing associations and the Training Commission) within their own region, thus providing the opportunity to construct development programmes for areas which cross administrative boundaries such as local authority areas. Large development projects, for example, will affect not only the areas in which they are located but surrounding areas as well. This will be the case for airports, large industrial estates, port development schemes, large office complexes, science parks and exhibition centres. When projects have significant economic and social effects in a number of areas, and when a variety of government departments and other organisations is involved, there is a strong case for taking a regional view. Regional development agencies are well placed to take on such a task.

A strong case can be made for establishing regional development agencies in English regions along the lines of those already in existence in Scotland and Wales. These regional agencies could play an important role in helping to *co-ordinate* the activities of those involved in regional economic development (including the local authorities). The agencies could also help to obtain more finance from the private sector. The reluctance of commercial banks to provide long-term loans is a long-standing criticism of the British banking system. Regional agencies can provide a pipeline for private finance, particularly for small and medium-sized firms.

EEC Regional Policy

Finally, the EEC has been developing a more aggressive regional policy during the 1980s. This includes an extension of the powers and financial resources of the European Regional Development Fund

(ERDF), which was established in 1975 to provide financial support to a wide range of investment projects in assisted areas. A significant feature of the ERDF is that development grants are provided not only to *private* sector firms but also to *public* authorities which invest in new economic infrastructure (such as roads and telecommunications).

In recent years the European Regional Development Fund has been switching its support from individual investment *projects* towards regional development *programmes*. The Fund is therefore encouraging designated assisted areas to submit comprehensive development programmes rather than large numbers of individual applications for unrelated projects. The switch in emphasis away from *individual projects* and towards *development programmes* is beginning to have a further beneficial effect: it is helping the EEC to gain more control over its Regional Development Fund. Since 1975, assistance to individual projects provided by the Fund has been channelled through national governments. In Britain, the government has tended to use this money as part of its own regional policy spending. A tight grip on assistance from the Fund has therefore been maintained by the central government. Assistance for entire programmes, however, is more directly influenced by the EEC and can be used to increase *total* spending on regional projects. The growth of programme assistance is therefore helping to weaken the grip that individual governments have on the Fund's spending activities.

One of the problems with the European Regional Development Fund is that it has to develop regional policies for the European Community as a whole at the same time as the individual member states are competing against each other in the race to attract mobile multinational investment. The EEC has therefore found it necessary to create powers to prevent member states from using their own regional policy incentives to out-bid each other for multinational investment. The powers have so far been applied with only partial success.

The European Regional Development Fund is about to receive a major boost. The twelve member countries of the EEC have recently agreed to remove the remaining barriers to free trade within the EEC. The Single European Act, which all member countries have signed, means that by 1992 almost all of the remaining barriers to trade (such as customs duties, different safety standards for individual products and so on) will have gone. In addition, work has now begun on the Channel Tunnel. When this is completed in 1993, it will be even easier for British firms to transport their goods to the continent and for goods to be imported into Britain.

The boost to trade which will occur in the early 1990s has important implications for the British assisted areas. Their geographical isolation from the main markets on the continent means that it will be more difficult for them to share in the benefits of the increase in trade. As a result of these fears, the EEC has announced that the European Regional Development Fund is to be *doubled* between 1988 and 1992. Just how much of this extra money will go to the British assisted areas remains to be seen.

The emergence of new actors on the regional policy stage in recent years has important implications for the future development of regional policy. Local authorities, enterprise boards, development agencies and the European Regional Development Fund are increasingly influencing the geographical pattern of economic development in the United Kingdom. It is therefore essential to make sure that these various agencies are pulling in the same direction since there is a grave danger that much of the effort will be wasted unless the activities of these various agencies are closely co-ordinated.

PROPOSALS FOR STRENGTHENING REGIONAL POLICY

By far the most effective way of reducing the substantial regional disparities in employment opportunities which now exist in the United Kingdom is to improve the growth in the number of jobs *nationally*. Historical experience indicates with striking clarity that regional unemployment differences are at their narrowest when the national unemployment rate is low. As national unemployment rose during the 1970s and 1980s, the unemployment rate gap between regions widened at an alarming rate. This is illustrated in Figure 7.6. Previous experience therefore suggests that policies to reduce regional unemployment disparities are very heavily dependent upon the national employment situation. Unless the national unemployment rate can be substantially reduced, regional differences in unemployment will remain very high. A sustained increase in national employment is therefore needed. This will require a sustained growth of national output of over 3 per cent per year since anything less than that will

Figure 7.6 Regional differences in unemployment and the UK unemployment rate, 1974–87

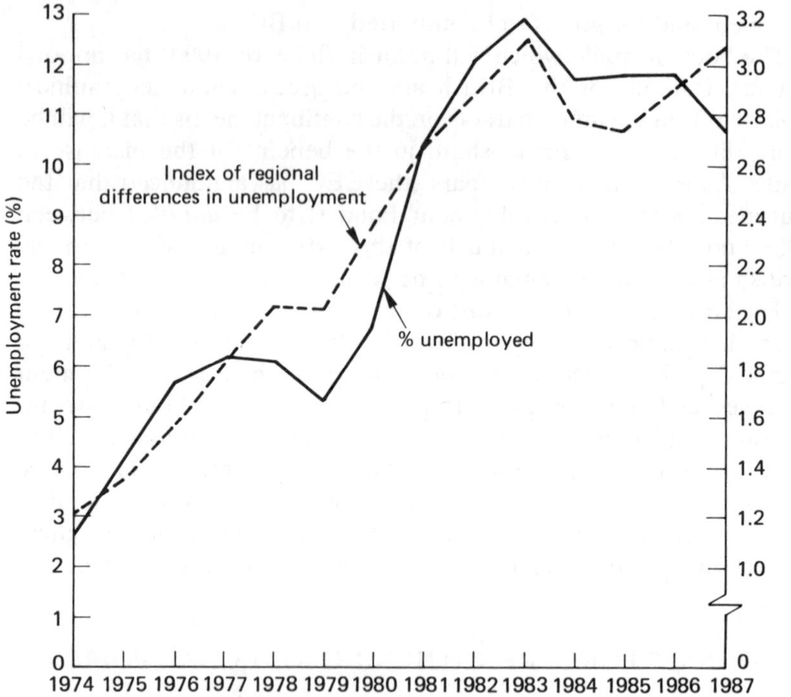

Notes

1 The index of regional differences in unemployment is the (unweighted) standard deviation of regional unemployment rates.

2 The unemployment rate for 1984–7 is calculated on a different basis to the pre-1984 unemployment rate. The sharp fall in UK unemployment between 1983 and 1984 is largely due to a change in the method of calculating the unemployment rate.

Source: Employment Gazette.

mean that national employment will decline. This is because a constant labour force can produce about 3 per cent more output each year as a result of productivity improvements.

A strong national economic expansion is therefore necessary if regional unemployment differences are to be substantially reduced. The problem with this strategy is that the UK economy will run into serious inflationary problems unless the expansion can be diverted to areas where labour is not scarce. A stronger regional policy could therefore help to sustain the period of rapid growth which we have seen since the mid-1980s by helping to reduce the inflationary pressures that this growth has helped to create.

Four ways in which regional policy can be strengthened are suggested here. Taken together, they could convert regional policy into an effective force for reducing regional differences in unemployment. Our proposals are as follows:

Proposal 1: The geographical impact of all government fiscal policies should be carefully and continuously monitored so that the regional effects of the government's own activities can be clearly seen

What little we know of the regional distribution of government expenditure suggests that some regions benefit much more than others. This applies to many areas of government spending from health through to defence. Estimates of government spending in the UK regions during the 1970s, for example, indicated that the West Midlands fared very badly compared to other regions (Short, 1981). Up-to-date information is therefore required of the regional distribution of government expenditure. Similar comments apply to taxation. It is known, for example, that indirect taxes (such as value added tax) tend to increase regional differences in disposable income whereas income tax has the opposite effect. The government ought therefore to consider the regional effects of tax changes very carefully before they are introduced. The replacement of domestic rates by a community charge (or poll tax) provides an excellent example of an occasion where very little consideration, if any, has been given to the regional impact of an important change to the tax system.

An excellent opportunity to improve matters is provided by the annual projections of public expenditure. As well as providing the public expenditure plans for each department, it would be useful to see the regional distribution of these planned expenditures so that each department can be asked to justify the regional allocation. At the very least, detailed information on the regional distribution of government spending would focus attention on the regional impact of the government's own activities.

Every policy undertaken by the government has a regional impact and should therefore be regarded as a potential instrument of regional policy. This does not mean that regional policy goals should override other policy goals, but an annual assessment of the impact of government expenditure in all regions would permit regional policy objectives to be considered at an early stage in policy formulation.

Proposal 2: All regional development initiatives should be co-ordinated

Our second proposal is that there should be greater *co-ordination* between the many different organisations and agencies now involved in economic development in depressed regions. As explained earlier, the near-monopoly which the central government has had over regional policy is gradually disappearing. At one end of the spectrum, local authorities have become increasingly involved in promoting the creation of new jobs within their own boundaries; and at the other end of the spectrum, the EEC has become increasingly involved in financing regional economic development. The regional policy initiatives of local government, central government, regional agencies and the EEC need to be carefully co-ordinated if they are to achieve their objectives efficiently.

To be effective, the co-ordination of regional policy must be extended to cover a wide range of activities. This will involve:

1. co-ordinating the activities of different local authorities;
2. co-ordinating the activities of different government departments;
3. co-ordinating the activities of all other organisations which have significant effects on a region's economic development, such as enterprise agencies and boards.

Considerable thought needs to be given by policy makers and their advisers to the best way in which the activities of all those involved in regional policy can be better co-ordinated. A start in this direction could be made by appointing a Minister with special responsibility for regional economic development.

Proposal 3: Regional development agencies should be created for all regions

Three arguments can be advanced in support of establishing regional development agencies for English regions alongside those already in existence in Scotland and Wales. First, regional agencies are in a better position than Whitehall to operate regional development policies on a day-to-day basis. The recent switch in regional policy from *automatic* to *discretionary* assistance, the provision of special help to small firms, and the construction of individually-tailored packages of advice and financial help for small firms, all require strong local involvement and local knowledge.

Secondly, regional development agencies offer an excellent opportunity for co-ordinating the activities of the many different organisations now involved in regional development. In particular, regional agencies could construct development plans for areas which cross local authority boundaries. This would involve the co-operation of all local authorities affected by such plans and the regional development agency would help to achieve the necessary cooperation.

But should regional development agencies be established in *all* English regions or should they be restricted only to the most depressed regions? One reason for setting up regional development agencies in the south as well as in the north is that the economic health of the north is closely tied to that of the south. All regions are heavily dependent upon each other. A prosperous and fast growing south, for example, generates a demand for the products of firms located in the north. Moreover, a strong growth in the south would create more opportunities for transferring jobs (through location controls or taxes and regional financial inducements) from the south to the north. It should also be noted that parts of the south are still suffering from very high unemployment rates. As we saw in Table 7.4, for example, Essex, Kent and Greater London all had unemployment rates of over 8 per cent in February 1988 in spite of several years of rapid national growth.

There is a real danger, however, that setting up regional development agencies in the relatively prosperous south could have harmful effects on the north–south divide. The south already has a head start on the north in the scramble for new jobs and there is a danger that regional development agencies in the south would be too successful relative to the north. It is therefore absolutely essential that the lion's share of regional aid should be steered (by the central government) towards the most depressed regions. The establishment of regional development agencies could therefore be counter-productive unless there were strict control over the allocation of central funds to these regional agencies.

A further problem with the creation of regional development agencies for English regions is that numerous tasks which such agencies would undertake are currently in the hands of existing organisations. If the English development agencies are to be given powers such as providing financial assistance to firms, buying shares in small firms, advising firms on technical, commercial and financial matters, developing environmental and reclamation projects, and constructing new industrial sites and premises, it will be necessary for the regional agencies to acquire some of the powers currently held by organisations such as the Department of Trade and Industry, the Department of the Environment, the Development Commission, local authorities and English Estates. Without the full co-operation of these organisations, the creation of regional development agencies will be a worthless exercise.

The success of regional development agencies rests upon two main factors. First, the agencies must draw heavily upon local knowledge, experience and enthusiasm. The answer to regional problems ultimately lies in the hands of the regions themselves. They cannot be solved from Whitehall. Secondly, the agencies must instill confidence in those investing in the depressed regions so that development becomes a self-perpetuating and self-reinforcing process. Those with funds to invest must be convinced that the region in which they are investing is a profitable location or will soon become one.

One of the primary functions of regional development agencies is therefore to attract private investment funds from the South-East. This applies particularly to venture capital. (Venture capital is the investment of funds in high risk, usually small, businesses which cannot obtain funds from the capital market in the way that public limited companies are able to do.) At the moment, the South-East gets the lion's share of venture capital (see Figure 7.7). This is reflected by the higher birth rate of new firms in the south than in the north (see Table 7.15). Regional development agencies need to help the northern regions to raise the birth rate of new firms by attracting more venture capital northwards.

Proposal 4: Regional policy expenditures should be substantially increased

The steady decline in regional policy expenditure since the mid-1970s is only partly due to deliberate action by successive governments. The abolition of the Regional Employment Premium at the beginning of 1977 was bound to cause a sharp reduction in regional spending; so too were the reductions in the Regional Development Grant from 22 per cent to 15 per cent in 1984, the reduction in the number of areas eligible for these grants, and the ultimate abolition of Regional Development Grants in 1988. But regional expenditure has also fallen as a result of the long-term decline of the manufacturing sector. The fall in expenditure on investment grants since the

Figure 7.7 Number and distribution of venture capital investments in the United Kingdom

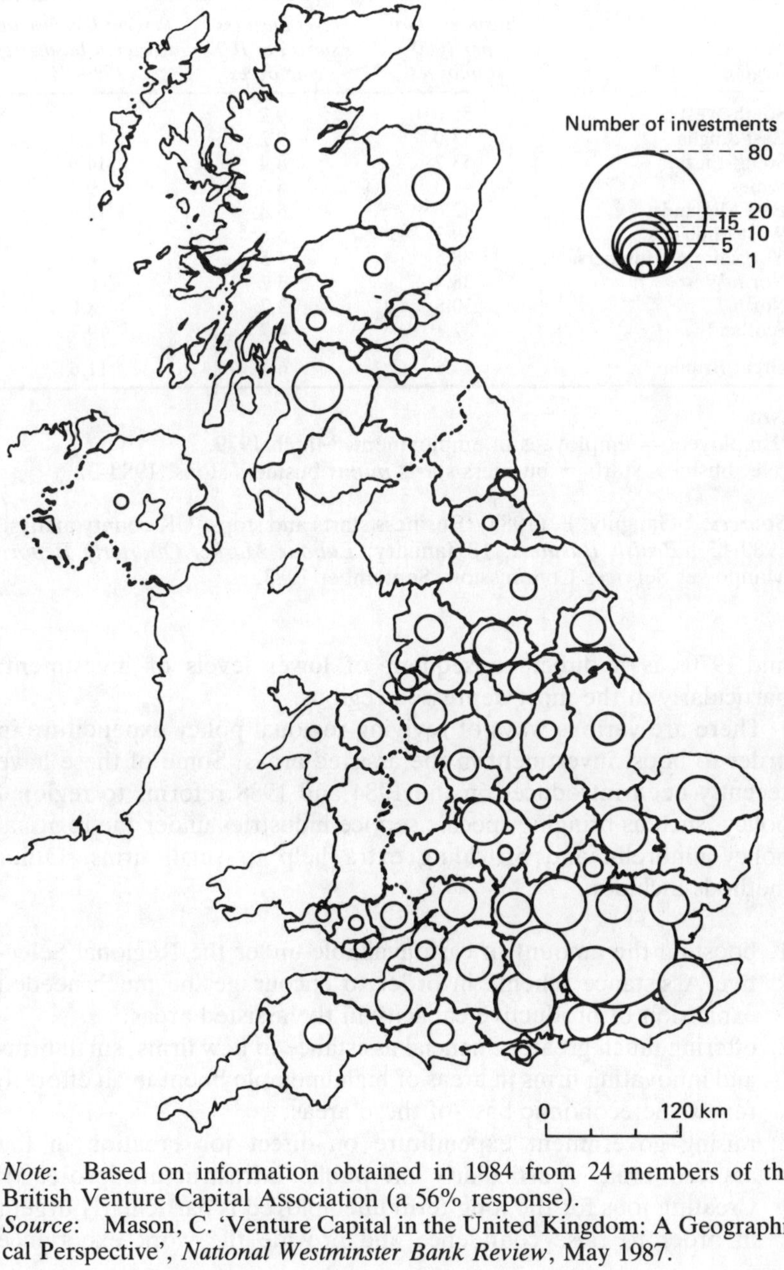

Note: Based on information obtained in 1984 from 24 members of the British Venture Capital Association (a 56% response).
Source: Mason, C. 'Venture Capital in the United Kingdom: A Geographical Perspective', *National Westminster Bank Review*, May 1987.

Table 7.15 New firm formation in the GB regions, 1980–3

Region	*Business starts per 1000 employees*[1]	*Net business starts per 1000 employees*[2]	*Percent increase in registered businesses 1979–83*
South-West	56.0	9.2	11.7
East Anglia	53.0	9.2	12.4
South-East	53.2	8.4	14.9
Wales	44.3	6.3	9.1
East Midlands	42.6	6.8	12.0
West Midlands	39.3	5.6	11.3
Yorkshire & Humberside	38.5	4.5	8.5
North-West	38.4	3.2	6.6
North	30.8	3.7	8.6
Scotland	32.1	4.7	9.7
Great Britain	44.6	6.4	11.6

Notes:
[1]Employees = employees in employment, March 1979.
[2]Net business starts = business starts *minus* business stops, 1980–3.

Sources: Ganguly, P. (1985) 'Business starts and stops: UK county analysis 1980–83', *British Business*, 18 January; *Labour Market Quarterly Report*, Manpower Services Commission, September 1983.

mid-1970s is a direct consequent of lower levels of investment, particularly in the most depressed regions.

There are various ways of reviving regional policy expenditure in order to boost investment in the assisted areas. Some of these have recently been introduced in the 1984 and 1988 reforms to regional policy, such as bringing specific service industries under the regional policy umbrella and providing extra help to small firms. Other methods include:

1. boosting the amount of cash available under the Regional Selective Assistance scheme in order to encourage the much needed expansion of productive capacity in the assisted areas;
2. offering much greater financial assistance to new firms, small firms and innovating firms in areas of high unemployment in an effort to renew the economic base of these areas;
3. raising government expenditure on direct job creation in the assisted areas (particularly on public infrastructure projects). Creating jobs for the long-term unemployed is particularly urgent in order to raise confidence and provide the work experience

which those unemployed for long periods require. Special employment subsidies for the long-term unemployed would help to equip workers with skills as well as stimulating employment growth. The benefits of such a policy would be particularly favourable to the high unemployment regions since a higher proportion of unemployment in the north is long-term compared to the south.

There is no shortage of jobs which need to be done and there is no shortage of willing hands to do those jobs. Many of Britain's schools, hospitals, houses, recreational amenities and public buildings are badly in need of repair, reconstruction and replacement. What seems to be lacking is the political will to carry through an exercise which inevitably involves a substantial increase in government spending.

CONCLUSION

For over forty years, successive governments have unreservedly committed themselves to the principle of reducing regional differences in job opportunities. Unfortunately, policy makers have not always lived up to these commitments in practice. This is aptly demonstrated by the steady fall in regional policy expenditure since the mid-1970s whilst regional differences in unemployment have moved very rapidly in the opposite direction.

The substantial widening of regional unemployment rates, however, was caused not by the decline of regional policy but by the plunge of the UK economy into its most serious slump since the 1930s. The recent strong growth in the economy (since 1984) is helping to reduce unemployment rates across all UK regions, but regional differences in unemployment have hardly changed in spite of this stronger national growth. Achieving a faster growth of jobs nationally is undoubtedly by far the best tonic for the depressed areas. A continuation of the national expansion of output and jobs is needed if regional unemployment differences are to be significantly reduced.

The first priority is therefore to keep up the national rate of output growth. This would bring the national unemployment rate down and eventually reduce regional unemployment. But this will not in itself eliminate the underlying problems facing the most depressed regions. Their fundamental problem is that they have weaker and far less resilient economies than the South-East. They cannot ride the storms of national and international recessions as easily as the South-East and they do not have the same growth potential. There is also evidence that the situation may get worse if left unchecked. Companies in the depressed regions are coming increasingly under the control of firms with their headquarters in the South-East and overseas (see Ashcroft, Love and Scouller, 1987). This loss of local control further weakens regional economies because of the consequent loss of top management jobs (Research and Development activities, marketing and other high skill functions) to parent organisations located elsewhere.

What needs to be done to regional policy in order to revitalise the depressed areas? The first and most obvious policy action is to reverse the downward trend in regional policy expenditure. Revitalising the economic base of the depressed areas cannot be done without a substantial increase in capital investment. The reduction in investment grants since the early 1980s should therefore be reversed – and as quickly as possible. But this is only a beginning. Several other policy initiatives will have to be assimilated as well. The following policies should, in our view, take priority:

1. *The regional impact of all government expenditure should be estimated and published* in order to focus attention on the government's own contribution to each region's economic activity. The regular publication of this information would act as a spur to government departments by forcing them to justify the regional impact of their spending plans. Britain's depressed areas may ultimately get a better deal from what are currently regarded as distinctly non-regional policies (such as government spending on defence, education, health and the civil service).
2. *The regional policy effort needs to be more closely co-ordinated.* Since the mid-1970s, there has been a steady increase in the involvement of a wide range of new organisations in regional economic development. The activities of these various agencies would make regional policy more efficient and more effective if they were more closely co-ordinated.
3. One way of achieving better co-ordination between the organisations involved in regional policy (such as local authorities, the central government and the EEC) is to follow the lead set by Scotland and Wales: *each region should have its own regional development agency*. The activities of these agencies would themselves need to be co-ordinated. This could be done through a

department of central government which would also be responsible for devising the overall regional economic development policy (and hence the allocation of funds between the individual regional development agencies).

4. Once they have been set up, *regional development agencies should be given a wide range of powers and responsibilities*. One of their main functions would be to construct financially attractive development programmes for their own regions in order to boost the confidence of potential private investors.

Finally, the revitalisation of the depressed areas will not occur unless these areas make a major contribution to their own future development. Regional policy will only succeed if the depressed areas respond to the challenge of the long haul that lies ahead with imagination and enthusiasm.

Notes

1. Jim Taylor and Harvey Armstrong are respectively Professor and Senior Lecturer in the Department of Economics at the University of Lancaster. They also edit *Regional Studies*, the journal of the Regional Studies Association. This is an updated and revised version of a text first published in January 1987 and reissued in September 1988.
2. (i): Department of Trade and Industry (gross) expenditures include: regional development grants; regional selective assistance; regionally-differentiated investment grants; loans, grants and factory building under the Local Employment Act 1972; regional employment premium; and land/factory expenditure by English Estates. Regional assistance administered through the Scottish and Welsh Offices is also included.
(ii): European Regional Development Fund: expenditures are allocations (Support and Specific Measures) for Great Britain. Since payments lag allocations, this series overstates the value of ERDF aid. On the other hand, EEC assistance from other sources (e.g. European Investment Bank, European Coal and Steel Community) is not included which means that total EEC assistance is greater than that shown.
(iii): Regional Agencies: Scottish Development Agency; Welsh Development Agency; Mid-Wales Development; Highlands and Islands Development Board. These expenditures refer to grants-in-aid. In addition to grants-in-aid paid to these agencies by central government, the regional agencies also raise income from their investments, sale of assets, etc. They also draw upon EEC finance and on national sources (e.g. National Loans Fund). This series therefore understates actual expenditure. On the other hand, not all of the agencies' expenditures are confined to the assisted

areas of Scotland and Wales. The regional policy component of this expenditure is therefore overstated.

Sources: Annual Reports of Industry Act; Economic Trends; Annual Reports of Scottish and Welsh Development Agencies, Mid-Wales Development, Highlands and Islands Development Board; Annual Reports of the European Regional Development Fund.

3. (iv): Wherever possible, expenditure refers to expenditures actually incurred rather than to commitments made.

Note 2: Expenditure on general infrastructure projects not directly tied to industrial development (such as roads and telecommunications) is excluded, as is expenditure on land reclamation and environmental improvements. This has been done to enable expenditures by different organisations to be directly compared. It means, however, that the expenditures in this table are not directly comparable to those given in Figure 7.4 (which include infrastructure expenditure).

(iii): Expenditure includes only deliberately geographically-discriminating assistance to industry. It includes the provision of sites and factories.

(iv): Local authority expenditure has been estimated from data supplied by the Chartered Institute of Public Finance and Accountancy. These estimates overstate the true expenditure made by local authorities since they include funds made available to councils by higher-order organisations (e.g. urban programme assistance from the Department of Environment and European Regional Development Fund grants).

Source: H. Armstrong (1988). Estimating the Degree of Central Control of Spatial Industrial Policy: Great Britain 1983/84. Annals of Regional Science 22.

8 Are Small Firms the Answer to Unemployment?

David Storey and Stephen Johnson[1]

INTRODUCTION

In a White Paper entitled *Building Business . . . not Barriers* (Department of Employment, 1986) the UK government made the following statement (our emphases):

> The prime aim of the Department of Employment is to encourage the development of an enterprise economy. *The way to reduce unemployment is through more businesses, more self-employment and greater wealth creation*, all leading to more jobs.
> The key aspects of the Department's work are to:
> – Promote enterprise and job creation in growth areas such as small firms, self-employment and tourism.
> – Help businesses to grow by cutting red tape . . .
> – Improve training arrangements . . .
> – Help the young and those out of work for some time to find work . . .

It is clear from this statement that the present government views new and small firms as a major part of the solution to the current high levels of unemployment in the United Kingdom. This view partly reflects an ideological commitment to a free market economy, but also appears to be justified by the results of a number of independent academic studies in North America and Europe.

The most notable contribution was that of David Birch of the Massachusetts Institute of Technology, who found that two-thirds of the net new jobs which were created in the United States between 1969 and 1976 were in firms with less than 20 employees (Birch, 1979). In the United Kingdom, two studies carried out by the Department of Industrial Management at the University of Newcastle-upon-Tyne also found that small firms played an important role in the creation of new jobs (Gallagher and Stewart (1986) and Doyle and Gallagher (1986)). In particular, it was found that small firms, together with the self-employed, created around one million new jobs between 1982 and 1984 in the United Kingdom (*Employment Gazette*, November 1986). A review of 'job generation' studies throughout the EEC countries found, with only one exception, that small firms experienced positive employment growth, whereas large firms suffered a loss of employment (Storey and Johnson, 1987a). Finally, a survey carried out for the Occupations Study Group by the current authors predicted that small independent firms in the United Kingdom would increase their level of employment by between 700 000 and 1 300 000 during the years 1985–90 (Rajan, 1986, Chapter 14).

At first sight, these statistics appear to provide strong support for the government's view that employment growth in small firms makes a major contribution to reductions in UK unemployment. The purpose of this chapter is to examine this evidence carefully and to provide a critique of the government's small firm policies. The chapter is structured in the following way. We first provide a detailed statement of the objectives of the UK government for its small firm policies and the evidence which it cites in support both of the objectives and of the effectiveness of its policies. This evidence is then appraised. This is followed by a critique of the general direction of government policies. An alternative approach is then described and justified. Finally we strip it down to its key elements.

THE IMPORTANCE OF SMALL FIRMS: THE GOVERNMENT'S PERSPECTIVE

Since no single statement of government policy exists (at the time of writing) it is necessary for outsiders to infer objectives of policy either from ministerial statements or from the policy instruments currently in operation. In this situation it is always possible for outsiders to point to (real or imaginary) inconsistencies between such statements. Even so, it does appear that there is a lack of certainty about the objectives of policy in this area.

On some occasions the government emphasises that, since it cannot create jobs directly, particularly in the small firm sector, its only function is to create the conditions under which firms may flourish. Policies are therefore directed towards reducing business burdens, training labour, providing free information and advice, and changing attitudes to business and enterprise. In short, whilst the government believes that it can create the conditions for the 'enterprise culture' to flourish, it stops short of claims that these conditions will actually create jobs. No estimates are therefore provided of the period over which job creation might occur. Nor are any attempts made to *quantify* the likely net effects of policies towards small firms.

On other occasions, however, the ministers responsible have been quick to attribute good employment news to the effects of their policies. This produces almost a reverse Catch 22 position whereby government is unable to lose: by claiming that it cannot create jobs, but merely acting as a scene-setter, it can blame everybody else if jobs fail to materialise – trade unions, high wages, entrenched social attitudes and so on – whereas if jobs do occur the government can claim them as proof of the success of its policies.

For these reasons our comments upon government small firm employment policies will discuss specific items which have been extensively publicised by the government. We believe that the coverage given to these items indicates that the government *does* believe that small firms have been and are likely to be a major source of new job creation in the United Kingdom. It also highlights the political and economic philosophy underlying its policies.

We investigate the following four items derived from ministerial statements or government publications:

(a) Most of the new jobs in the United States are created in small firms. ('Big place of small firms in job generation – the US experience', *British Business*, 19 October 1984).
(b) In the 1970s, in the United Kingdom, small firms were an important source of new jobs. In the 1980s they are the major source. ('Look to small firms for new jobs', *Employment Gazette*, November 1986).
(c) There has been, during the 1980s, a major increase in both the birth rates of small firms and a net increase in the total stock of UK businesses. The period has also seen a major increase in self employment. (*Lifting the Burden*, Cabinet Office, 1985, para 1.4).
(d) Britain has a lower proportion of its employment in small firms than its competitors, many of which have lower rates of unemployment. Hence increasing the importance of small firms in an economy is one way of reducing unemployment. ('Jobs before profits', *Chief Executive*, September 1985).

(a) 'Most of the new jobs in the United States are created in small firms.'

In 1979 David Birch, then at the Massachusetts Institute of Technology, produced a report which had a major impact upon not only the government of the United States, but also on many other developed countries (Birch, 1979). Using data supplied by the credit rating agency Dun & Bradstreet, Birch claimed to show that two-thirds of the increase in employment in the United States between 1969 and 1976 was in firms employing less than 20 workers. Several inferences were drawn from Birch's report:

1. The small business sector was a major creator of new jobs;
2. Similar factors were at work in other countries where it was probably also true that small firms were a major source of new jobs;
3. If small firms were the major source of new jobs world-wide, then policies to promote their development should be pursued, particularly in areas experiencing high unemployment.

It is no exaggeration to say that the Birch report provided the statistical underpinning for the recent profusion of policies to help small firms which have occurred in Europe and North America.

Whilst many governments grasped the Birch report with enthusiasm, the response from his fellow researchers varied from a lukewarm acceptance to outright rejection and hostility. First on the scene in the United States were Catherine Armington and Marjorie Odle, then of the Brookings Institute (Armington and Odle, 1982, pp. 14–17). Like Birch, they used Dun & Bradstreet data, but looked instead at the period 1978–80. In stark contrast to Birch's results, they found that firms with less than 100 workers provided only 39 per cent of all new US jobs. As at that time about 40 per cent of US employment was in such firms anyway, their work indicated that small firms were creating jobs *no faster* than large firms.

A furious debate followed. It was eventually agreed that Birch and his associates at MIT should be provided with the identical data tape used by Armington and Odle to enable them to make their own calculations. After conducting his analysis Birch made the claim that in fact 70 per cent of the increase in employment over these years had been in firms with less than 100 workers – compared with the 39 per cent figure obtained by Armington and Odle (Birch and McCracken, 1983).

We have investigated, in detail, the basis of these wildly different results (Storey and Johnson, 1987b, Chapter 3). The story is not straightforward but for present purposes it is sufficient to say that the difference in the results stems mainly from the different adjustments that each group made to the raw data to allow for known biases. It will be recalled that the data are derived from Dun & Bradstreet which is a credit-rating agency. Whilst in absolute terms the data base is massive (five million establishments and four million enterprises – see United States Small Business Administration, 1985, page 21) many individual firms are not included. Most importantly, it is certain that the coverage of *new* firms is incomplete and biased. Birch estimates that only about *one-quarter* of firms which are two years old actually appear in the data file. Furthermore those which do appear are likely to be those which are of most interest to the agency. This boils down to those firms most in need of credit – which of course means, above all, those which are growing the fastest.

To illustrate these differences in approach, and their importance to the final result, take the example of the way in which the two research teams allowed for the incomplete enumeration in Dun & Bradstreet files of new firms. Recognising that only a proportion of the new firms formed over the 1978–80 period were actually incorporated into Dun & Bradstreet files, Armington and Odle allowed all new firms founded over the five-year period 1976–80 to be included. On the other hand Birch created a set of 'absorption factors' which were meant to reflect the speed with which new firms had been incorporated into Dun & Bradstreet records in the past. Unfortunately the basis of these 'absorption factors' has never been made available, but the key result is that the different approaches of the two groups to this single element of the overall employment calculation leads to a difference of nearly 2.2 million jobs in small firms over two years.

Hence much of the difference between the Birch studies on the one hand, and those by Armington and Odle on the other, lies in the different ways in which they estimate the growth of employment in firms, *not* in the data base. Broadly we believe that the estimation techniques used by Birch substantially *overestimate* the contribution made by small firms, whilst those used by Armington and Odle lead to an *underestimate*. We reach a similar conclusion over other areas of debate between the two groups. In our, we hope informed but nevertheless subjective, view we conclude that about 50 per cent of net new jobs in the USA during the 1978–80 period were in firms with less than 100 workers. In the same period, roughly 40 per cent of *existing* jobs were in firms of this size.

Our analysis of research in the USA suggests that small firms were creating jobs faster than other sizes of firm but not on the scale initially suggested by Birch. It also demonstrates that 'sensational' summary figures should be treated with extreme caution.

(b) 'In the 1970s in the United Kingdom small firms were an important source of new jobs. In the 1980s they are a major source.'

In the UK there have been two main groups of studies which have examined the extent to which job creation takes place in different sizes of firms or establishment. The first group are local or regionally-based studies of changes in manufacturing employment mainly during the 1960s and 1970s. The second group are based on the UK Dun & Bradstreet data files and are subject to the uncertainties discussed for the US studies above. Nevertheless Dun & Bradstreet files cover service industries as well as manufacturing, and results have recently been produced for the 1980s.

Similar studies have also been undertaken in Western Germany, France and Ireland (see Storey and Johnson, 1987a). The results are summarised in Table 8.1. The table shows that establishments with less than twenty workers have generally shown an increase in employment. In the thirteen studies only that of Northrhine–Westfalia in Germany shows very small firms exhibiting a decline in employment. The table also shows that firms/establishments with more than 500 workers consistently experienced a decline in employment. Only in the study of Ruhr and Frankfurt in Germany does this group shown an increase in employment. Indeed Table 8.1 demonstrates the clear effect of size, with almost all the employment growth (+ signs) being on the left of the table (small firms). It also shows that these trends are not limited simply to the manufacturing sector but occur also in studies where the service sector is included.

While the evidence presented in Table 8.1 appears to provide impressive support for the view that small firms are the major source of job creation in Europe we would urge caution for several reasons:

1. The methodology used in some studies tends to be biased in favour of small firm job creation.
2. In terms of absolute numbers of jobs a large percentage rise in employment in the small firm sector (that is, less than twenty workers) will not 'compensate' for a very small percentage decline

Table 8.1 Job generation studies in Europe: employment growth by firm/establishment size

Country/area	*Period*	*Coverage*	*Under 20*	*20–49*	*50–99*	*100–499*	*500+*	*Total*
			Number of employees					
			Percentage change in employment (at annual rates as percentage of base year employment)					
United Kingdom								
East Midlands	1968–75	Manuf.	+0.4	+0.3	+0.2	−0.3	−0.9	−0.3
Northern England	1965–76	Manuf.	+0.2	+0.1	+0.0	−0.1	−1.0	−0.8
Northern England	1976–81	Manuf.	+0.2	−0.0	−0.2	−1.6	−3.8	−5.4
United Kingdom	1972–75	Manuf.	−0.0	−0.0	−0.0	−0.0	−0.1	−0.1
United Kingdom	1971–81	All Sectors	+0.8	−0.1	−0.0	−0.1	−1.4	−0.7
United Kingdom	1982–84	All Sectors	+2.0	+0.3	−0.0	−1.0	−2.2	−0.9
Northern Ireland	1971–81	Manuf.	+0.1	−0.0	−0.2	−1.2	−1.9	−3.2
Germany (Federal Republic)								
Germany (Sample)	1974–81	All Sectors	+0.2	+0.2	+0.2	+0.2	−0.5	+0.3
Germany (4 regions)	1974–80	All Sectors	+0.8	+0.7	−0.0	−0.2	−0.5	+0.8
Northrhine-Westfalia	1978–84	Manuf.	−0.2	−0.3	−0.3	−0.9	−1.3	−3.0
Ruhr & Frankfurt	1975–80	All Sectors	+1.1	−0.4	−0.4	−0.5	+0.5	+0.3
France								
Poitou-Charentes	1972–84	All Sectors	+1.0	+0.7	−0.1	−1.9	−2.4	−2.6
France	1981–83	All Sectors	+0.0	−0.1	−0.1	−0.4	−0.4	−1.0
Ireland								
Ireland	1973–80	Manuf.	[+0.7]		+0.3	−0.3	−0.2	+0.6

Source: Storey, D. J. and Johnson, S. (1987a) *Small and Medium-Sized Firms and Employment Creation in Europe*, Commission of the European Communities.

in employment in the large firm sector (500+ workers).

3. Figures presented in this way inevitably paint small firms in a good light. If a very small firm goes out of business the maximum number of jobs which can be lost is twenty, whereas there is no upper limit to the number of jobs they can create. A few rapidly growing small firms may therefore easily 'compensate' for a large number of deaths. This is not the case for existing large firms.
4. For this reason it should not be thought that the 'typical' small firm is experiencing growth in employment and the 'typical' large firm is experiencing decline. In fact, significant small firm employment growth actually takes place in only a very few cases.

To demonstrate the presence of methodological bias in studies we can take the recent work by Doyle and Gallagher which has been subject to high Ministerial acclaim. Doyle and Gallagher (1986) used UK Dun & Bradstreet data for the period 1982–4, and concluded that, whilst there was an overall decline in employment in the United Kingdom of 280 000 jobs, firms with less than twenty workers experienced an increase of 600 000 jobs. The analysis, however, is subject to some of the same pitfalls as the United States studies which use Dun & Bradstreet data. In particular Doyle and Gallagher recognise that only about 12 per cent of firms with less than twenty employees are included in the Dun & Bradstreet file. Hence they scale up the employment change over the 1982–4 period in the firms which are in the data base.

We believe, however, that the Doyle and Gallagher scaling leads to a major *overestimate* of the contribution of small firms to employment change because, as we noted earlier, employment growth in small firms takes place in very few firms. It will also be recalled that Dun & Bradstreet are likely to include more fast-growing small firms than a random sample.

To illustrate the sensitivity of the results we have reworked the Doyle and Gallagher figures purely by assuming that Dun & Bradstreet had a complete enumeration of the fastest growing 61 *small* firms out of a total number of 152 000 small firms on the data base, that is, that employment growth in the 61 fastest growing firms does not need to be scaled up. By making this minor adjustment we find that employment growth in the very small firm sector (less than twenty employees) falls from 600 000 to 210 000 (Storey and Johnson, 1987b, Chapter 4).

The 'results' of job generation studies are highly sensitive to relatively minor methodological changes. In the UK it appears that small firms are creating new jobs, but not on a scale which will compensate for job shedding amongst large firms.

(c) 'During the 1980s there has been a major increase in both the birth rates of small firms and a net increase in the total stock of UK businesses. The period has also seen a major increase in self-employment.'

When faced with statistics on rising levels of unemployment, government ministers have frequently responded by quoting statistics on the increase in the number of businesses in the United Kingdom. Government data on VAT returns show that the stock of businesses in the United Kingdom has grown from approximately 1.29 million in 1980 to 1.44 million in 1985. Table 8.2 shows that this increase in stock (Column 3) reflects both the formation of new businesses (new registrations) and deregistrations (primarily traders going out of business). It is interesting to note that, while the number of deregistrations remained broadly constant over the period 1980–3 at around 140 000, the number of new registrations climbed annually from about 160 000 in 1980 to 183 000 in 1984/5. In 1985, however, the increase in new registrations appeared to level off, while there was an increase in deregistrations. Nevertheless there was, even in that year, an increase in the total number of businesses (stock).

Table 8.2 Growth of businesses in the United Kingdom (figures in thousands)

Year	*New VAT registrations*	*De-registrations from VAT*	*Stock of firms*
1980	158.2	142.3	1 288.3
1981*	152.0	120.5	
1982	166.0	146.0	
1983	180.0	146.0	
1984	182.0	153.0	
1985	183.0	163.0	1 439.0

*Figures for this year are affected by a lengthy strike by Civil Servants.

Source: *British Business*, 19 September 1986, pp. 6–7.

Figure 8.1 Employment distribution in manufacturing by firm size, 1971–82

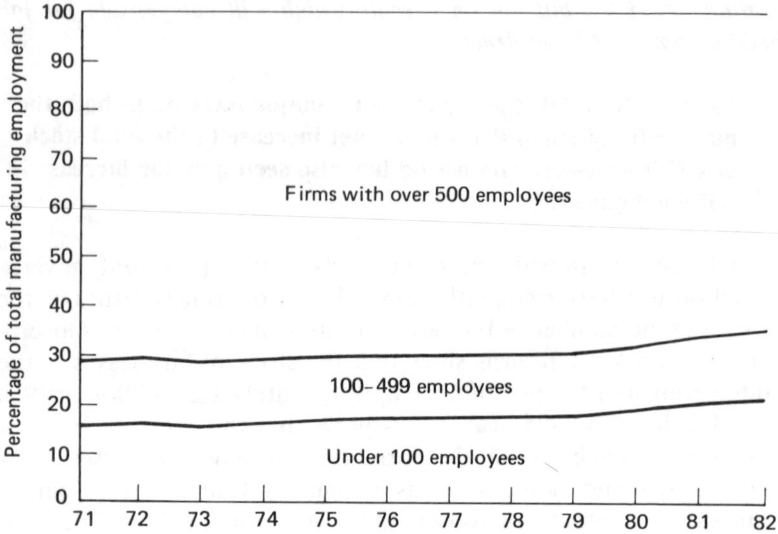

Source: *Annual Census of Production* (various years).

The increase in both the stock of businesses and the formation rate of new firms is seen by government as a desirable development, indicative of a more enterprising economy in which people are prepared to take risks. These new firms are seen as the seed corn which will provide the basis of the revival of the British economy. Our interpretation of these statistics is, however, very different. We believe that the increase in the birth rate and hence the stock of businesses *in the UK context* is a reflection of the poor economic performance of large firms. In other words it is the mirror image of the recession which the British economy has been experiencing and therefore presents a much weaker case for optimism.

Our explanation is reflected in Figures 8.1 and 8.2. Figure 8.1 shows how the proportion of employees in manufacturing who work in small firms has been increasing relative to employment in large firms. This increase has been occurring for most years from the early 1970s onwards. However Figure 8.2 shows that this increase has *not* occurred because manufacturing employment in small firms has increased, but simply because it has remained stable *at a time of massive reductions in large firm employment.*

Figure 8.2 Manufacturing employment by firm size, 1971–82

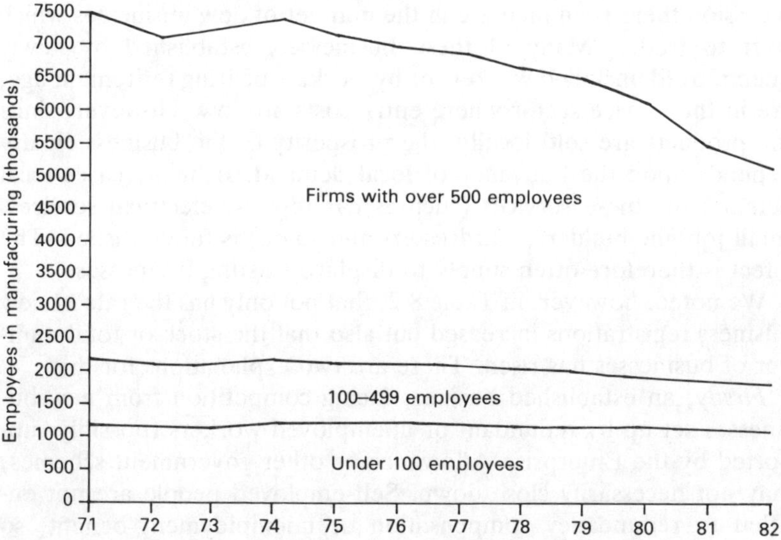

Source: *Annual Census of Production* (various years).

There can be little doubt that this job shedding amongst large manufacturing firms has occurred primarily because of poor international competitiveness. It is, however, relevant to consider how this reduction in manufacturing employment has been reflected in the *type* of employment within and outside existing firms and what impact this may have had on the growth of small firms.

Few large firms actually die. It is therefore more appropriate to discuss contractions in their activities than their disappearance during recession. The major change which has taken place amongst large UK companies has been the shedding of unskilled workers. In many cases these were full-time male workers and, where recruitment has taken place, the jobs have tended to be taken by part-time female workers. Since unskilled male workers have considerable difficulty in obtaining employment within the conventional labour market many turn, through lack of an alternative, to starting their own businesses.

Research has shown that between 25 and 50 per cent of all businesses established are by workers who are unemployed or likely to be unemployed immediately prior to starting the businesses.[2] Even amongst those establishing a high technology business approximately one in five claimed either to be unemployed or likely to become unemployed. For these reasons it is not surprising that during times of recession there is an increase in the number of new businesses which start to trade.[3] Many of these businesses, established by newly unemployed unskilled workers or by workers nearing retirement age, are in the service sector where entry costs are low. However, since the products are sold locally, the prosperity of the business clearly depends upon the buoyancy of local demand. In many cases local demand for these services (such as car repairs, electrical services, small jobbing builders, hairdressers and so on) is fully satisfied. The effect is therefore often simply to displace existing businesses.

We noted, however, in Table 8.2, that not only has the rate of new business registrations increased but also that the stock or total number of businesses has risen. There are two explanations for this.

Firstly, an established business facing competition from new businesses set up by redundant or unemployed workers (possibly supported by the Enterprise Allowance or other government schemes) may not necessarily close down. Self-employed people are not entitled to redundancy compensation or unemployment benefit, so there will be little reason to close the business, even if there is no longer much income coming in. However, the established business *is* likely to reduce employment levels with the result that there will be more businesses but *not* more employment. The *Annual Census of Production* reports an 18 per cent increase in the number of manufacturing firms with less than 100 employees from 68 455 in 1971 to 80 782 in 1982. However the level of employment in this group of firms remained approximately constant over the same period.

It seems that the result of recession has been to spread the available work amongst a larger number of businesses, with no discernible impact upon total employment in small manufacturing firms. The shedding of unskilled or low-skill (primarily male) labour and the partial replacement by part-time female labour is shown in Figure 8.3. This illustrates the corporate hierarchy in the form of a triangle with the managing director at the apex and the least skilled/lowest paid worker at the base. It shows that the original triangle (firm) has contracted primarily by the shedding of unskilled labour – with some of the displaced workers starting their own businesses.

A *second* element is also illustrated in Figure 8.3 – the transfer of functions. It is now well documented that virtually all large companies have responded to the recession by eliminating 'peripheral' functions and concentrating upon 'core' activities. This has been achieved by a

Figure 8.3 Job changes in a contracting company

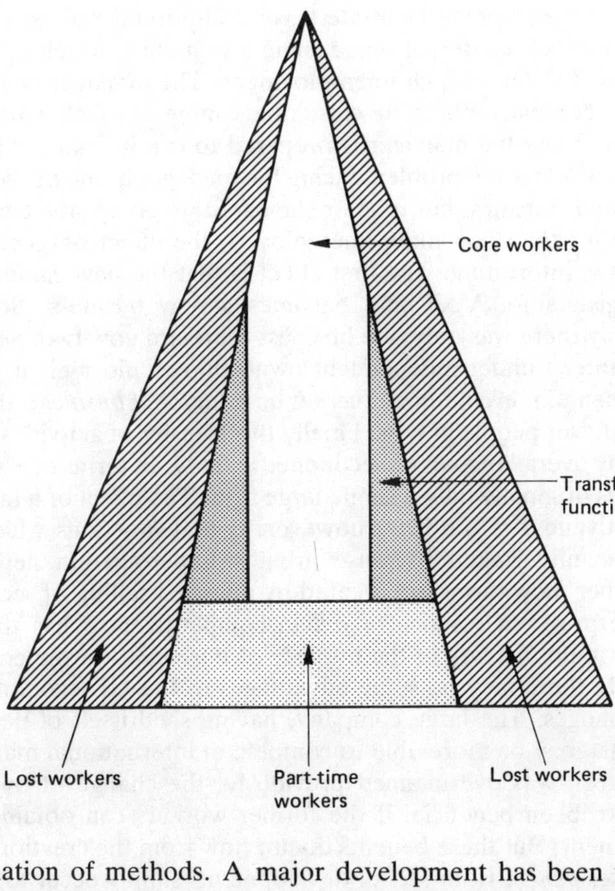

combination of methods. A major development has been the promotion of management buy-outs, whereby existing management purchase from the parent company a plant or factory which is judged to be surplus to requirements. Many large companies have also transferred functions which previously were conducted 'in-house' to outsiders. This is achieved in a variety of different ways such as promoting home-working or using 'networkers' who undertake computing functions at home, often with a base load of orders from the parent company. In other cases services such as transportation, cleaning, catering and security are transferred either to new organisations, or to former members of staff who are encouraged to run the operation as their own business. Finally, growth in sub-contracting also illustrates the greater emphasis upon 'core' activities amongst larger firms.

These developments illustrate several important points. Consider the example of a catering manager in a large firm which operates a factory in an area of high unemployment. The manager is informed that the company plans to close the canteen, which employs 10 workers, unless the manager is prepared to run it as his or her own business. Clearly the problem facing the manager is one of economics rather than statistics, but if he or she agrees to accept the company's offer rather than becoming unemployed, the effect on government statistics is interesting. The first effect is that the new canteen business registers for VAT and becomes a new business. So where previously there was only one business there are now two. Secondly, if the canteen under independent ownership employs eight workers rather than ten, *even though there is an additional business*, there are actually fewer people in jobs. Finally this transfer of activities has not led to any overall increase in economic activity. In terms of Figure 8.3 there was originally only a single large firm. The effect of a fall in the competitiveness of the firm, however, is that functions which were previously undertaken 'in-house' are now undertaken in 'new' firms, while other 'new' firms are created by a formal selling of sections of the enterprise. In essence, a *fall* in competitiveness has therefore resulted in an *increase* in the number of businesses in the economy.

Clearly there may be some advantages to the UK economy from these changes. The large company, having shed itself of peripheral functions, may be more able to compete in international markets. If the canteen was overmanned previously, the change of ownership may have been beneficial if the former workers can obtain gainful employment. But these benefits do not flow from the creation of new businesses *per se*. Both sets of developments simply occur together – and both *reflect* the recession.

Our argument is that there is no intrinsic benefit to the UK economy from having more firms and particularly more small firms. The increase in the number of firms since 1980 is likely to be more a reflection of recession than a source of rejoicing.

(d) 'Britain has a lower proportion of its employment in small firms than its competitors which have lower unemployment. Hence increasing the importance of small firms in the economy is one way of reducing unemployment.'

If small firms were the major source of new jobs in the economies of the developed countries then it would be reasonable to infer that those countries where small firms were relatively more important would, in some sense, perform better than economies which were more dominated by large firms. Some intuitive support for this view may be obtained by examining the cases of Britain and Japan. The British economy has been dominated by large firms and, within the manufacturing sector, has only about one-quarter of employment in firms with less than 200 workers. On the other hand Japan has more than half of its manufacturing employment in firms with less than 200 workers. Recognising the vastly superior performance of the Japanese economy some commentators have been tempted to infer that an increase in the relative importance of small firms could lead to superior economic performance, because small firms are assumed to be more flexible, more innovative and more entrepreneurial.

This intuitive plausibility is not, however, supported when data for developed countries other than the United Kingdom and Japan are included. In Figures 8.4 and 8.5 we look at data for 14 industrial economies. The diagrams relate the percentage of manufacturing employment in small firms to unemployment levels in 1983 (Figure 8.4) and to manufacturing employment changes between 1980 and 1982 (Figure 8.5). Both figures show broadly similar results. There is no apparent relationship between the relative importance of small firms in an economy and the performance of that economy. It is unfortunate that only data for the manufacturing sector are available for all 14 countries. For five countries data are, however, available for both the service and manufacturing sectors. They suggest that countries having a high proportion of small firm employment in services also have a high proportion of small firm employment in manufacturing. Hence the relative importance of small firms in the manufacturing sector may be an adequate proxy for their relative importance in the economy as a whole.

In Figure 8.4 unemployment rates in 1983 were chosen for comparative purposes, but varying the year chosen makes little difference to the observed pattern. The year chosen for employment data for small manufacturing firms also varies slightly from one country to another but again this is unlikely to alter results derived.

We conclude that there is no clear evidence to support the view that economies with more small firms 'perform' better in terms of job creation than those dominated by large firms. These results offer no justification

Figure 8.4 Unemployment rates and share of small firm manufacturing employment in the OECD countries, 1983

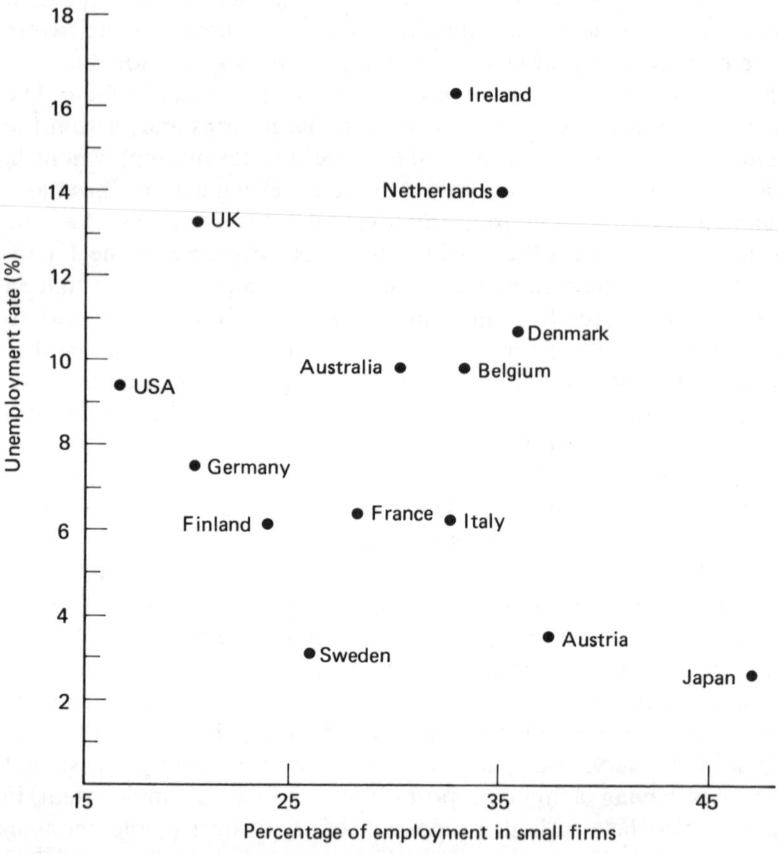

Source: OECD (1985).

for regarding an increase in the absolute or relative importance of small firms as desirable in and of itself as a way of improving the overall performance of a national economy.

POLICIES TOWARDS SMALL FIRMS: THE OTHER SIDE OF THE COIN

We have identified in terms of specific statements those elements which the current UK government has emphasised in justifying its

Figure 8.5 Manufacturing employment changes, 1980–2 and percentage employment in small firms in the OECD countries

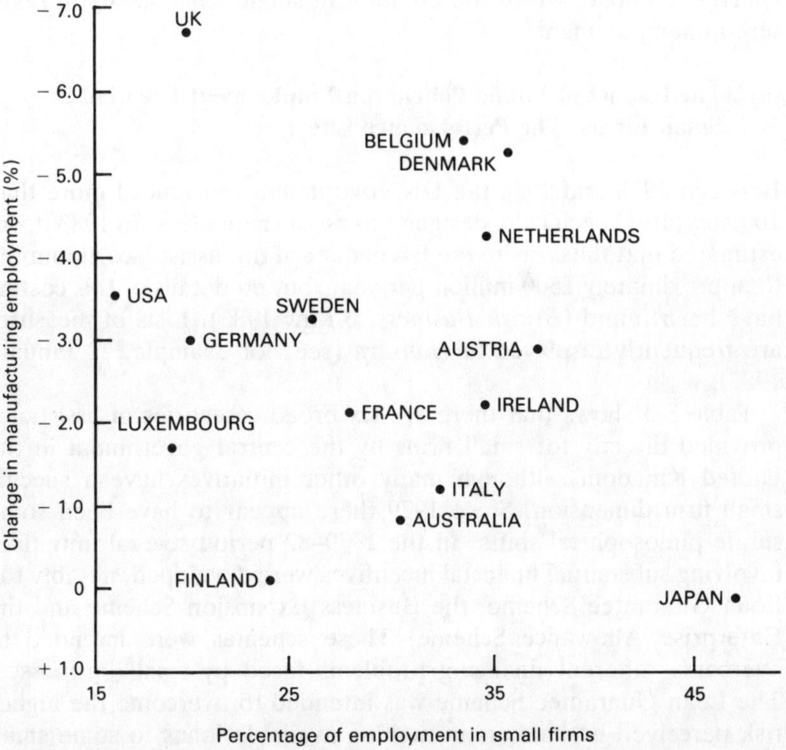

Source: OECD (1985).

policies to promote new and small firms. On closer inspection, many of these statements have proved to be somewhat questionable.

We now turn to a second set of issues relevant to policies towards small firms which the government chooses either to ignore or set aside:

(a) The impact of public policies on the performance of small firms.
(b) The regional divisiveness of small firm policies.
(c) The type of jobs created and the impact on registered unemployment.

In discussing these issues we will identify two major uncertainties inherent in current small firm policies: *the performance effect*, the impact which public assistance to the firm has upon the performance of the firm, paticularly in terms of job creation; and *the labour market effect*, the impact which job creation in small firms has upon registered unemployment.

(a) The Impact of Public Policies on Employment Creation in Small Firms: The Performance Effect

Between 1979 and 1986 the UK government introduced more than 100 measures specifically designed to assist small firms. In 1983 it was estimated that the costs to the Exchequer of this assistance amounted to approximately £500 million per year, but no details of this costing have been found (*British Business*, 6 May 1983). Lists of measures are frequently displayed in *Hansard* (see, for example, 22 January 1987).

Table 8.3 shows that there are six broad categories of assistance provided directly for small firms by the central government in the United Kingdom, although many other initiatives have a specific small firm dimension. Since 1979 there appear to have been some subtle philosophical shifts. In the 1979–82 period several initiatives involving substantial financial incentives were developed, notably the Loan Guarantee Scheme, the Business Expansion Scheme and the Enterprise Allowance Scheme. These schemes were intended to overcome different financing problems faced by small businesses. The Loan Guarantee Scheme was intended to overcome the higher risk perceived by bankers in making available loans to some small firms by guaranteeing to the bank 70 per cent (originally 80 per cent) of loans made, subject to an interest premium charged to the firm, to cover the additional risk. The Business Expansion Scheme was designed to provide tax relief to individuals making an equity investment in an eligible small business either directly or through a financial institution. Finally the Enterprise Allowance Scheme provided a guaranteed £40 per week to individuals who had been unemployed for some time and who had £1000 to help start a business.

Since 1982, rather less emphasis has been placed upon financial schemes and no major new initiatives have been undertaken although modifications to these schemes have been implemented. Instead greater reliance is now placed upon enabling small businesses to prosper without the regulatory burdens of 'red tape' or complying with government regulations and the rest. In its own research the government claimed:

Table 8.3 Small business assistance in Britain

Direct Financial Assistance	→ Business (Start-up) Expansion Scheme → Loan Guarantee Scheme → Enterprise Allowance Scheme
Indirect Financial Assistance	→ Raising VAT threshold → Reducing corporation tax liability
Premises & Planning	→ Government factory building particularly of small premises → Enterprise Zones
Red tape/ Business Burdens	→ Reduced form filling → Relaxing health & safety (under consideration) → Relaxing employment protection (under consideration)
Provision of Advice	→ Establishment of counselling services → Enterprise Agencies (Trusts)
Education Training	→ Youth enterprise → Business in schools → Start your own business programme

> Reductions in . . . compliance costs would be likely to feed through into profits and prices; the end result being . . . a higher level of employment in the whole economy'. (*Burdens on Business*, Para 2.5.3.)

This form of logic permeates government small firm policy. Broadly it appears that the initiatives outlined in Table 8.3 are designed to reduce the operating costs of small firms below those which would have existed in the absence of the initiative. In some cases such as the Loan Guarantee Scheme the financial benefits to the firm are clear in the sense that it obtains a loan when this would otherwise have been impossible. In other cases where, for example, information is provided free of charge to small firms, the benefit to the firm is indirect in the sense that it may either have had to obtain the information commercially, through the payment of a fee, or more probably would have been less well informed and so been less efficient.

The initiatives are designed to reduce the costs of operating the business and are paid for out of the public purse. In this sense they are public *subsidies* and so must be justified on grounds of market failure. The precise mechanism by which the government believes that these subsidies lead to additional employment in the small firm sector is rarely specified. The closest we have come to any such description is found in the quotation above from *Burdens on Business*.

It will be noted that the statement does not distinguish between direct and indirect job creation, so that it is unclear whether the reduction in costs, which the assisted firm receives, leads to job creation within that firm (direct) or whether the jobs would be expected to occur more generally as a result of an overall reduction in the price level in the economy (indirect). It is our inference that the main thrust of policy is to reduce the operating costs of a given firm or, perhaps in the case of industries dominated by small firms, a given industry, so that these firms or industries will themselves be able to increase their profits. Small firms, however, have considerable discretion in the use of these profits as shown in Figure 8.6. For example, some firms may regard the increase in profits as a once and for all 'windfall' gain. They may therefore remove the money from the business directly in the form of additional salaries (emoluments) for the directors or perhaps indirectly by repaying some of the Directors Loan Account. Although it is true that such additional income for the directors may be spent and so lead (indirectly) to additional jobs it would be inconsistent with the government's overall approach to economic strategy to rely on this route to stimulate demand and hence jobs.

A second possible result of public assistance, also shown in Figure 8.6, is that it could lead to increased profits which *are* reinvested in the firm in the form of new plant and machinery. The effect of this additional investment upon employment depends upon the nature of the firm's production function, but there is no automatic linkage between new investment in plant and machinery and additional employment within the firm.

Figure 8.6 also shows a number of other possible outcomes of the provision of subsidies to small firms. For example, the subsidy could merely lead the firm to become less efficient in an operational sense (so-called X-inefficiency). Once removed, the subsidy could therefore simply leave the firm unable to compete in the market-place. It could also lead to workers obtaining higher rates of pay without

Figure 8.6 The impact of subsidies on small businesses

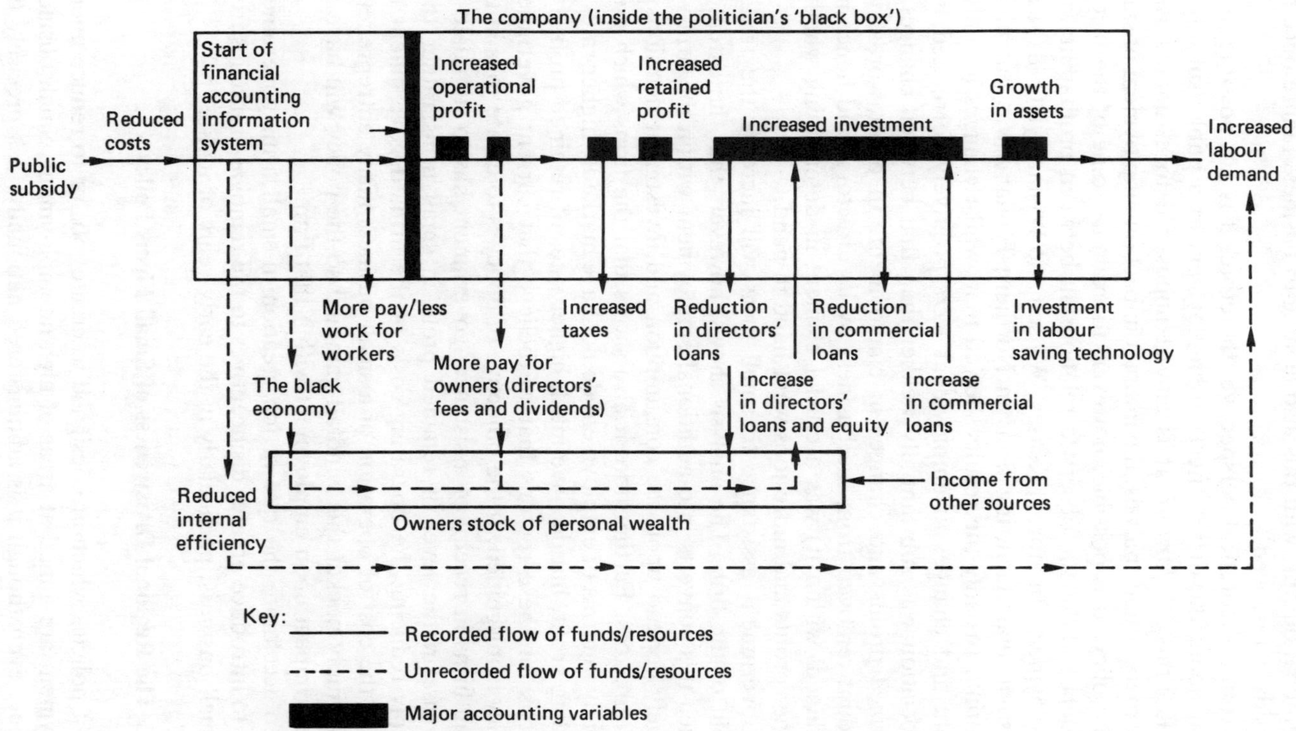

Source: Storey, D. J., K. Keasey, R. Watson and P. Wynarczyk (1987) *The Performance of Small Firms* (London: Croom Helm).

additional output, with this also leading to business failure once the subsidy is removed.

From a theoretical perspective, therefore, it is not possible to be clear about the direct effect on employment of a public subsidy to small firms. *A fortiori*, it is almost impossible to estimate, using macroeconomic analysis, the indirect impact on employment of small firm policy. It is possible, however, to examine some of the factual evidence about the observed relationship between profitability and employment. In Storey, Keasey, Watson and Wynarczyk (1987) a set of small manufacturing firms in Northern England was put under scrutiny. Broadly the results showed that, whilst changes in trading profit and changes in employment *were* positively correlated, the association was substantially weaker than that between changes in *retained* profits and changes in employment. In other words, the amount removed from the business by its directors (and hence not 'retained' within it) was a crucial element in determining whether higher profits and more jobs went hand in hand.

Government assistance to small firms will increase the trading profit of the firm. The analysis shows, however, that the extent to which this converts into additional employment within the firm will largely depend upon the consumption and investment decisions of the directors. Furthermore it also shows that the firms which grow rapidly in terms of employment do not have markedly higher rates of trading profit, but do have much higher rates of retained profit.

It is for these reasons that we believe that current government policy is misguided. If the objective of policy is to create jobs in the small firms in receipt of assistance, government has to stimulate an *increase* in the level of retained profit in small firms rather than simply reducing the operating costs of the firm. If government reduces the cost of operation of a small business many entrepreneurs will simply pocket this windfall gain and so the policy will have no direct impact upon employment within that firm.

To accelerate the rate of job creation in small firms government has to introduce greater disincentives to the removal of monies from a small business, particularly in the early years of its life.

(b) The Regional Divisiveness of Small Firms Policy

Most policies which are designed to create jobs or to reduce unemployment are aimed at areas of high unemployment. Small business policy, even though it is administered nationally, has precisely the opposite effect. It creates jobs primarily in the areas with *low* rates of unemployment and has the least impact in areas of high unemployment. By so doing it increases the economic divisions between the UK regions.

The government is fully aware of this criticism but has chosen to ignore it. In 1982 a 'Regional Index of Entrepreneurship' was produced by one of the current authors (Storey, 1982). The index was constructed on the basis of factors which had been shown to be correlated with both the propensity to form a firm and the propensity of that firm to grow once established. The factors were:

- previous experience of employment in a small firm,
- managerial experience,
- educational attainment,
- access to capital,
- previous job experience in the chosen market,
- buoyancy of local markets.

Since these factors vary regionally within the United Kingdom it was possible to construct a composite index which combined the above elements, allowing the UK regions to be ranked in order of entrepreneurship. Not surprisingly the South-East obtained the highest score and was therefore classified as the most entrepreneurially fertile. Northern England was the lowest, closely followed by Wales.

The index served firstly to demonstrate that real differences existed between UK regions in their ability to generate entrepreneurs and respond to small business incentives. The index was designed to predict not only the regional distribution of entrepreneurship but, given that small business policy is administered nationally (that is, without spatial considerations), the distribution of assistance under the policy.

It is not possible to identify the beneficiaries, on a regional basis, of many of the policy initiatives identified in Table 8.3, since data are not available. Nevertheless for four elements of policy it is possible to obtain regional distribution data. These are payments to firms under:

- The Loan Guarantee Scheme,
- The Business Expansion Scheme,
- The Enterprise Allowance Scheme,
- The Small Engineering Firms Investment Scheme.

Data on payments made until 1985 have been collected and analysed by Mason and Harrison (1986). They have produced a set of 'location quotients' (LQ) reproduced in Table 8.4. A region having an LQ above unity has an above-average level of assistance under the policy instrument and a region with one below unity has a below-average level of assistance. Table 8.4 shows that a number of criteria for constructing the LQs are possible, depending for example on the particular years chosen or whether assistance is weighted by the number of loans or by value. Even so it is clear that, irrespective of the criteria for its construction, the entrepreneurship index in column one is positively correlated with the LQs of the payment. When, however, take-up rates for the four schemes are collapsed into a single index the current authors show that the regional entrepreneurship index and the regional distribution of small firm policy instruments are *very* highly correlated. (Storey and Johnson, 1987c)

Hence the entrepreneurship index, constructed in 1982, predicted almost perfectly the subsequent regional distribution of small firm financial assistance. The warnings of one of the current authors, issued in 1980, have been shown to be true.

> Until the incentives are greater in the assisted areas small firms policies risk being regionally divisive, in the crude sense that the rate of responsiveness or take-up will be greater in the South than in the North, i.e. in areas which require the employment least. A regional dimension to small firm policy is essential. (David Storey, *The Banker*, 1980)

The 'regional divisiveness' argument may initially appear to conflict with the earlier observation that much of the growth in the number of small firms was induced by the recession. Surely, it may be argued, if this is the case then why is most assistance to small firms not found in areas of high unemployment? However the formation and growth of small firms is positively related to *both* 'push' factors (such as unemployment which affects primarily the number of firms established) and 'pull' or structural factors (such as those identified in the entrepreneurship index). The elements within the index affect not only the number of firms which start in business but also their performance once established. Clearly an increase in unemployment will lead to an increase in business formation in all regions, but the take-up of assistance depends upon both push and pull factors, and at any given level of unemployment the structural or pull factors consistently favour the existing prosperous areas.

Table 8.4 Regional index of entrepreneurship and location quotients for four instruments of small firms policy

		Loan Guarantee Scheme (LGS)				*Business Expansion Scheme (BES)*		*Enterprise Allowance Scheme (EAS)*	*Small Engineering Firms Investment Scheme (SEFIS)*	
		(1) 1981–4		*(2) 1984–4*						
Region	*Entre-preneurship index*	*No. of guarantees*	*Value of loans*	*No. of guarantees*	*Value of loans*	*No. of companies*	*Amount of finance*	*Participation rate*	*No. of firms*	*Value of finance*
	ENT	*LGS1N*	*LGS1V*	*LGS2N*	*LGS2V*	*BESN*	*BESV*	*EAS*	*SEFISN*	*SEFISV*
South-East/ East Anglia	8.05	1.04	1.14	1.06	1.18	1.30	1.69	1.05	1.13	1.02
South-West	7.54	0.95	0.91	1.11	0.91	1.05	0.65	1.22	1.82	1.88
West Midlands	5.18	1.00	0.97	0.90	0.88	0.97	0.93	1.13	0.90	0.97
East Midlands	6.09	0.93	0.95	0.83	0.77	1.24	0.74	1.13	0.97	0.98
Yorkshire and Humberside	4.64	1.02	0.88	0.85	0.73	0.72	0.71	0.97	0.78	0.84
North-West	6.64	1.36	1.28	1.04	0.98	0.72	0.49	1.38	0.73	0.82
North	3.45	1.06	0.96	0.99	1.16	0.37	0.07	0.72	0.97	1.10
Wales	3.70	0.85	0.78	0.61	0.57	0.70	0.94	1.12	0.68	0.68
Scotland	5.11	0.95	0.83	1.51	1.39	1.17	0.67	0.75	0.83	0.89
Northern Ireland	4.44	0.32	0.38	0.70	0.76	0.12	0.06	0.92	2.11	2.22

Note: The location quotients are calculated as follows:

LGS1N, LGS1V, LGS2N, LGS2V : BESN, BESV

$$LQ = \frac{\text{Regional share of number of loans/companies/value}}{\text{Regional share of UK stock of VAT registered businesses}}$$

$$\text{SEFISN, SEFISV} : LQ = \frac{\text{Regional share of firms receiving SEFIS grant/amount of grant}}{\text{Regional share of manufacturing units with less than 100 employees in Division 3 of the 1980 SIC}}$$

$$\text{EAS} : LQ = \frac{\text{Participation rate per 1000 unemployed in November 1984}}{\text{UK average participation rate per 1000 unemployed in November 1984}}$$

Source: Storey, D. J. (1982); Storey, D. J. and S. Johnson (1987c); Mason, C. and R. Harrison (1986)

Figure 8.7 Self-employment in Britain, 1965–86

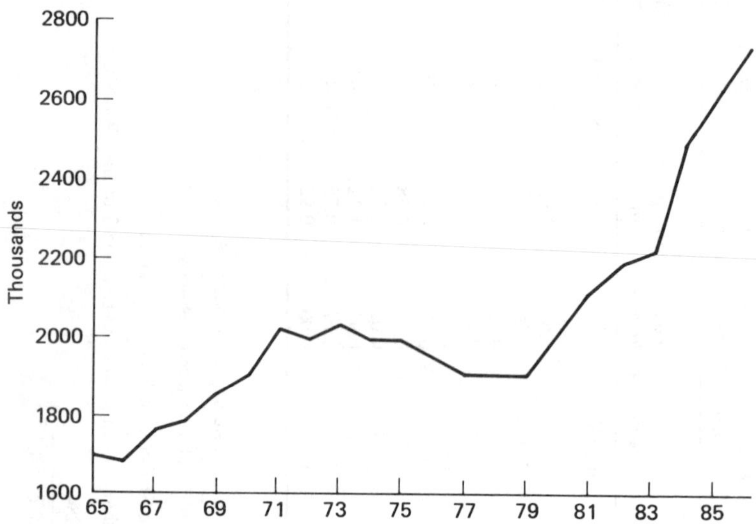

Source: *Department of Employment Gazette.*

(c) The Impact Upon Registered Unemployment: The Labour Market Effect

Our earlier review of the evidence established that small firms had been responsible for many new jobs in the United Kingdom in the recent past, although the precise contribution is unclear. We saw also that there has been a substantial increase in the number of companies registered for VAT. Finally, the number of self-employed people has risen dramatically since 1979. Figure 8.7 shows that there were over 800 000 more self-employed people in the United Kingdom in June 1986 than there were in June 1979. Almost one-tenth of the working population is now self-employed.

Thus those characteristics which the government sees as indicative of the 'enterprise economy', and which are necessary to reduce unemployment – 'more businesses, more self-employment . . .' – have been exhibited in the United Kingdom in the first half of the 1980s. Moreover, the government is extremely proud of its job creation measures, often claiming that the United Kingdom has created more jobs in recent years than the rest of Europe put together (see, for instance, Cabinet Office (1985) para. 1.4). The

Figure 8.8 Registered unemployment in Great Britain, 1965–86

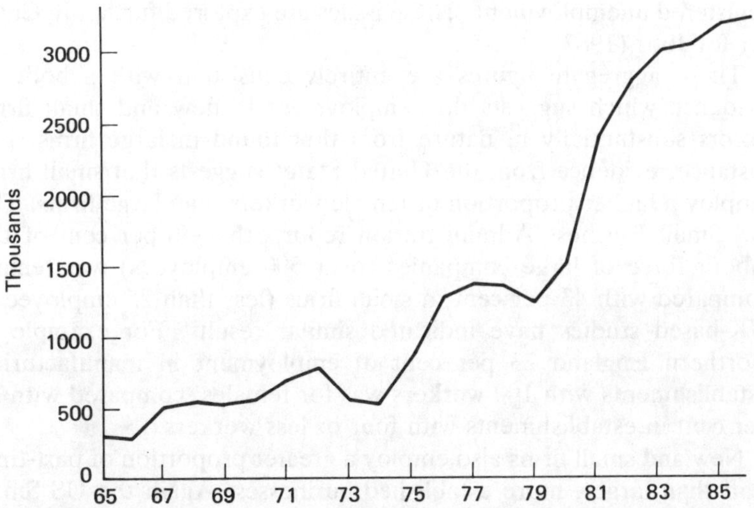

Source: *Department of Employment Gazette.*

claim appears to be corroborated by the evidence of Department of Employment figures (*Employment Gazette*, April 1987) which show that there was a growth of more than one million jobs in the British economy between March 1983 and September 1986, nearly half of which was accounted for by self-employment growth.

This apparently phenomenal level of job creation is not, however, reflected in the unemployment figures. Figure 8.8 shows that, contrary to the predictions of the government's 'model', registered unemployment *increased* by almost a quarter of a million between June 1983 and June 1986. This paradox of increasing employment coupled with higher levels of unemployment clearly requires some explanation. Part of this explanation undoubtedly lies in demographic factors, with an increase (until recently) in the number of young people seeking work. However, this is not the whole story.

A more detailed examination of the employment figures reveals that a substantial proportion of the new jobs has been taken by women, approximately half of whom work part-time. Indeed, male employment fell by 93 000 between 1983 and 1986. Thus, in terms of *full-time equivalents*, the employment growth is not as impressive as it first appears. Also, since a substantial proportion of female workers do not register as unemployed, an increase in female employment is unlikely to be reflected in a corresponding reduction in the level of registered unemployment. These issues are explored further in Charter for Jobs (1987).

These aggregate figures are entirely consistent with a body of evidence which suggests that employment in new and small firms differs substantially in nature from that found in large firms. For instance, evidence from the United States suggests that small firms employ a higher proportion of female workers than large firms. The US Small Business Administration reports that 36 per cent of the labour force of large companies (over 500 employees) was female compared with 43 per cent in small firms (less than 25 employees). UK-based studies have indicated similar results. For example in Northern England 23 per cent of employment in manufacturing establishments with 100 workers was for females, compared with 31 per cent in establishments with four or less workers.

New and small firms also employ a greater proportion of part-time staff than larger, more established businesses. Again the US Small Business Administration (1984, ch. 4) reports that 26 per cent of workers in firms with less than 25 workers were part-time compared with 10 per cent of workers in firms with more than 500 workers. Amongst Northern England manufacturing establishments 22 per cent of employment in establishments with less than five workers was part-time compared with 4 per cent in establishments with more than 100 workers. (See Storey and Johnson (1987b), Chapter 6)

Evidence from Canada and United States indicates that small firms tend to employ relatively high proportions of young workers (less than 25 years old) and old workers (more than 65 years old). For example in the United States 12 per cent of workers in firms with less than 25 workers were under 19 years of age, compared to only 6 per cent of workers in firms with more than 500 workers. At the other extreme, 4 per cent of workers in very small firms were beyond the retirement age compared to 0.5 per cent of those in large firms.

Analysis of the occupational structure of small firm employment in several countries suggests that small firms tend to employ a higher proportion of managerial, professional and clerical staff than large firms. Conversely, they employ fewer unskilled manual workers. Clearly these occupational differences are partly due to the presence of the owner working within the very small firm.

Finally there is extensive evidence that 'quality' of jobs in small firms is lower than in large firms, although there is some debate over

Table 8.5 Firm size and job quality

United States	*Enterprise size*	
	Less than 25 workers	*More than 1000 workers*
Proportion of employees covered by health insurance coverage (%)	35	86
Proportion of employees covered by pension or retirement plan coverage (%)	17	88
Average tenure with current employer (years)	4.5	9
Proportion of employees working part-time (%)	32	12
Japan	*Enterprise size*	
	Less than 100 workers	*More than 5000 workers*
Employer payments for pension schemes (%)	71	100
Provision of company housing, canteens, recreational facilities (%)	29	100
Retirement allowance at mandatory retirement (%)	22	100
Average years of tenure with current employer (years)	8	12
Part-time employment (%)	9	8

Source: OECD.

whether there may be compensating differences in job satisfaction amongst the workforce. The evidence for job quality being lower in small firms is based primarily on data produced by the OECD. These show that in the United States and Japan, according to the variety of indices of job quality shown in Table 8.5, small firms provide significantly fewer non-wage benefits than large firms. For example health insurance coverage, pension entitlements and provision of non-statutory facilities such as canteens, are found in generally less than one-third of small firms but in virtually all large firms.

OECD data also show that the less frequent provision of non-wage benefits is *not* compensated by the payment of higher wages in small firms. Indeed the opposite is the case. Table 8.6 shows that, amongst the eight OECD countries listed, only in Denmark are wage levels in firms with less than 100 workers similar to those in firms with more than 500 workers. In most cases average wages in small firms are

Table 8.6 Average wages by firm size (as percentage of wages in enterprises with 500 persons or more in 1978)

	Enterprise/establishment size (number of persons employed)		
	10–99	*100–499*	*500+*
Belgium	78.1	85.7	100.0
Denmark	93.2	97.3	100.0
France	82.9	86.3	100.0
Germany	89.7	92.2	100.0
Italy	85.4	92.7	100.0
Japan (1982)	77.1	82.9	100.0
Luxembourg	74.5	78.7	100.0
United States (1983)	57.0	73.8	100.0

Source: OECD: *Employment Outlook*, 1985.

between 70 per cent and 90 per cent of those in large firms, but in the United States average wages in small firms are only 57 per cent of those in large firms.

According to all these 'objective' criteria the quality of jobs in small firms is inferior to that in large firms. Even so it is sometimes argued that job satisfaction levels are higher in smaller firms. This view was given strong support by the Bolton Committee (1971) which suggested that work-place conflicts were minimised in the small firm (see also Curran, 1986). Furthermore workers in small firms were more likely to feel a greater sense of belonging, to experience higher levels of job satisfaction and more likely to participate in decision making. This appeared to be reflected in lower levels of strike-proneness and absenteeism in small firms.

Subsequent research has seriously questioned this rather 'cosy' view of the work-place environment in the smaller firm. The Bolton perspective was derived exclusively from discussions with the owners, with no reported discussions with the workforce or their representatives. Absenteeism rates do not appear to be closely related to size and the most authoritative recent review by Curran and Stanworth (1986) is at best agnostic about the job satisfaction benefits of employment in small firms.

In conclusion therefore it appears that, according to most objective criteria, the quality of jobs in smaller firms is lower than that in large firms. The inferior job quality offered by small firms, according to objective criteria, does not appear to be compensated by other subjective factors. It may therefore be argued that small firm employment growth is unlikely to absorb more than a small proportion of workers from the large firm sector. Instead, small firms take a relatively high proportion of their labour from the 'secondary labour market', primarily married women and others who were previously outside the labour force.

It can be argued in a similar vein that the characteristics of the self-employed population do not match those of the unemployed in several important respects, in particular their age and occupational profiles. There is also evidence to suggest that a significant proportion of the growth in self-employment which has occurred since 1979 is accounted for by married females working on a part-time basis. In addition, around two-thirds of the self-employed population do not employ others, and this proportion appears to be growing (Johnson, 1986).

It may be concluded from the evidence presented here that small firm employment growth and self-employment is likely to have a smaller effect upon registered unemployment than the same number of jobs created in large firms. Furthermore the jobs themselves may be less attractive to workers.

AN ALTERNATIVE APPROACH

Thus far we have reviewed the government's own case for support for small firms, showing that the majority of its arguments are either not supported by the facts or, at best, unproven. We have also shown that in reviewing public policies to support small firms there are key elements which are rarely discussed by government. These elements lead the objective analyst to take a rather less euphoric view of the role of small firms in wealth and job creation than is currently fashionable.

Nevertheless small firms in most developed countries provide more than one-quarter of employment in the manufacturing sector and in some cases more than half of employment in the service sector. Furthermore in most developed countries small firms are becoming relatively more important, partly because of the growth of the service sector, partly because of changes in the structure of demand, partly because of technological change and partly because of increasing unemployment. For all these reasons the small firm sector cannot be ignored as a source of new wealth and job creation and appropriate public policies have to be constructed in order to promote its development.

In constructing such a policy, one key result should be borne in mind by policy-makers: *the performance of small firms is extremely diverse*. Significant job creation takes place in very few small firms but these few firms are responsible for a substantial proportion of job creation in the small firm sector. To illustrate this point, it has been shown that, of the 1991 wholly new manufacturing firms known to have been established in the Northern region between 1965 and 1981, 1187 were still trading and independent in 1981. At that time, total employment in these firms was 13 313. Out of these 1187 firms the largest 34 employed 3439 and the largest 118 firms employed 6320 workers. Hence 6 per cent of the firms which are known to have started after 1965 provided 47 per cent of all jobs. (Storey and Johnson, 1987b, chapter 7). Adjusting for the known under-representation of short-life firms in the data set the evidence is as follows. ***Out of every 100 manufacturing businesses which begin, 30 cease to trade within two to three years. A further 30 cease to trade over the next seven to eight years, so that after a decade only 40 businesses will survive. Of these 40 businesses, four will provide half the jobs.***

This concentration of employment growth in a small number of firms is even more clearly illustrated in the results presented by Doyle and Gallagher (1986) on the manufacturing and service sectors. It will be recalled from our earlier discussion that reservations were expressed over whether it was appropriate to scale up employment in those small firms within the data base to compensate for small firms not included in the data base. However it should be more valid to examine the contribution to job creation *within* the small firm sector of the fastest growing set of firms. According to Doyle and Gallagher there were 560 250 firms which in 1982 had less than 200 employees. Over the next two years 120 grew in employment to having more than 500 employees. These 0.02 per cent of small firms actually created 45 per cent of new jobs in the expansion of firms of this size. Although there are reservations about interpreting these figures it remains clear that job creation amongst small firms is heavily concentrated within very few such firms.

It is our observation that current policy is focussed, not upon specific small firms or groups of firms, but upon small firms in general. For example, information services are provided for all firms wishing to take advantage of them either directly through the Small

Firms Services or through public financing of bodies such as Enterprise Agencies. Similarly the government's efforts to reduce red tape, bureaucracy and other 'unfair' impediments to small firms will benefit all small firms, not simply those wishing to expand. Equally the Enterprise Allowance Scheme can be used by any registered unemployed worker capable of assembling £1000 to indicate his or her serious intention of starting a business. Even the Loan Guarantee Scheme is 'responsive' in the sense that the bank will frequently await a request from a customer and then make a decision on whether to issue a loan on normal commercial criteria or through the Guarantee Scheme. Indeed, if anything, the scheme is tailored towards less successful firms (or at least more risky firms as far as the banks are concerned), which are less likely to be amongst the tiny minority which will succeed in a major way.

The major lesson to be learnt from the observation and tracking of small firms in Britain and overseas is that the relatively poor performance of the British economy, if it is related at all to the performance of the small firm sector, is *not* related to a shortage in terms of *numbers* of small firms. Policy has to be directed towards improving the *quality* rather than the *quantity* of small firms. There appears to be a strongly held view within UK government that, while some small firms are good, more small firms are better. The high profile of the Enterprise Allowance Scheme within the package of Job Schemes suggests that one indication of 'success' is an increase in both the formation of new businesses and of the total number of businesses in the economy. We do not accept this view for reasons outlined earlier. In our view the fundamental problem within the UK small firm sector is a shortage of *quality* rather than quantity.

The problem in Britain is that it has too few businesses which are able and willing to grow into large firms, and that current policy is insufficiently directed towards facilitating the growth of such businesses. *The objective of small business policy should be to enable more small businesses to grow into large businesses*. Current policies designed to maximise the number of individuals starting in business could even inhibit the growth of these potentially rapid growth firms, since lowering the entry barriers to business formation could result in cut-throat competition for businesses in their early and vulnerable stages of life. In this respect much can be learnt from the experience of the West Germans where, since 1953, regulations have required individuals in many crafts and trades to hold proficiency certificates before they are allowed to practise. The Germans recognise that, during periods of high unemployment, large numbers of unemployed workers attempt to become small business owners. Since such individuals are able to compete only on the basis of price they can lead to reduced standards, a decline in customer confidence and to both their own bankruptcy and that of established traders. For all these reasons the Germans maintained high barriers to entry in trades whereas in the United Kingdom the current administration has been attempting to reduce barriers, and hence the quality of service, even further. The enshrinement of 'quality' throughout all aspects of German business life is a lesson which should be learnt in the United Kingdom.

Finally there is also a 'moral' case against encouraging unemployed workers to risk their modest savings in establishing a business where the chances of success are small and the chances of bankruptcy much higher.

To summarise, we believe there is a strong case for placing much greater emphasis upon facilitating and enabling the growth of those small businesses which are currently experiencing rapid growth but which could grow even faster. Such businesses are likely to be selling overseas. Their growth will have minimal local displacement effects and could, through sub-contracting and local sourcing, promote the growth of other small firms. Such policies would require a recognition that assistance would be highly selective, since few firms would qualify. It would constitute a major reversal of current policy. For these reasons selective small firms policies have been criticised on several grounds.

SELECTIVITY: THE CASE FOR AND AGAINST

Four arguments are generally presented against a selective small firms policy:

(a) Successful small firms, because they are successful, do not need assistance.
(b) The public sector has a particularly bad record of identifying successful firms.
(c) It is better/easier to increase the number of those starting in business since each new business creates employment.
(d) A selective policy is inequitable and complex to administer.

(a) Successful firms do not need assistance

Our survey results indicate the opposite to be the case. The small firm which is expanding and attempting to grow rapidly is likely to be experiencing a shortage of suitable premises, problems with a conservative bank manager (fears of over-trading), problems with recruiting skilled labour, problems with exporting and so on. It is quite understandable that firms which have the greatest number of such problems are those which are growing fastest. The slow growth, or no-growth, firm does not have these problems since it is not trying to export, obtain new premises or skilled labour.

If policy can therefore relax these constraints upon further growth for relatively few firms the return in terms of net job creation is likely to be much higher than can be obtained, for example, by spreading assistance thinly across many firms, many of which will not respond.

(b) The public sector has a poor record in implementing selective policies

This is a somewhat complex argument which comprises two separate elements: (a) it is technically not possible to identify fast growth firms; (b) it is politically unacceptable to identify and assist such firms.

From a technical viewpoint it is clear that helping small firms yields an uncertain return. Small firms have high failure rates and any assistance policy has to recognise this. There are, however, ways in which these uncertainties can be minimised. For example, failure rates are high in the early years of a business's life. Furthermore there is no effective tool to distinguish successful businesses at, or prior to start-up. This suggests that it would be preferable to direct assistance resources more towards existing established small businesses with a track record. Here it is possible to identify potential failures from potential non-failures with a tolerable degree of accuracy. There are certain characteristics of businesses which are associated with success and indeed these businesses are seen as different from the 'norm' after two or three years of trading. Again it has to be emphasised that there is always a risk involved in assisting small firms but, using professional appraisal techniques, it is possible to limit these risks to an acceptable degree. The growth of venture capital in the United Kingdom in recent years provides an eloquent testimony to the potential returns from a selective policy.

Even if it is technically possible to implement a selective policy, however, some may raise political objections. Perhaps the most familiar is that if businesses are successful and growing rapidly then they should attract assistance from the private sector – banks, venture capitalists, accountants – so obviating the need for public assistance. Such reasoning is misguided because it fails to recognise that the objectives of public and private organisations differ markedly. For example the banks, accountants and venture capitalists measure success in terms of *financial* performance. In crude terms the venture capitalists are looking for businesses which will show rapid growth in profitability and (perhaps) assets. The accountants are interested in small businesses which will grow rapidly so as to demand the increasingly wide range of services provided by the major practices. Although the major clearing banks may not place such weight upon growth they will need to be satisfied about the financial viability of the business. On the other hand the public sector agencies will be more interested in *employment* growth and, although financial and employment performance are associated, the two measures are not coincident. There will therefore be cases of firms which could experience rapid employment growth, but which are not necessarily the focus of attention from the private sector.

A second, again essentially political argument is that selective industrial policies have in the past been associated with providing assistance to businesses with no prospect of commercial viability. In the United Kingdom, for example, many of the National Enterprise Board investments are now viewed as not having been made on commercial criteria, but rather upon judgements of politicians about which firms to 'save' and which to allow to die. Memories of that era have tended to tarnish the image of selective policies, but in no way are these valid parallels. In the past, decisions were made by politicians upon *large* firms which were in danger of closure and where there were many jobs (and votes!) at stake. Under the present proposals decisions will be made, perhaps even ultimately by politicians, but without the same pressures since there are less votes in deciding to support or not support businesses with twenty or less employees. In our view it is *not* a solution to this problem to attempt to exclude politicians from decision taking. Since it is public resources which are at stake, it is appropriate for politicians to take the ultimate decisions, even if the grounds for this decision are commercial.

(c) It is better/easier to increase the number of start-up businesses

The argument here is that if there are approximately four highly successful small businesses in every 100, then policy should be directed towards increasing the number of businesses to 200 as this would produce eight successes. As noted earlier, we reject this argument on the grounds that policies which artificially raise the number of business formations lead to higher death rates of businesses and to a radical reduction in the number of successful firms and hence of employment. In short, whilst it may be possible to increase the birth rate of businesses quite sharply, especially in a recession, this will reduce the number of successes perhaps to one or two per hundred, primarily because of the difficulties of such firms earning sufficient profits in their early years to finance subsequent expansion. A sharp reduction in the number of fast growers from four per 100 to one or two per 100 without compensating employment increases in large firms would mean a catastrophic drop in the numbers of jobs created. It is for these reasons that an increase in the rates of new firm formation can lead, perhaps paradoxically, to fewer jobs.

(d) A selective policy is inequitable, bureaucratic and difficult to administer

This argument does carry considerable power. It has to be recognised that selective policies mean that, by definition, many businesses will not receive public support when otherwise similar businesses are assisted. To the owner of a non-assisted business such policies will appear unjust and, particularly if an assisted firm performs poorly, totally misguided.

Some public servants may prefer to administer non-discretionary, automatic grants, since these require less judgement to be exercised. 'Automatic' policies, however, are acknowledged to lead to instances where businesses receive assistance to undertake actions which they would have undertaken in the absence of the policy (deadweight). Indeed the high deadweight element perceived to exist in much regional policy expenditure has been a major factor influencing the recent switch towards greater selectivity. If greater selectivity is acceptable to government in its administration of regional policy we see no reason, in principle, why it cannot be applied to small firm policy.

THE PROPOSED POLICY

A selective policy of small business support has to recognise that the particular problems facing individual small firms vary widely. Some have problems over production, others over obtaining payments from large debtors, others over premises or recruiting skilled labour. In other cases key items of information, building into a local network of advice, are crucially absent. The variety of problems is endless whereas the ability to solve such problems is sometimes very limited.

Small business policy makers have to recognise this diversity of problems and recognise that there is no standardised problem-solving package which is available. In many cases the small firm itself may not correctly identify the nature of its own problem, with this only coming to light after an in-depth appraisal by an experienced professional. Unfortunately, because of the cost involved, this in-depth assistance/counselling cannot be provided to all firms. Yet it *is* needed by many firms if they are to overcome the constraints upon their growth. For these reasons we believe that there should be a fundamental reappraisal of small firm policy in the United Kingdom along the following guidelines:

1. *No* public assistance should be given to start-up businesses – although no impediments should be placed in the way of those wishing to start a business.
2. A comprehensive package of assistance should be available *only* to those businesses with worthwhile growth prospects. Assistance could include finance, advice, marketing assistance – using a 'hands on' approach.
3. Only existing businesses which could demonstrate both a good track record and good prospects should be selected for assistance.
4. An assisted business should also demonstrate that it was not merely displacing other local businesses. It should show a capacity to sell outside its own region, and preferably outside the United Kingdom.
5. Assistance should be provided by local agencies.[5]

CONCLUSION

This chapter has shown that small businesses make an increasingly important yet nevertheless modest contribution to the creation of new jobs in the United Kingdom. Small business growth is certainly *not* the 'answer' to the problem of high unemployment, and it is seriously misleading to suggest that this could ever be the case. It must be recognised that current small business 'growth' in much of Britain is a reflection of recession rather than of entrepreneurial revival. Finally severe reservation should be expressed over the quality of the jobs created (many are part-time, low-paid, in poor working conditions) and the fact that small firm jobs are not being created in areas of high unemployment. Instead, job creation in small firms is regionally divisive with most of the jobs being created in the existing prosperous areas.

If government wishes to use small firm policies as a way of creating employment several major changes are required. Firstly it has to be recognised that over a decade half the jobs created in every 100 small firms occur in the four firms which grow fastest. Only by enabling these few firms fully to realise their potential will the job-creating potential of the small firm sector be maximised. This means a reversal of current policies of promoting 'the enterprise culture' in which every redundant worker is encouraged to gamble his or her redundancy money in starting a business. Instead it means a policy of selectivity in which only a few chosen firms are eligible for support, but where the support makes a significant contribution to the growth and development of the business.

Even these changes would not be sufficient for the small firm sector to become the 'answer' to unemployment in Britain. In our view, however, it would constitute a significant improvement upon current policies.

Appendix

Research on Small Firms

The views which we present have drawn upon the results of numerous studies of small businesses in all sectors and all regions of the United Kingdom and overseas. Six items of research with which we have recently been involved are frequently referred to:

1. A study of the employment and financial performance of 636 small manufacturing companies in Northern England during the 1965–81 period. Full results of this study are reported in Storey, Keasey, Watson and Wynarczyk, (1987).
2. An international review of job generation studies – stimulated initially by

the influential work of David Birch which claimed to show that two-thirds of the increase in employment in the United States between 1969 and 1976 was in firms with less than 20 workers. The results of our review are published in Storey and Johnson (1987b).

3. A review of the role of small and medium-sized enterprises (SMEs) in European job creation. This study was undertaken with collaborators in Italy, Germany, France, Spain, Portugal, Belgium and Holland and covers the contribution to job creation of SMEs and an assessment of the effectiveness of different policy instruments in *all* EEC countries. This is published in Storey and Johnson (1987a).
4. A survey of 298 UK small businesses covering all sectors in six locations. The sample of firms surveyed was designed to replicate the pattern of development of UK small businesses. The survey was conducted as part of the review undertaken by the Occupations Study Group of projected employment change in Britain until 1990. The small firm employment projections are found in S. Johnson and D. J. Storey, 'Small Firms' in Rajan (ed) (1987) *Special Studies in the UK's Employment Prospects*, Butterworth.
5. A major interview study of 239 small high-technology firms in Britain, about 60 per cent of which are located on Science Parks. The study was financed and undertaken in conjunction with United Kingdom Science Park Association (UKSPA) and Peat Marwick. The results of this study were presented to the UKSPA Annual Conference on 10 December 1986 and are available from the Association.
6. Finally an interview study of 301 businesses new to Cleveland during the 1970s was conducted by one of the present authors. The results of these interviews were published in Storey (1982).

Notes

1. David Storey is Director of Research, Small Business Centre, University of Warwick and Stephen Johnson is Research Associate of the Centre for Urban and Regional Development Studies, University of Newcastle-Upon-Tyne. A version of this text was first published in April 1987.
2. See, for instance, Storey (1982), Mason (1986), Binks and Jennings (1986).
3. A similar pattern of new firm foundation in the United Kingdom during the inter-war years is revealed in Foreman-Peck (1985).
4. Of particular note is the work of the Institute of Manpower Studies. See Atkinson (1985). See also Shutt and Whittington (1987).
5. These might operate in a similar way to the United States 'National Development Council' described in Storey (1986).

9 A Job Guarantee for Long-Term Unemployed People

Richard Jackman[1]

(with assistance and contributions from: John Cahill, Mark Cornelius, Richard Disney, Jonathan Haskel, Richard Layard, Sir Richard O'Brien)

INTRODUCTION

This concluding chapter proposes a remedy for the most serious economic and social problem of our time. At its peak in the summer of 1986, the number of people who had been unemployed for a year or more in the United Kingdom exceeded 1.3 million. Over half a million had been unemployed for a continuous period of three years or more. The scale of this problem is without precedent in our history and the consequences therefore incalculable, but few imagine that the detachment of so many people from normal working life can have other than devasting social and economic effects.

The recovery of economic activity which continued quite steadily from early 1981 failed for a long period to cut the numbers of long-term unemployed. On the contrary, as the recovery proceeded so in each year long-term unemployment increased. The assumption that long-term unemployment would fall as an *automatic* consequence of economic growth was clearly not valid.

The costs of this high level of long-term unemployment are immense. We describe in this chapter the experience of long-term unemployment and some of its human and social effects. The evidence indicates very clearly that the experience of long-term unemployment is a miserable and demoralising one. We believe that no civilised society can go on ignoring such costs for ever.

The government has recognised the need for special measures to assist the long-term unemployed, instituting for instance the Community Programme and the Restart Programme. While useful in themselves, these measures are totally inadequate to the scale of the problem. What is needed is a clear commitment by the government to provide work, or training, for the long-term unemployed, taking the form of a *job guarantee*. There are always defeatists who believe that the massive investment of resources that such a guarantee would require would be wholly impractical. To allay such doubts we shall briefly describe the situation in Sweden where the government does provide a job guarantee to the unemployed as part of its policies for maintaining full employment.

But we have first to understand the causes of the growth in long-term unemployment and the economic consequences of policy actions which might be taken to reduce it. We shall argue that long-term unemployment is the consequence of a deep-rooted failure of the labour market which the present government's economic policies have exposed. The long-term unemployed have been separated from the labour market, and bringing them back into it will improve the efficiency of the market and allow economic expansion while at the same time helping to restrain pressures for excessive wage increases. The economic costs of unemployment are to be seen as much in the work that has not been done (the decaying infrastructure, the poor quality of the housing stock and so on) as in the depressed state of the unemployed themselves.

Our proposals for Britain are then set out. They follow the outline scheme recommended by the House of Commons Select Committee on Employment in January 1986 (House of Commons, 1986), but we add to their scheme. We have examined these proposals more thoroughly than the Select Committee had the opportunity to do, and while we make some suggestions for modifications, the main themes of the Committee's proposals stand up to scrutiny. We estimate that, at a *net* annual Exchequer cost of £1.3 bn, schemes providing 750 000 places a year could be implemented. Clearly this represents a large investment of resources, but we are confident that it would achieve the desired results and that the economic and social benefits from reinvigorating the long-term unemployed and restoring them to the normal working world would far outweigh the costs.

We conclude that a job guarantee is not only desirable and practical but that in present labour market conditions it is the only non-inflationary policy that offers any hope of substantially reducing long-term unemployment. Clearly the costs are substantial but it is better to face up to the problem and the costs of solving it than to do nothing and close one's eyes to the consequences.

LONG-TERM UNEMPLOYMENT AND THE INDIVIDUAL

Historical Experience

During the Great Depression of the 1930s, the number of people who had been out of work for a year or more rose to a peak of 483 000 in May 1933. The number of long-term unemployed then declined steadily and had halved by the outbreak of the war in 1939 (*International Labour Review*, 1942). After the war, the numbers of long-term unemployed continued to fall, and by the mid-1950s the figure was as low as 20 000. During the 1960s and 1970s, long-term unemployment rose, along with the general level of unemployment. By 1979, more than 300 000 people had been unemployed for a year or more. Since 1980, the numbers of long-term unemployed have shot up, reaching half a million in 1981, over one million by July 1982 and continuing to rise thereafter, though at a slower rate, to the summer 1986 level of 1.35 million. Even allowing for differences in coverage, definition and so on, the present scale of long-term unemployment is entirely without precedent in our historical experience.

The recent growth of long-term unemployment has been obscured by the fact that the definition of unemployment has been changed so often since 1982. In Figure 9.1 we have made an attempt to correct for these changes to give a consistent postwar series of male unemployment. It is virtually impossible to produce a comparable chart for female long-term unemployment because of changes in work habits and benefit entitlements.

The 'Hidden' Long-Term Unemployed

The peak figure of 1.35 million long-term unemployed is derived from records of claimants of benefit held at Unemployment Benefit Offices who have been continuously unemployed for a period of 52 weeks or more. The term 'claimants' includes those who claim unemployment benefit, supplementary benefit (income support) or national insurance credits, although unemployment benefit is not normally paid after twelve months. Whether or not this figure gives a

Figure 9.1 Male unemployment and long-term unemployment rates

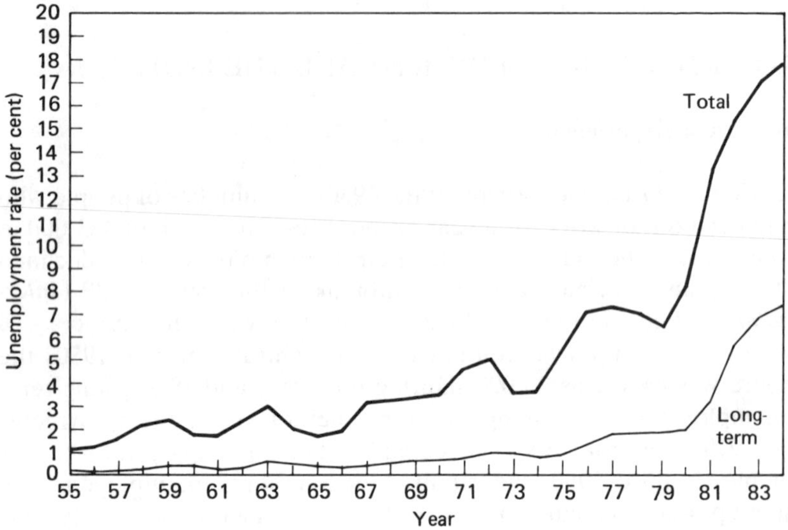

true representation of the number who are available and would like to work is subject to debate. It has been suggested that it might be an overestimate, because some people on benefit work in the black economy or do not want to work. The best available evidence on this comes from the *Labour Force Survey*, which is an independent official statistical survey carried out by the Office of Population Censuses and Surveys for the Department of Employment. According to the *Labour Force Survey*, the number of people actively looking for work – both claimants and non-claimants – plus those who would like a job, but have stopped looking for work because they believe no jobs are available, exceeds the total number of benefit claimants.[2]

It is thus more likely that the official total for *long-term* unemployment is at least representative if not an underestimate of the problem. Married women represent the main group of unemployed who are not counted in the official statistics as they are not entitled to separate supplementary benefit. Almost all men aged over 60 are excluded from the long-term unemployment count. They are eligible for a higher long-term rate once they go onto supplementary benefit. Those who receive the long-term rate do not register in the unemployment statistics.

A further consideration is that if someone who has been unemployed for a number of years takes a temporary job – even for only a week or so – and then, when the job comes to an end, returns to the unemployment register he/she will be classified as short-term unemployed for twelve months. There is little recent evidence on such repeat spells of unemployment, but data from the 1978–9 DHSS Cohort Study suggest that 55 per cent of the unemployed men who found work were unemployed again within a year (Stern, 1986).

Who are the Long-Term Unemployed?

While in the past long-term unemployment was a problem confined to particular groups within the community – the elderly, disabled and sick (see, for example, Daniel 1974) – today the long-term unemployed can be found in every section of the population. Figure 9.2 shows the proportion of long-term unemployment in the labour force

Figure 9.2(a) Male unemployment and long-term unemployment rates by age, 10 July 1986

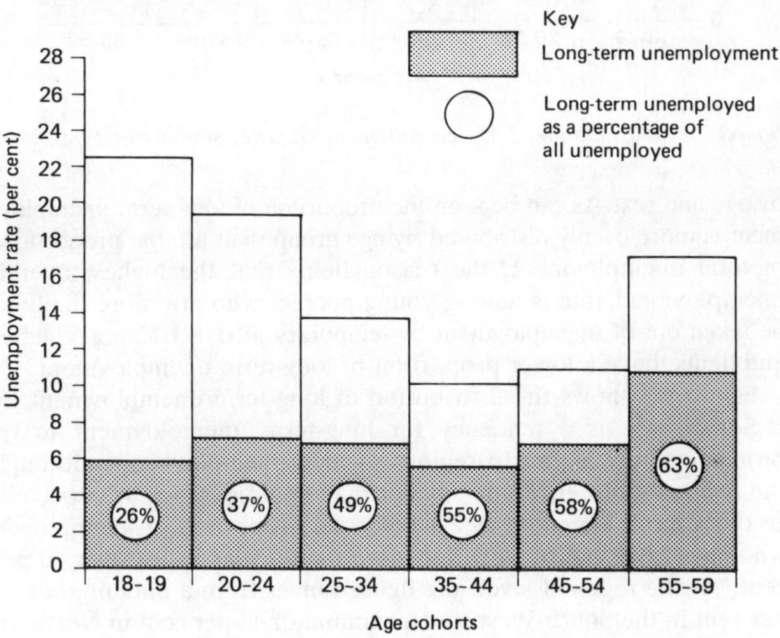

Source: Tables 2.6 and 2.15, *Employment Gazette*, September 1986.

Figure 9.2(b) Female unemployment and long-term unemployment rates by age, 10 July 1986

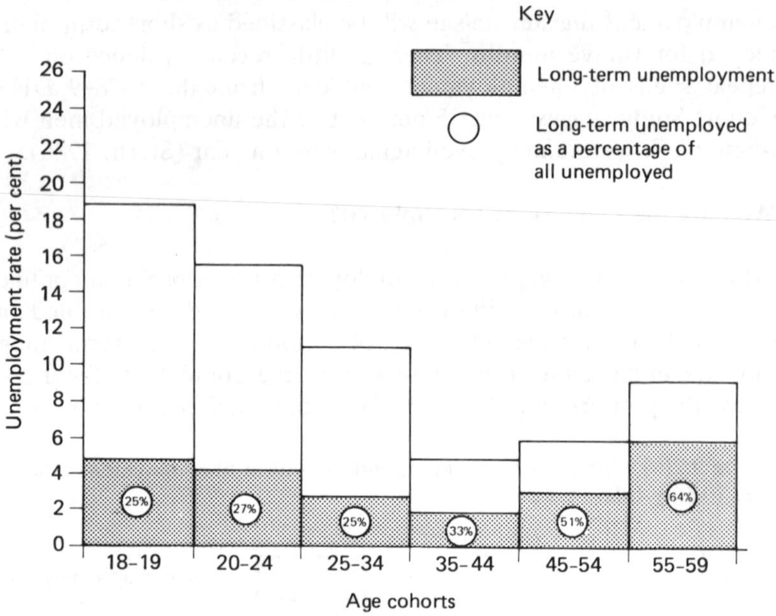

Source: Tables 2.6 and 2.15, *Employment Gazette*, September 1986.

by age and sex. As can be seen the proportion of long-term unemployment is more evenly distributed by age group than are the proportions of total unemployment, the reason being that the highest overall unemployment rate is among young people, who are more likely to be taken out of unemployment by temporary jobs or training schemes and hence have a lower proportion of long-term unemployment.

Figure 9.3 shows the distribution of long-term unemployment by region. There is a tendency for long-term unemployment to be proportionately higher in regions of high unemployment, although the regional differences are smaller than might perhaps be expected. In the United Kingdom as a whole, the proportion of unemployed who have been out of work for more than a year is just over 40 per cent. At the regional level, the figure ranges from a minimum of 34 per cent in the South-West to a maximum of 48 per cent in Northern Ireland.

Turning to skills, the 1983 *Labour Force Survey* showed a slightly

Figure 9.3 Regional unemployment and long-term unemployment rates 10 July 1986

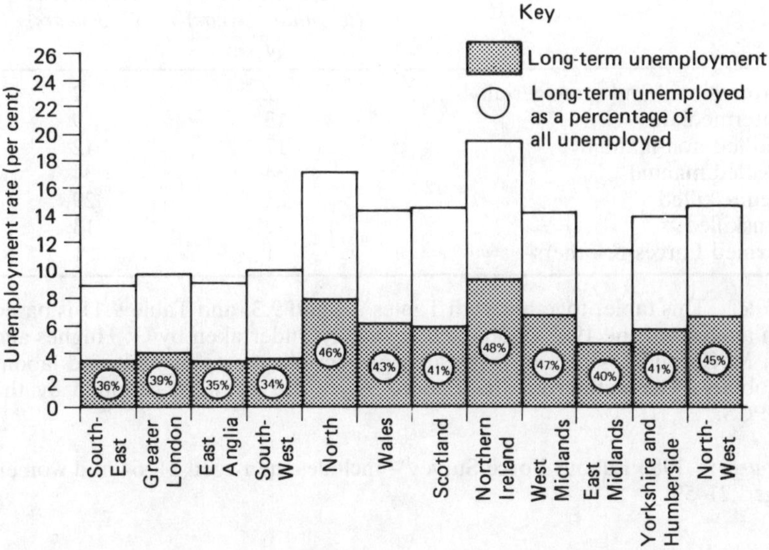

Source: *Employment Gazette*, September 1986.

higher proportion of unskilled and semi-skilled manual workers among the long-term unemployed than among the short-term unemployed (Table 9.1). The main conclusion to be drawn from Table 9.1, however, is that the long-term unemployed do not appear to differ at all significantly from the unemployed as a whole in terms of skills. Moreover the survey only gives information on the last occupation before unemployment which does not necessarily correspond to the longest job the person has held. Michael White (1983), in his survey of the long-term unemployed, found that the longest jobs were on average at a higher level of skill than the most recent.

The 1983 *Labour Force Survey* also shows that the long-term unemployed typically have fewer formal qualifications than the short-term unemployed (Table 9.2). Again, though, the differences between the long-term unemployed and the unemployed as a whole seem quite small. Finally, a finding of many studies has been the high proportion of single, rather than married, men amongst the long-term unemployed. In Michael White's survey, 35 per cent of long-term unemployed men were unmarried, as against 25 per cent of the

Table 9.1 Skill levels of the unemployed by last occupation

	Short-term (less than 1 year) %	*Long-term (1–3 years)* %
Professional and managerial	2	2
Intermediate	13	9
Skilled non-manual	17	12
Skilled manual	34	34
Semi-skilled	25	29
Unskilled	9	13
Armed Forces & others	1	1

Note: This table, together with Tables 9.2 and 9.3, and Table 9.11 is based on analysis of the 1983 *Labour Force Survey* undertaken by G. Hughes and B. McCormick as part of a research project on unemployment and labour mobility. The data from the *Labour Force Survey* were supplied by the OPCS.

Source: 1983 Labour Force Survey – includes men aged 21–64 and women aged 21–59.

Table 9.2 Qualifications of the unemployed

	Short-term (less than 1 year) %	*Long-term (more than 1 year)* %
Degree/professional qualification	7	4
O Levels +	25	15
Other qualifications	12	10
None	55	71

Source: 1983 *Labour Force Survey* – includes men aged 21–64 and women aged 21–59.

population as a whole (weighted according to the age distribution of the long-term unemployed). Of the married men, only half had dependent children, but, where there were children, family size tended to be large.

The Experience of Long-Term Unemployment

The experience of long-term unemployment is for most people a miserable and depressing one. In general, it is characterised by poverty, boredom and a loss of self-respect. Harrison (1976) provides a full and evocative account of its characteristics and problems.

Long-term unemployment is a trap which exerts a tightening grip over time. Erosion of skills and employer prejudice combine to reduce the prospects of the long-term unemployed finding work. Often long-term unemployment can lead to harmful and measurable effects on a person's physical and mental health. Moreover all these consequences are felt not only by the unemployed themselves, but also in many cases by their spouses and children.

Poverty

Poverty is often slow to strike. Many people who become unemployed receive tax rebates or redundancy payments and some have savings they can draw on. Most have a reasonable stock of household goods which they can continue to use without incurring out-of-pocket expenses. Some also find work again before this cushion of reserves is exhausted and never confront the difficulties of living off the dole without any other source of support.

After a year without a job a person will have become significantly worse off. The long-term unemployed are not eligible for unemployment benefit, but only for means-tested income support which is reduced if one has savings (of over £3000 in 1986) or other household income. The available evidence suggests that the level of supplementary benefit (income support) has not been adequate to provide for basic needs. This is particularly so when there are children in the family. Richard Berthoud's study (1984) found that out of the non-pensioner householders without children receiving supplementary benefit 30 per cent ran out of money most weeks, 39 per cent lacked a complete standard set of clothing and 36 per cent were in debt when interviewed (excluding credit arrangements they were keeping up to date with). The picture was much worse for couples with children where the figures were 50 per cent, 60 per cent and 52 per cent respectively.

Campbell (1984) gives a vivid description of what these statistics mean in human terms.

> One man and woman in their early 20s living in Coventry with one child, mostly unemployed since leaving school, have a total income of £63 (prices are for 1982–3), including £5.25 child benefit. Weekly bills total £46.36 (rent £27.36, loan payment £3, sheets and

> blanket club £5, television hire purchase £2, electricity £4, gas £3, and bike payments £2). Their food bill averages £15 per week. Their average diet is toast and porridge for breakfast, nothing at midday (the child has school dinners), sandwiches or beans on toast at tea time, cooked meals only at weekends, usually sausages or chicken and vegetables. Sometimes the woman gets vegetables from her father's garden. This is what she spent on her last three pairs of shoes: £3.99 in 1977, £9 in 1980 (when she was working), and £4.99 in 1982. She has never possessed boots or winter shoes: 'I can't afford closed-in shoes, so I always wear sandals and in the winter I just put on two pairs of socks.' She never buys a paper and never goes out in the evening.

Such testimony is very common. Indeed the typical experience of the long-term unemployed is not that of the contented dole scrounger but rather one of real financial hardship.

Lack of anything to do

Initially, unemployment can be a busy time. Not only do newly unemployed people tend to search around for jobs quite actively, but often they take the opportunity of a break from work – which may turn out to be short – for dealing with things that need doing round the house. Most people in full-time work feel they could do with a little more leisure time and initially are able to make good use of it.

As time passes, however, some of these activities lose their appeal. Moreover opportunities become exhausted. In particular financial stringencies discourage activities that involve going out of the house, and indeed many (such as decorating) within it. Many of the unemployed find boredom the most difficult problem to cope with.

Loss of self-respect

To lose a job may be regarded as a misfortune, but to be unable to find another one tends to be seen as a mark of personal failure. The longer a person has been unemployed, the more difficult it becomes to explain away being unable to get a job in terms of luck or circumstances. Most of the unemployed want to work, both for the income it brings and to enable them to use their time productively. These pressures are particularly severe for the long-term unemployed, so that their loss of self-respect for failing to find work is correspondingly greater.

Quite apart from the individual's own motivation, he or she will be confronted with the attitudes of other people. There is a deep-rooted, and in itself quite reasonable, attitude amongst people in work that they do not see why they should exert themselves to support people who are sitting around doing nothing. This attitude appears to be persisting despite the experience of sustained high levels of unemployment.

Reduced prospects of finding work

The long-term unemployed have greater difficulty in finding work for a variety of reasons. First, making job applications costs money. Even if 'Jobclubs' now provide help with stationery and other needs, there are still the bus fares and the expense of presenting oneself at interviews suitably dressed. These are costs which the long-term unemployed can ill afford. Second, if they are depressed and demoralised they will appear unattractive to potential employers. And thirdly, employers may be wary of employing people who have been unemployed for a long time on the grounds either that long-term unemployment is a sign of the individual's inadequacy or that the individual will have lost work habits such as punctuality while unemployed.

Job Search

The unemployed in Britain do not search for jobs very actively. Only about half of all unemployed people are involved in job applications in any month. Perhaps surprisingly, however, given the reduced likelihood of their getting a job, job search by the long-term unemployed does not fall off in the way one might have expected. As Table 9.3 shows, the proportion actively seeking work does not change significantly until after three years. A similar conclusion was drawn by White in his survey of the long-term unemployed. White's survey revealed that the number of jobs applied for held up remarkably well (see White, 1983, p. 118). However he also asked about the degree of effort which people expended in their search for work. More people said that they had reduced the time they had spent looking for work than said that they had increased it since they had lost their job. This trend continued and was more pronounced when the same people were interviewed again one year later (see Table 9.4).

It is apparent then that, despite the many obstacles in their way,

Table 9.3 Job search

	Unemployment duration (months)			
	0–12 %	*13–24* %	*25–36* %	*37+* %
Engaged in active* job search in the last month	58.9	53.2	48.7	32.5

* Active job search includes:

- placing newspaper advertisements,
- answering newspaper advertisements,
- direct applications to employers,
- awaiting outcome of job applications.

Thus job searching activities such as reading newspaper job columns or visits to the jobcentre are excluded.

Source: 1983 *Labour Force Survey* – includes men aged 21–64 and women aged 21–59.

Table 9.4 Time spent looking for work*

	First interview %	*Second interview (one year later)* %
Women		
More than last year	23.6	14.1
Less than last year	29.7	32.0
Same or don't know	46.7	53.8
Men		
More than last year	20.3	10.8
Less than last year	32.0	42.4
Same or don't know	47.7	46.9

* The question asked was worded as follows: 'Would you say that, in general, you're spending more time looking for work than you were about a year ago, or are you spending less time now, or has the time you spend remained about the same?'

Source: White, M. (1983) *Long-Term Unemployment and Labour Markets*, Policy Studies Institute.

the long-term unemployed are typically still anxious to find work. This is despite the fact that people are significantly more pessimistic about their chances of getting a job as time goes on (see again White, 1983).

Health

The unemployed are more prone to ill-health, both physical and mental, and have higher suicide and mortality rates than people in work. However statistical association on its own is no proof that unemployment is a cause of ill-health. For it may be due to the fact that people in poor health are more likely to become unemployed, and have greater difficulty in finding work again once they have lost their job.

Physical health

It seems fair to conclude that no study has been able to demonstrate a clear causal relationship between unemployment, or more particularly long-term unemployment, and physical health. Thus, whilst one might expect the experience of long-term unemployment to lead to a deterioration in the health of those affected through the increased stress it places on the individual and the prolonged poverty which it exposes them to, there is as yet no incontrovertible evidence to support this proposition.

However prolonged unemployment might not only affect the health of the jobless themselves, it could also affect their dependents. In this instance the direction of causation is less easy to deny. A study by Moser *et al.* (1984) using longtitudinal data, found that over the ten-year period 1971–81 the standardised mortality rate of the wives of men seeking work at the time of the 1971 Census was some 20 per cent higher than that of other married women in the sample. Thus, although one might argue that men might have become unemployed on the basis of health problems, it is more difficult to argue that they could have become unemployed on the basis of their wives' health. Indeed the leading cause of this high mortality was a heart condition often brought on by stress. This could be taken as evidence that the ill-health of the jobless themselves is due to the stress induced by unemployment.

Equally disturbing is the apparent effect prolonged unemployment has on the children of the jobless. Various (Payne 1984, Rona *et al.* 1979) have shown that the height of children with unemployed fathers, after allowing for social class, is significantly less than those whose fathers have jobs – in one study by an average of 4 cm.

Thus, whilst we are still unable to say conclusively that long-term unemployment does cause a deterioration in physical health, the weight of evidence is supportive of such a conclusion.

Mental health

The causal link between unemployment and mental health is better established. Particularly telling in this respect has been the study of school leavers in Leeds by Banks and Jackson (1982). They showed not only that those who became unemployed scored higher on the General Health Questionnaire (and so had a higher probability of being a psychiatric case) than those who found work but also that the two groups had scores on the Health Questionnaire that were not significantly different when they were still at school. Thus it cannot be argued that poorer mental health was the cause of their unemployment.

Although it has proved difficult to find a relationship between duration and psychological ill-health amongst young people (see for example Warr, Banks and Ullah, 1985) a significant relationship in samples of older people has been established (see Jackson and Warr, 1984). This can perhaps be attributed to the relatively higher financial and other pressures on older people with families, which build up the longer unemployment lasts (see above).

Suicide and parasuicide[3]

The statistical association between unemployment, suicide and parasuicide is well documented. However epidemiologists are unwilling to commit themselves on causation. No study has attempted to link the length of unemployment with suicide. However Platt and Kreitman (1984) found that the risk of parasuicide amongst the unemployed relative to the risk among the employed was related strongly to length of unemployment: it was nine to one among those unemployed for fewer than four weeks; five to one among those unemployed for five weeks to six months; ten to one among those unemployed for six to twelve months and nineteen to one among those unemployed more than a year. These figures are consistent with anecdotal evidence of how the unemployed are affected over time. The initial shock of losing a job causes much distress and then people adapt only to become more demoralised if they do not find a job after many months.[4]

Family Breakdown

Prolonged unemployment can also have a detrimental effect on family relationships. Studies of the unemployed which enquire into the impact on family relationships report an increase in friction, stress and tension particularly between spouses and to a lesser extent between parents and children. Indeed there is evidence (reported in Hakim, 1982) to suggest that unemployment and divorce are causally related. Long or repeated spells of unemployment are related to other stress factors (financial difficulties, housing problems and frequent housing moves) which are invariably more pronounced among divorcing couples than those maintaining a stable marriage.

Assessment

The scale of long-term unemployment in the mid-1980s is the highest in our historical experience. It is a problem which even the most prosperous areas of our country, such as the South-East, seem unable to avoid. Also in terms of qualifications and skills long-term unemployment does not appear to discriminate. The short- and long-term unemployed are almost indistinguishable on these lines.

The experience of long-term unemployment is a corrosive and unhappy one, which damages a person's self-respect and financial well-being and can lead to more permanent scars through family breakdown and a deterioration in physical and mental health. It is clearly not a condition which most people endure willingly.

SPECIAL EMPLOYMENT MEASURES IN THE UNITED KINGDOM

Background

The United Kingdom has over 75 years' experience of public sector programmes to help the unemployed find work. Special employment and training measures were introduced in the 1930s to help relieve mass unemployment. Immediate postwar schemes successfully resettled millions of returning servicemen. In the fifties and sixties special schemes were maintained for some particular groups – disabled people, ex-Regulars and others with special needs.

We now have more than a decade of experience of measures designed to combat the sharp rise in unemployment which followed the oil price shock of 1973. None the less, for much of this period, unemployment continued to increase in numbers and in duration. A variety of measures has been introduced, expanded, contracted, amended, withdrawn or replaced as Secretaries of State for Employment have come and gone, and with almost equal rapidity. What can we learn from this experience? What are the strengths and weaknesses of the current schemes? Why have they so often failed?

Recent Programmes

All employment and training services – including those provided in the private sector – are of potential benefit to the long-term unemployed as well as to others. Arguably all help to create jobs by improving the functioning of the labour market and raising the productivity of individuals within it. We shall look here primarily at measures which seek directly to create employment opportunities, partly or solely for the long-term unemployed. Chief of these have been:

- the Community Programme (CP);
- the Enterprise Allowance Scheme (EAS);
- the Restart Scheme, particularly the Jobstart Allowance (JSA);
- the New Workers Scheme (NWS).

We shall not look at the Voluntary Projects Programme (which is essentially 'CP on Benefit'), Community Industry (which is limited to young people with particular social problems) or the Job Release Scheme or Job Splitting Scheme (which are essentially work-sharing schemes). Nor shall we cover youth or adult training initiatives. Although these are designed – in conjunction with the education system and employers' own training schemes – to improve the productivity and adaptability of the workforce and hence to help create jobs and to prevent long-term unemployment, they do not themselves directly create employment.

The Community Programme

The Government's main programme for long-term unemployed in the mid-1980s has been the Community Programme (CP), administered by the Manpower Services Commission (MSC). The estimated cost in 1986/7 was forecast at about £1100m at cash prices. It provided some full-time, but mostly part-time, opportunities for work of up to a year's duration on projects of practical community benefit. The CP was open to those receiving State benefit, who had been unemployed for the last two months and, if aged between 18 and 24, had been out of work for at least six of the last nine months or, if aged 25 and over, had been unemployed for at least twelve of the last fifteen months.

The work was on projects, designed primarily to benefit the community, which would not otherwise have been undertaken within two years, but could be sponsored by any organisation or group of individuals, including (rarely in practice) private companies. Participants were paid the hourly rate for the job but the *average* weekly wage for each project could not exceed £67 (from April 1986). In consequence the great majority were employed only part-time, and typically received *less* than £67 per week. For less than one in ten concurrent training was provided under the MSC's Wider Opportunities Training Programme.

The main *strength* of the CP was that it provided a long-term unemployed person, for up to twelve months, at low net cost, with something more acceptable than continued unemployment. In 1985/6 the annual gross cost per filled place was just under £4500. Net of savings in benefit and flow-backs in tax and national insurance it was £1800 (Normington, *et al.*, 1986, p. 12). It has been claimed (*Employment Gazette*, January 1985) that on leaving the Programme participants were two or three times more successful in obtaining jobs than those of the long-term unemployed who had not had a place on the CP. But this higher success rate cannot be attributed wholly to the effects of the programme. Those attracted to CP had higher than average qualifications and probably a higher degree of commitment to job search than the long-term unemployed as a whole (Normington *et al.*, 1986, p. 37). The work done has some community, even some economic value. But as a matter of policy it was work that no one would otherwise be prepared to pay for within the next two years, and to ensure that this was so the work was in practice well down the list of economic priorities.

The main *weakness* of CP was its inadequate size. Its peak size was 255 000 places for some 300 000 entrants a year (some participate for less than twelve months). There is no exact estimate of the total size of the client group. In July 1986 there were 569 000 claimant unemployed under 25 who had been *continuously* unemployed for six months or more and 1 026 600 aged 25 or over *continuously* unemployed for a year or more. The client group was therefore certainly in excess of 1 595 600 and the chances of securing a place, less than one in five and perhaps much less.

But the constraint on size came less from a shortage of places (except in some localities) than from a shortage of applicants. Even the *maximum* average CP project wage of £67 (and many actually got less) offered little incentive over benefit levels for married couples on their own or with teenage children. (Normington *et al.*, 1986, Table 5, p. 28). The maximum wage payable to supervisors, £110 per week, was a further serious limitation on the size of the programme in many places. Small wonder that the over-25s – by far the larger number in the client group – were seriously under-represented on CP, which became 'increasingly a programme for the single under-25s' (Normington *et al.*, 1986, p. 29). In consequence, despite the numerical disparity between places and potential applicants, there was little competition for places save in certain areas. In London and the South-East there was particular difficulty in filling places despite the large numbers of long-term unemployed in the region (so that the greater difficulty experienced in *providing* places in this region has not in fact been a constraint).

There was no obvious solution to this problem within the constraints of the CP concept. Because of the 'poverty trap' a very substantially higher wage would have been required. But since participants' wages already account for nearly two-thirds of the cost of the scheme and every increase in wages of £1 a week costs more than £10m annually in total gross expenditure, this would raise costs beyond the currently acceptable level for a product which is not *at*, but way *beyond*, the margin of commercial return.

Related to this is the artificiality of the work atmosphere of CP, in particular the use of outdated labour-intensive methods and slow pace of work. As a result, many believe, employers were often reluctant to hire people previously employed on Community Programme projects. Yet to seek to reduce costs by increasing efficiency and productivity would have run counter to the aim of providing the maximum number of job opportunities for labour often lacking relevant skills.

In sum, if we employ 'a million men with teaspoons' to do the work of one giant caterpillar tractor we cannot afford to pay them much above the level of benefit for a single person – particularly if the work is not even in the next tranche of our economic priorities.

The Enterprise Allowance Scheme

The Enterprise Allowance Scheme (EAS) provides an allowance of

£40 a week for up to a year to unemployed people who would like to become self-employed or start their own small business. They must have been out of work for at least eight weeks and receiving benefit. They must also be able to invest at least £1000 in their business – by loan if need be. Advice and training are available. The cost in 1986/7 was forecast at about £150m.

The *strength* of the EAS is the very low net cost (actually negative if one assumes benefit would otherwise have been paid) and its success in resettlement. Some 87 per cent of entrants complete their year on the scheme and 86 per cent of those are still trading three months later. There is some evidence that by 1986 well over half were still trading three years after entering the scheme (that is, after two years on their own), and that for every 100 businesses still trading 99 additional jobs had been created (50 full-time and 49 part-time).

Its *weaknesses* are, first, its scale in relation to the problem. There were in July 1986 some two million people unemployed for more than six months (let alone the eight weeks required to qualify for this scheme). This is not just a matter of providing more places. Not all the unemployed are suited by temperament or ability to run their own businesses, nor have the relevant experience, and though the scope for a larger programme must remain open to debate the fact that an advertising campaign is needed to fill a mere 100 000 places suggests the existing demand is not that great.

More importantly, much of the apparent success may in fact reflect deadweight – in other words many of these people would have started up on their own anyway (something which, in the present changing pattern of employment it is virtually impossible to prove or disprove). Finally, those applicants whose businesses fail end up worse off than they were before, since they return to unemployment having lost their capital or, in some cases, having acquired an additional burden of debt.

Restart Programme

From July 1986 the pilot scheme operating in certain areas since January was extended nation-wide. By March 1987 all those who had been unemployed for a year or more on Budget Day 1986 had been offered a jobcentre interview. The aim of the interview was to assess whether the person could:

– be placed in a suitable job;

- take a place on the CP or an MSC training course;
- participate in a Jobclub;
- enter the EAS;
- be placed on a Restart course (see below);
- be placed in work with a Jobstart Allowance (see below);
- be helped in any other way.

(Some 1.3m people had been unemployed for a year or more on Budget Day, 1986, but not all will still be unemployed by the time they are called to interview. An extra 2000 staff were being allocated and an extra £91m in 1986/7.)

This part of the programme is essentially designed to help the long-term unemployed take advantage of the job, training or other opportunities open to them. It does not of itself increase those opportunities and, according to the Department of Employment, of 260 000 people interviewed by autumn 1986, jobs had been found for only 1650, a success rate of only 0.6 per cent.

The *Restart courses* are one- or two-week courses to help people assess what they are good at, and to show them how to look for jobs more effectively. As such they are essentially an extension of the counselling process described above. *The Jobstart Allowance* – £20 per week for six months for those taking jobs at less than £80 per week – is a subsidy to encourage the unemployed to take jobs offering low wages. It has no mechanism to discourage deadweight, which may therefore be very high. After six months those for whom benefit would otherwise be more attractive will, presumably, return to unemployment – incurring the usual penalties if they quit voluntarily. Or they may progress to higher-paid jobs.

The New Workers Scheme

Like the former Young Workers Scheme (YWS) this scheme is end-on to the YTS but extends up to age 21 with a wage limit of £55 per week for those under 20 and £65 per week at age 20. It is not limited to the long-term unemployed but could help some young long-term unemployed people. It is essentially an employer subsidy of £15 per week limited to young people. As with YWS, the NWS is liable to high deadweight and/or substitution for older workers. It will however help to ensure good placing results for YTS.

THE JOB GUARANTEE IN SWEDEN

The rapid growth in unemployment, and in particular in long-term unemployment, in recent years has not been confined to the United Kingdom. Most countries of Western Europe have faced similar problems and most, like the United Kingdom, have instituted various special employment measures in the attempt to stem the rise in unemployment. But in most countries, again like the United Kingdom, the scale of these programmes has been too small to have had more than a marginal impact on the growth of unemployment. Within Western Europe only one country, Sweden, has committed resources on a large scale to special employment measures, and has as a result been able to deliver a job guarantee.

World Growth in Long-Term Unemployment

Across the world, as unemployment has increased in recent years, the numbers of long-term unemployed have tended to rise disproportionately. Increased unemployment typically takes the form of longer durations of unemployment spells, rather than increased numbers of people becoming unemployed for short spells. In Table 9.5 the unemployment rate and the proportion of the unemployed who have been out of work for more than 12 months are set out for a number of countries for 1979 and 1984, together with the average duration of unemployment spells for adult males for 1984. Table 9.5 shows that the unemployment rate in each of the 15 main OECD countries went up between 1979 and 1984, and with it the proportion of long-term unemployed in each country, except Japan.

Comparing across countries, it is clear that there is a tendency for countries with high unemployment rates to have a higher proportion of long-term unemployed. But there is also a great deal of variation in long-term unemployment that cannot be accounted for in this way. In particular, long-term unemployment is lower than might be expected in Canada, the United States, Norway and Sweden and higher than might be expected in most of the EEC countries (Belgium, France, Italy and the Netherlands). This relationship is illustrated in Figure 9.4.

At the risk of over-simplification, two main factors appear to contribute to the explanation of these inter-country differences. First, there is the social security system. Most countries have contributory

Table 9.5 Unemployment and the proportion of long-term unemployed

	1979		*1984*		
Country	*Unemployment (% of labour force)*	*Long-term unemployment (% of total unemployment*	*Unemployment (% of labour force)*	*Long-term unemployment (% of total unemployment*	*Average duration (adult males) (months)*
Australia	6.2	18.1	8.9	31.2	13.4
Austria	2.1	8.6	3.8	12.9	7.4
Belgium	8.2	58.0	14.0	68.0	20.3
Canada	7.4	3.5	11.2	9.9	6.0
France	5.9	30.3	9.7	42.3	14.4
Germany	3.2	19.9	8.6	32.7	12.6
Ireland	7.1	31.8	16.0	39.1	8.6
Italy	7.5	35.8	10.2	41.9[1]	11.6[1]
Japan	2.1	16.5	2.7	15.2	9.9
Netherlands	5.4	27.1	14.0	55.5	13.5
Norway	2.0	3.8	3.0	10.8	6.2
Spain	8.5	27.5	20.1	54.2	17.8
Sweden	2.1	6.8	3.1	12.3	6.3
UK	5.3	24.8	13.0	39.8	19.4
USA	5.8	4.2	7.4	12.3	5.8

[1] 1983

Source: OECD *Employment Outlook*, September 1985, Table 17 and Appendix Tables H and I. The unemployment figures are OECD standardised rates. Measures of long-term unemployment are collected in different ways in different countries.

unemployment insurance schemes which pay benefits to the unemployed, but for only a limited length of time. In the United States, unemployment insurance is paid for up to six months; in Sweden for on average ten months; in France, Germany and the United Kingdom for twelve months; in the Netherlands for 30 months and in Belgium without limit. As Table 9.5 shows, the proportion of long-term unemployed is much lower in countries where benefit is paid for only a short period (United States and Canada) than in countries where it is paid for much longer (Belgium and Netherlands). But as important as the duration of the benefit payments is the social security entitlement of a person who has exhausted his or her unemployment benefit. In some countries, such as the United States, there is very little public assistance available to people in this position. At the opposite extreme, in the United Kingdom supplementary benefit (income support) provides benefit at rates no lower than unemployment benefit (though, unlike unemployment benefit, it is means

Figure 9.4 Unemployment and the proportion of long-term unemployed, 1984

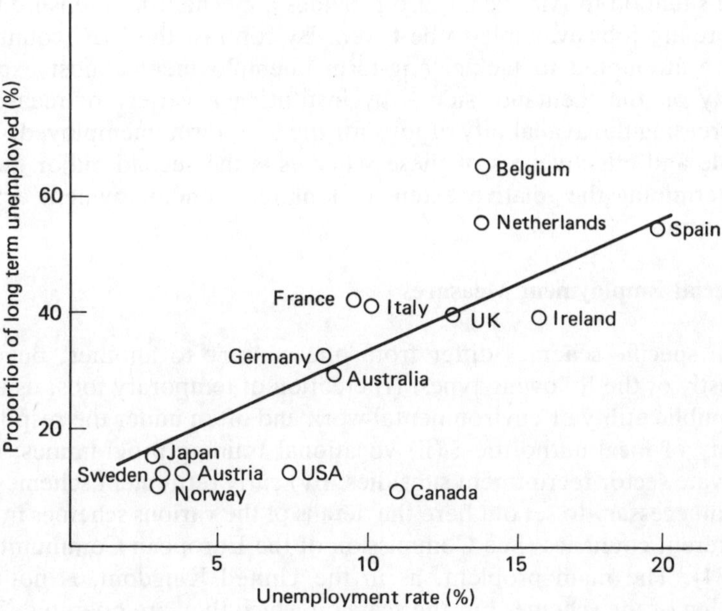

Source: 1983 *Labour Force Survey*–includes men aged 21–64 and women aged 21–59

tested). Most European countries, like the United Kingdom, effectively provide unlimited social security support of some kind for the unemployed.

In Sweden, as in the United States, an (able-bodied) unemployed person is entitled to only a minimal income from the state after his or her unemployment benefits are exhausted,[5] but in Sweden the government, in the form of the Labour Market Board, makes it its business to ensure that all unemployed people receive a job offer or a place on a training scheme before their unemployment benefit runs out. Furthermore unemployed people who turn down job offers or a place on a training scheme automatically lose their entitlement to unemployment benefit. Since in Sweden unemployment benefit can be as much as 80 per cent of income in work, the threat of removal of benefit provides a very strong financial incentive for people to take up job offers and return to work.

Thus, while the Swedish system, like those of North America, puts strong financial pressures on the unemployed to take work, unlike the situation in America it also provides a mechanism to ensure that there are jobs available to be taken. By contrast the EEC countries have attempted to tackle long-term unemployment almost exclusively on the 'demand' side – by instituting a variety of measures increasing the availability of jobs for the long-term unemployed. The scale and effectiveness of these schemes is the second major factor determining the relative extent of long-term unemployment across countries.

Special Employment Measures

The specific schemes differ from one country to another, but are mostly of the following types: (i) creation of temporary jobs, usually in public utility or environmental work and often under the responsibility of local authorities; (ii) vocational training programmes; (iii) private sector recruitment subsidies; (iv) early retirement schemes. It is unnecessary to set out here the details of the various schemes in the different countries (See Commission of the European Communities, 1984). The main problem, as in the United Kingdom, is not the design of the schemes but the scale on which they are operated. The numbers of people involved are too small to have had more than a marginal impact on the growth in long-term unemployment.

There seem to be two main reasons for the limited scale of special employment measures in most European countries. Many governments were taken by surprise by the sharpness of the rise in unemployment after 1979, and by the persistence of the long-term unemployment created by it. Many of the schemes now in operation were not introduced until 1982 or 1983. If only on administrative grounds, it is hardly surprising that they do not yet cover the multitudes of long-term unemployed.

A more fundamental reason, perhaps, is that long-term unemployment has emerged at a time of fiscal retrenchment in many countries. Governments have been attempting, not always very successfully, to cut back their expenditure, and thus have been very reluctant to launch into new and potentially hugely expensive programmes of job creation. They have preferred to rely on the private sector to create more jobs and bring the unemployed back to work.

A consequence of these restrictive fiscal attitudes has been that special employment measures have been limited to the least costly. The Community Programme in Britain, as noted earlier, has very low costs, but this has meant producing output of equivalently low worth and, more importantly, work experience of low commercial value.

Labour Market Policy in Sweden

In contrast to the limited scale of expenditure on special employment measures in most European countries, in Sweden there is an immense investment in programmes of this type. In 1984, there were over 218 000 people (5 per cent of the labour force) involved in various special employment schemes as compared with 136 000 people (3 per cent of the labour force) unemployed. The total gross expenditure of the Swedish Labour Market Board, which is responsible for these measures, amounted to 23 billion Swedish Kroner (about £2.1 billion) in 1984/5 which is 7.5 per cent of total Swedish government expenditure and no less than 3.2 per cent of Swedish GNP (Johannesson and Persson-Tanimura, 1984 Table 2). But this figure includes in addition to the direct costs of special employment measures a variety of other measures including provision of labour market information, some regional development and industrial assistance grants, payments of unemployment benefits and various vocational rehabilitation and similar schemes. To complicate matters further, a substantial part (over 40 per cent) of the gross cost of special employment measures is borne not by the Labour Market Board but by other organisations, in particular local authorities. Making these adjustments, the gross cost of special employment measures was calculated in 1983/4 as just over 15 billion Swedish Kroner (2.3 per cent of GDP) (Johannesson, 1985). The implicit gross cost per job, or training scheme place, is thus 84 000 Swedish Kroner (about £8000).

While these costs are large in gross terms, the net costs are very much smaller and the benefits of the programme are very considerable. In the absence of the programmes one might need to pay unemployment benefit for up to another 5 per cent of the labour force. The savings of government expenditure on benefits together with the flowback from higher taxes for 5 per cent of the labour force could easily account for 2 per cent of GDP. Further, the programmes have direct benefits in terms of the value of the work done, the retraining of the workforce, and in preventing the growth of long-term unemployment and all its associated costs.

The main types of programme are set out in Table 9.6, together with their cost to the Labour Market Board. Since Sweden is able to deliver a job guarantee with these programmes, it is perhaps useful to describe them in a little more detail. *Temporary jobs* (relief work) are

Table 9.6 Special employment measures in Sweden

Programme	*Number of people on programme*[1] *(thousands)*	*(% of labour force)*	*Cost of programme (SKr millions)*	*Cost per person (SKr thousands)*	*Cost per person*[2] *(£)*
	1984		*Current prices 1984/5*		
Training schemes	39.7	0.90	3 991	100.5	9 350
Temporary jobs (relief work)	43.6	0.99	3 612[3]	82.8	7 700
Sheltered work	67.5	1.53	–[4]	–	–
Youth team	46.9	1.07	1 541[3]	32.9	3 060
Recruitment subsidy	20.6	0.47	n.a.	n.a.	n.a.

Notes:
[1] Annual average (i.e. the average of the numbers on the schemes at any point in time. Since the duration of many of the schemes is less than a year, and in many cases six months, it follows that the total number of people entering the schemes in a year is about double the numbers given above).
[2] Converted at the average daily rate of exchange for 1984/5 (£1 = 10.75 SKr)
[3] A significant part of the cost of these programmes is borne by local authorities (see text). In 1983/4 about two-thirds of the public expenditure cost of relief work was borne by the Labour Market Board, the rest mainly by local authorities.
[4] This programme is funded by local authorities. In 1982/3, expenditure on it was 5210 million SKr providing 64 000 places at a cost per place of 81.4 thousand kroner (£7600) at 1982/3 prices.

Sources: Johannesson, J. (1985) *On the Composition and Outcome of Swedish Labour Market Policy 1970–85*, Stockholm, and Johannesson, J. and Persson-Tanimura (1984) *Labour Market Policy under Reconsideration*, Swedish Ministry of Labour, Stockholm

jobs provided mostly by local authorities to people put forward by the Labour Market Board. The jobs last for six months and are paid at the negotiated wage for the job. The Labour Market Board provides a 75 per cent subsidy to the employment cost of the person put forward, the remaining 25 per cent together with any other costs associated with the placement being borne by the local authority. Private employers can also offer temporary jobs and receive the wage subsidy, but very few do so. In placing people on temporary jobs, the Labour Market Board gives priority to the long-term (that is, over 6 months) unemployed, and guarantees a job of this type to any unemployed person for whom nothing else has been found before their unemployment benefit entitlement runs out. Because there are separate programmes for young people (see below), relief work is now confined to those aged 20 and over. Temporary jobs are seen in Sweden primarily as a form of counter-cyclical policy, and the number of people involved fluctuates with the business cycle (see Figure 9.5). The jobs are mostly unskilled as the main purpose of the programme is to provide temporary activity for people who will return to their normal work when the economy recovers.

Training. The Labour Market Board places people at training establishments. The Labour Market Board pays people on training courses an amount approximately equal to their unemployment benefit entitlement (In Sweden, as noted above, people who turn down the offer of a place on a training scheme would lose their entitlement to unemployment benefit.) Some in-plant (on-the-job) training is included in this programme, but it amounts to only about 10 per cent of total placements. The number of places on training schemes has been relatively static, at about 40 000 a year, since the early 1970s.

Sheltered work. This programme provides work, including work training, for people with disabilities. The programme is operated and

Figure 9.5 Numbers on special employment measures and unemployment in Sweden

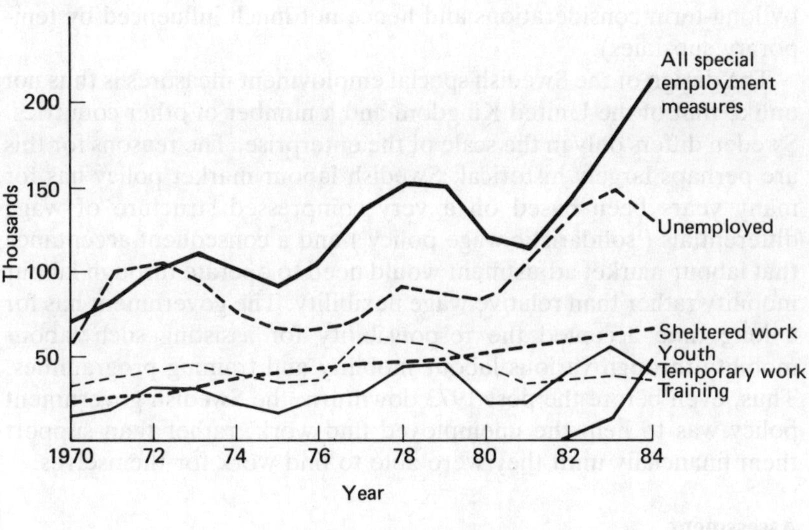

Source: Johanesson, J. (1985) *On the Composition and Output of Swedish Labour Market Policy 1970–1985, Stockholm.*

financed by local authorities. The number of people in this programme has risen steadily and quite rapidly since the early 1970s owing, it is thought, to better provision of jobs and higher rates of pay to those on the programme rather than to an increase in the proportion of disabled people in the population.

Youth Team. This programme consists of part-time jobs and training courses for people aged 16–19. Nearly all the jobs are in the public sector, mostly with local authorities. Young people on the programme are paid the negotiated wage for the job. Because young people are guaranteed a youth team job within a short period of becoming unemployed, the Youth Team programme takes the place of unemployment benefit entitlement for young people.

Recruitment subsidy. The subsidy pays 50 per cent of the labour cost to employers taking on unemployed people sent them by the Labour Market Board. The purpose of the subsidy is to encourage private employers to take on more unemployed people, particularly long-term unemployed, but the subsidy can also be claimed by public sector employers taking on the long-term unemployed. The subsidy was introduced in 1984, although there had been similar subsidies in 1978/9 and in 1982. The previous subsidies had been abandoned because it was thought that they had failed to stimulate additional recruitment by firms (whose hiring policies appear to be determined by long-term considerations and hence not much influenced by temporary subsidies).

The design of the Swedish special employment measures is thus not unlike that of the United Kingdom and a number of other countries. Sweden differs only in the scale of the enterprise. The reasons for this are perhaps largely historical. Swedish labour market policy has for many years been based on a very compressed structure of wage differentials ('solidaristic wage policy') and a consequent acceptance that labour market adjustment would need to operate through labour mobility rather than relative wage flexibility. The government has for a long time accepted the responsibility for assisting such labour mobility through various labour mobility and training programmes. Thus, even before the post-1973 downturn, the Swedish government policy was to help the unemployed find work, rather than support them financially until they were able to find work for themselves.

Assessment

It is perhaps unnecessary to stress that, notwithstanding its high level of public expenditure, the Swedish economy has been able for many years to deliver one of the highest standards of living in Western Europe, and a macroeconomic performance in terms of growth, export competitiveness and inflation which is very creditable by European standards and certainly not inferior to that of the United Kingdom (See Charter for Jobs, 1986).

Sweden's labour market policies, through their effects on training and maintaining a high degree of labour force participation, may have contributed to some extent to Sweden's relatively successful economic performance. In any event there is no evidence to suggest that the benefits of the policy in terms of reducing the suffering of the unemployed have been bought at a cost of worsened economic performance. Sweden shows what can be done when a government has the commitment and the determination to tackle the problems of long-term unemployment.

LONG-TERM UNEMPLOYMENT AND THE LABOUR MARKET

The Rise of Long-Term Unemployment

Why has long-term unemployment risen so sharply in recent years and why did it continue to rise throughout the five years of economic recovery from 1981 to 1986? There seem to be two main factors. First, the economic policies which were adopted by the government from 1979 involved running the economy with a lower pressure of demand in the labour market than had been the case under previous postwar administrations. It was, therefore, more difficult for anyone unemployed to find work. But, secondly, in recruiting workers employers tended to be reluctant to take on those who had been unemployed for a long time. As unemployment rose, long-term unemployment rose much more rapidly, and the proportion of the unemployed out of work for more than a year went up from 25 per cent in 1979 to 40 per cent in 1986.

To get a picture of the dynamics of the situation, between 1981 and 1986 about a million people a year entered long-term unemployment. This compares with a figure of about 200 000 a year in the late 1970s. The increased rate of entry into long-term unemployment was an almost inevitable consequence of higher unemployment rates in the economy as a whole. At the same time, in each year about 45 per cent

Table 9.7 The growth of long-term unemployment (illustrative example)

Year	*Inflow during year* (*m*)	*Numbers of long-term unemployed at beginning of year* (*m*)	*Numbers leaving long-term unemployment during year* (*m*)
0		0.35 →	
	1.0 →		→ 0.54
1		0.81 →	
	1.0 →		→ 0.72
2		1.09 →	
	1.0 →		→ 0.84
3		1.25 →	
	1.0 →		→ 0.90
4		1.35 →	
	1.0 →		→ 0.94
⋮		1.41	
10		1.50 →	
	1.0 →		→ 1.0
11		1.50	
⋮			

of the long-term unemployed escaped from unemployment, into jobs or onto training schemes or by leaving the labour force through retirement, invalidity or taking on increased family responsibilities.

Table 9.7 shows how the number of long-term unemployed would increase on the basis of these magnitudes. If initially, at the beginning of 'Year 0', there were 350 000 long-term unemployed (as was the case during the late 1970s), and during the course of each year from then onwards one million people enter long-term unemployment, and the *average* escape rate is 0.4, the numbers of long-term unemployed would increase gradually over a period of years, to a total of 1.5 million. For simplicity we have assumed the 0.4 escape probability in each year applies both to the stock of long-term unemployed at the beginning of the year and to the net inflow during the year. We discuss a more exact simulation, based on actual escape probabilities, below. While only an illustrative example, Table 9.7 shows how long-term unemployment can continue to increase for many years even when labour market conditions as a whole are not deteriorating.

Figure 9.6 Proportion leaving unemployment in a quarter by duration (first quarter 1984)

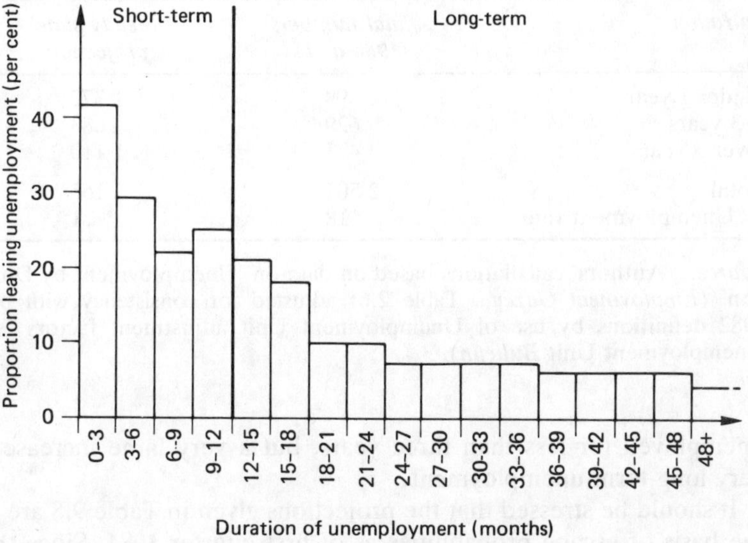

In reality the situation is bleaker than the simple example suggests. The actual escape probabilities at different durations of unemployment are plotted in Figure 9.6 (which is based on data for the first quarter of 1984). The figure shows not only that the long-term unemployed have a much worse chance of escaping unemployment than the short-term unemployed, but, among the long-term unemployed, the longer one has been out of work the worse one's chances are. Thus, three years after the sharp increase in overall unemployment in 1980/1, the inflow of people into very long-term unemployment started to rise and remained high. These people had a very low chance of escaping from unemployment so their numbers continued to increase. In Table 9.8 we have calculated the implications of the escape probabilities set out in Figure 9.6 for the levels of long-term unemployment that would ultimately be reached on the basis of the current inflow. This evidence relates only to unemployed men, since, for reasons of benefit entitlement, the data on long-term unemployment of women are particularly unreliable. The table shows that, in the absence of any changes in labour market conditions, we might expect little change in short-term unemployment, or in the numbers

Table 9.8 Male unemployment: actual and projected (pre-1982 definition)

Duration	*Actual numbers (1986 q. 1)*	*'Steady state' projection*
Under 1 year	1 399	1 372
1–3 years	629	683
Over 3 years	473	1 110
Total	2 501	3 165
% Unemployment rate	18	21

Source: Authors' calculations based on data on 'Unemployment by Duration' (*Employment Gazette*, Table 2.6) adjusted for consistency with pre-1982 definitions by use of Unemployment Unit adjustment factors (see Unemployment Unit *Bulletin*).

unemployed for less than three years, but a very large increase in very long-term unemployment.

It should be stressed that the projections given in Table 9.8 are on the basis of escape probabilities as of first quarter 1984. Since that time, the government has introduced a number of policy measures – the expansion of the Community Programme, the Restart scheme, 'Jobclubs' and so on – designed to improve the prospects of the long-term unemployed finding work. The point we want to make here is that these measures are operating against the background of a labour market in which long-term unemployment would otherwise have been tending to rise. We will argue that the measures the government is taking may be successful in arresting the upward trend in long-term unemployment, and may well achieve a reduction in the numbers, but the scale of the programme is far too small to achieve a really substantial reduction in long-term unemployment.

Returning to Table 9.7, it is apparent that in principle one can think of policies for reducing long-term unemployment as operating through two routes. One can reduce the inflow into long-term unemployment through aggregate measures to reduce the overall level of unemployment such as an expansion of aggregate demand or supply-side measures to encourage business expansion. If it is easier for people who become unemployed to find work, fewer will still be unemployed after a year and hence the inflow into long-term unemployment will fall. Second, one can take measures specifically aimed at improving the chances of the long-term unemployed finding work, that is measures aimed at increasing the escape rate from long-term unemployment. The policies proposed in this chapter follow the second of these routes, because we argue that the first route (through aggregate measures) risks rekindling inflation while the second route, through special employment measures, does not.

Wage Pressure and Long-Term Unemployment

While the factors influencing the size of wage settlements are many and various, and far from fully understood, there now seems little doubt that unemployment is an important restraining influence on wage increases. The effect of short-term unemployment appears, however, to be very much greater than that of long-term unemployment. In a recent study, Layard and Nickell (1986) have found that, while higher unemployment reduces wage pressure, an increase in the ratio of long-term to total unemployment tends of itself to increase wage pressure. While there are a number of complicated features of their estimates, the overall result is that the long-term unemployed have virtually no effect in restraining wage pressure.

The reason for this can be seen from Figure 9.6. We discuss the reasons for the low escape probabilities of the long-term unemployed in the next section, but the essence of it is that employers regard them as less good workers than those already in work or who have recently become unemployed. From the standpoint of influencing wage settlements, the long-term unemployed become effectively detached from the labour market. Unemployment can influence wage settlements through a number of channels: if unemployment is high, firms can recruit more easily and have less difficulty in retaining workers, and the fear of unemployment becomes a greater concern to existing workers which moderates their wage demands. But in each case what matters is short-term unemployment. For example if a firm is anxious to recruit more workers it may raise its wage notwithstanding a high level of long-term unemployment because it is reluctant to recruit from the long-term unemployed. Similarly, high levels of long-term unemployment may not deter union wage demands, because in the event of a prolonged strike or large-scale redundancies, union members looking for other jobs will see themselves to be in competition only with the short-term unemployed (some survey evidence on this point for Australia is quoted by Gregory 1986).

Policies to reduce unemployment in the economy as a whole – be they traditional policies of demand expansion or 'supply-side' measures encouraging new business enterprises – thus run into the risk that most of the jobs created will be filled by the short-term unemployed which will in turn risk inflationary wage pressures developing in the economy. By contrast, special employment measures directed at the long-term unemployed which reabsorb them into the labour force while leaving unchanged the level of short-term unemployment are unlikely to increase inflationary wage pressure. (It is, of course, also highly desirable to take measures which allow a non-inflationary reduction in short-term unemployment. However, the nature of the measures to be taken is a matter of extreme political contention. The present government is very firmly committed to an approach based on deregulation and encouraging competition and is equally firmly opposed to any form of 'incomes policy'. This chapter is written in the belief that the problem of long-term unemployment is too serious and too urgent to await a solution to the problem of short-term unemployment.)

The Duration of Unemployment and the Prospects of Finding Work

Figure 9.6 shows a systematic pattern. The longer a person has been unemployed the lower their chance of escaping unemployment. This section examines in more detail why this should be the case. We have already seen that the long-term unemployed suffer from lower morale, reduced means for job search and a much lower rate of offers of jobs from employers. However there are a number of distinct interpretations of this state of affairs.

The first possibility is that unemployment operates as a sorting process, with workers of higher productivity leaving unemployment more rapidly. Since the high productivity people tend to find jobs, and hence to leave unemployment quite quickly, almost of necessity the long-term unemployed consist mainly of low productivity people who have the greatest difficulty in finding work. (In this context low productivity may take the form of less energetic job search, low morale or lack of commitment to the labour market as much as of lack of relevant skills.) According to this way of thinking, the long-term unemployed have difficulty in finding work not because of the length of time for which they have been unemployed but because of their low productivity.

A second possibility is that the skills or motivation of people do in fact decline significantly during a period of unemployment. According to this explanation the prospects of any given individual finding work would decline the longer he or she is unemployed because his or her productivity would deteriorate.

Neither of these possibilities is altogether persuasive. Clearly the unemployed differ from one another in terms of their productivity to some extent. But in terms of the (possibly too crude) measures of skill and qualifications summarised in Tables 9.1 and 9.2 the long-term unemployed do not differ at all significantly from the short-term unemployed. Further, we have in the last few years experienced a vast increase in the numbers of long-term unemployed. This would have the effect of raising the average productivity of the long-term unemployed relative to the short-term unemployed as a relatively larger proportion of the short-term unemployed continued into long-term unemployment. If differences in individual productivity were the explanation of Figure 9.6, one would then expect the relative escape probabilities of the long-term unemployed to improve. But no such improvement has taken place (Jackman and Layard, 1986c). This argument seems to us more persuasive than the results of econometric studies, which are in any event inconclusive.[6]

Similarly, much evidence, most strikingly that of the trouble-free assimilation of long-term unemployed people into the war effort in 1940 (International Labour Review, 1942), shows that once back in work the long-term unemployed quickly establish the same work patterns, and are as reliable and as efficient as other workers.

A third possibility is that employers, often faced with many applicants for a particular job, simply 'screen out' the long-term unemployed. Even if they are aware that most of the long-term unemployed applicants they get would make good workers, they may well reason that the risk of taking on a bad worker is higher with the long-term unemployed, that it is not easy to sift out the bad worker at the time of recruitment and that, with plenty of job applicants, there is no need to take on that additional risk. This argument carries an important implication for policy towards the long-term unemployed. For if the long-term unemployed, typically, are no less productive than other workers but simply carry the stigma of long-term unemployment, then, if they find work, that of itself removes the stigma and the worker can then return almost automatically to a normal working life. By contrast, if the long-term unemployed were typically low quality workers, finding work would be little more than a temporary palliative. Workers of low quality (as we have defined it) would be likely to have difficulty in holding down a job, and once unemployed again would have minimal prospects of finding another job. Finally, if unemployed workers are not inherently of low quality but temporarily so because of a decline in their productivity while unemployed, finding work may cause their productivity to recover. Providing the employer is prepared to tolerate any difficulties of readjustment, the worker can again expect to return to a normal working life thereafter.

It is therefore important for our way of thinking that the low escape probabilities from unemployment of the long-term unemployed are consequential upon the length of time they have been out of work (that is, 'duration dependent') whether because of a decline in productivity during unemployment, or as we think more likely, screening out of the long-term unemployed in recruitment. Provided this is the case, all that is required to solve the problem of the long-term unemployed is to find work for them. Employers see themselves as taking an unnecessary risk in taking on long-term unemployed people. Clearly what is therefore needed is an incentive to compensate employers for taking that risk.

Labour Market Analysis of the Job Guarantee

We now analyse the implications of the government introducing a number of measures designed to help the long-term unemployed find work. If, to be specific, the government were to institute policies creating some given number of new jobs per year, each lasting for one year, what would be the effect on the overall level of long-term unemployment?

To answer this question we require a theory of what determines the level of long-term unemployment in the economy as a whole. This depends on the inflow into long-term unemployment and the escape rate from it (as shown in the example in Table 9.7). But what determines the inflow and the escape rate? The inflow into long-term unemployment depends essentially on the level of short-term unemployment. If the overall labour market is depressed, short-term unemployment will be high and many people will not have found work by the end of a year. They will thus enter into long-term unemployment. If, for whatever reason, there are more jobs available, short-term unemployment will fall and fewer people will remain unemployed for a year, so the inflow into long-term unemployment will diminish.

But what then determines the level of short-term unemployment? Our argument is that short-term unemployment is one of many factors influencing wage pressure in the labour market. Given the objective of stabilising the inflation rate it is necessary to hold down wage pressure in the labour market. The level of short-term unemployment needed to restrain wage pressure depends on the extent to which other variables are exerting upward or downward pressure on wage demands. During the late 1960s and the 1970s increased worker militancy and union power put upward pressure on wages and inflation, though from 1975 to 1978 this upward pressure was offset successfully by the Labour Government's incomes policies. We do not explore further here the causes of the increase in short-term unemployment in Britain over the past thirty years (for a comprehensive discussion, see Layard and Nickell, 1986). The conclusion in the present context is that, other labour market institutions and policies being taken as given, the level of short-term unemployment is determined by the need to restrain wage pressure. In economic terminology, we would argue that there is an 'equilibrium' rate of short-term unemployment, determined by labour market institutions, to which the actual rate of short-term unemployment will tend to gravitate. Attempts by governments to hold actual short-term unemployment below this equilibrium rate will lead to accelerating inflation while if short-term unemployment is above this rate, wage pressure will decline.

In analysing the consequences of the job guarantee we assume no other changes in policy (such as an incomes policy), and hence no change in the equilibrium rate of short-term unemployment. We further assume that the 1986 level of short-term unemployment (of around 1.9 million people) which has been associated with reasonable stability of wage inflation for three or four years is close to this equilibrium rate. We therefore assume that the inflow into long-term unemployment will continue at its present rate of about one million people a year.

The escape rate from long-term unemployment depends on three main factors: (i) the success of the long-term unemployed in competing for normal jobs; (ii) the provision of places on special employment programmes such as the Community Programme; (iii) the extent to which long-term unemployed people leave the labour market due to retirement or sickness. In the next section we will look at the factors determining the outflow through these different routes in more detail. The principle we want to emphasise at this stage is that *any measure which increases the overall escape rate from long-term unemployment will reduce, over a period of years, the numbers of long-term unemployed, while leaving the level of short-term unemployment unchanged.* In fact, in the long run, the number of long-term unemployed people will fall by the same proportion as the increase in the escape rate, since in equilibrium the inflow must by definition equal the outflow and the latter is again by definition equal to the number of long-term unemployed multiplied by the escape rate.

To take an example: In 1986 there were 1.35 million long-term unemployed people, and the escape rate was 0.185 per quarter so that the outflow of 0.25 million per quarter was equal to the inflow. If by new policy measures one had been able to raise the escape rate to 0.25, the outflow from long-term unemployment would have exceeded the inflow and the numbers of long-term unemployed would have fallen until the stock reached one million. At this point, with an escape rate of 0.25, the outflow would again have equalled the inflow. Thus, comparing the new situation with the old, the numbers leaving unemployment would have been the same in the two situations. The measures have the permanent effect of reducing unemployment (in this example by 350 000) and of increasing employment by the same number, and also the permanent effect of increasing the escape rate from, and hence reducing the expected duration of, long-term unemployment. But the measures would not have permanently raised the outflow from long-term unemployment.

A reasonable target for a comprehensive job guarantee programme (as detailed below) is *to raise the escape rate for the long-term unemployed to the same level as that of the short-term unemployed, that is, about 0.40 per quarter*. If this were achieved, the number of long-term unemployed would fall, over a period of years, to 0.60 million, implying a reduction in unemployment compared with 1986 of 750 000. For reasons to be discussed later, we will assume that once the new steady state is reached all recruitment of long-term unemployed people into work becomes part of the job guarantee programme.

The impact of the job guarantee in terms of labour market flows is illustrated in Figures 9.7 and 9.8. The boxes represent four states; employment, short-term unemployment, long-term unemployment and the Community Programme (CP). The numbers in each box represent the approximate numbers of people in that state at a point in time. The arrows indicate the flows of people each year between states.[7] The numbers in Figure 9.7 correspond approximately to the situation in the UK economy in 1986. About 250 000 people a year,

Figure 9.7 Stocks and flows in the labour market: current position

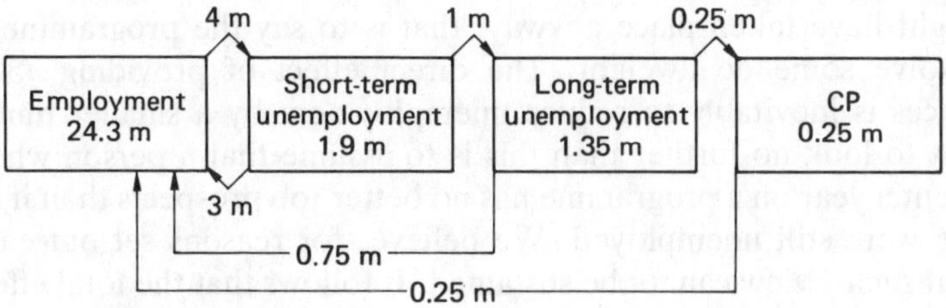

Figure 9.8 Effects of job guarantee

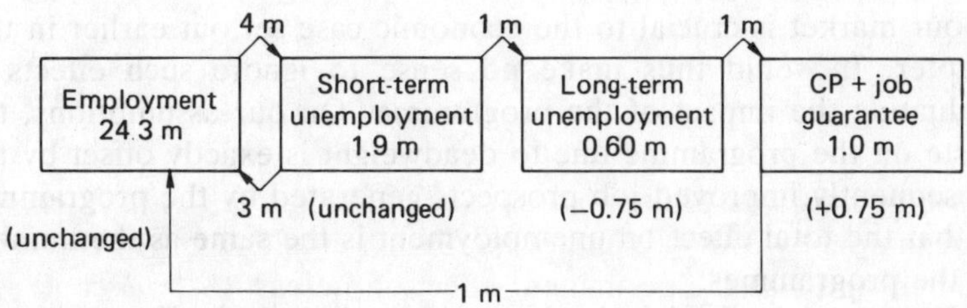

mostly from long-term unemployment, took places on the Community Programme and most of these people remained on Community Programme projects for a year. They are assumed thereafter to have gone into normal employment. (The fact that some returned to unemployment complicates the picture but does not affect the points we wish to make.) In the example in the figure, the flows into and out of each state are in balance so numbers in each state remain constant – approximately the situation in the United Kingdom in 1985 and 1986.

We now see what would have happened if we had introduced an expanded programme of special employment measures, involving the job guarantee (while retaining the expanded Community Programme). In Figure 9.8 we take the example of a job guarantee programme providing 750 000 jobs (or training places) a year. The figure shows the new pattern of flows, again on the assumption that inflows and outflows in each state balance.

On our assumption it so happens that the number of people on job guarantee programmes (750 000) is the same as the estimated reduction in unemployment due to the programme. But we are *not* assuming that unemployment falls by 750 000 because we are providing 750 000 places. Clearly, some of the places on the job guarantee might have taken place anyway, that is to say the programme may involve some deadweight. The direct effect of providing 750 000 places is inevitably to reduce unemployment by a smaller number. But to look no further than this is to assume that a person who has spent a year on a programme has no better job prospects than if he or she were still unemployed. We believe, for reasons set out earlier, that such a view cannot be sustained. It follows that the total effect of the programme in reducing unemployment is greater than the impact effects since a year on a programme also improves a person's subsequent job prospects.

The effect of the job guarantee in improving the efficiency of the labour market is crucial to the economic case set out earlier in this chapter. It would thus make no sense to ignore such effects in evaluating the impact of the programme. On our assumptions, the waste on the programme due to deadweight is exactly offset by the subsequently improved job prospects generated by the programme, so that the total effect on unemployment is the same as the number on the programmes.

Mention of deadweight leads to the possibility of other sources of inefficiency that may be associated with special employment measures. These could be of two types. First, the provision of jobs under a job guarantee programme may have displacement or substitution effects. We define and discuss these terms below. Second, the provision of a job guarantee may affect the search intensity of the unemployed. People may be more ready to give up searching for work if they know the government is obliged to find something for them.

Displacement means that, as a result of the job guarantee programme, an employer takes on a long-term unemployed person into a job which might otherwise have been taken by, say, a short-term unemployed person. This will make it more difficult for the short-term unemployed to find work, and hence, it might be thought, raise the inflow of people into long-term unemployment. But such a conclusion runs counter to our assumptions set out earlier. An increase in the numbers of short-term unemployed, with no change in the labour market institutions determining the equilibrium rate of short-term unemployment will reduce wage pressure and thereby encourage employers to take on more workers, until short-term unemployment returns to its equilibrium rate.

Substitution means that an enterprise which expands by taking advantage of the job guarantee programme increases its share of the market at the expense of other enterprises which may have to cut back employment or even close down. In terms of the overall labour market, substitution has the same effects as displacement.

Turning to the effect of the programme on the intensity with which the short-term unemployed search for work, we envisage that most of the jobs provided under the job guarantee will be relatively unskilled, and relatively low paid. Thus the unemployed are likely to prefer ordinary jobs and their attempts to find such jobs may not be much diminished by the job guarantee programme.

We now attempt some estimates of the effect of the job guarantee programme over time, assuming its introduction in 1986 at a lower level and a subsequent build-up over a period of years.

The Scale of the Programme

We start by recapitulating the factual background. There were in 1986 1.35 million long-term unemployed people according to our definition (that is, those who had been continuously unemployed for at least twelve months). Each year about a million people entered long-term unemployment, and, each year, with the assistance in particular of the Community Programme, about one million people left long-term unemployment.

In what follows, we assume that about 250 000 long-term unemployed people a year continue to be found places on the Community Programme, or found work or places on training schemes with the assistance of other existing employment policies. This number is of course smaller than the total of those assisted by the existing policies because not all of those assisted are long-term unemployed. (For example, as noted earlier, the Community Programme recruited mainly from those aged under 25, and the under-25s were eligible if they had been unemployed for six months out of the previous nine.)

We also need to make an estimate of the number of long-term unemployed who cease to be unemployed in any year because of leaving the labour market altogether, owing to retirement, invalidity or for family reasons. For technical reasons concerned with the administration of benefits most people in this category will have left the unemployment count when their unemployment benefit runs out at twelve months and thus will not enter long-term unemployment.[8] Even so, there is no doubt that some of the long-term unemployed do leave the labour force. (White (1983) found about half of those in his sample leaving long-term unemployment left the labour force altogether, but this survey was carried out before some of the administrative arrangements described above for taking people out of the unemployment count after one year had been introduced.) There is no recent evidence on the numbers of long-term unemployed leaving the labour force but, as the numbers seem likely to be small, we will ignore this category. Should it turn out that there are significant numbers in this category, however, the scale of the job guarantee programme can be correspondingly reduced.

It follows that, in the labour market conditions of 1986 about 750 000 long-term unemployed people found work of one type or another each year. (This figure is the difference between the total number leaving long-term unemployment each year and taking places on the Community Programme or on other government schemes.) The job guarantee programme must therefore be seen as adding to the already quite large numbers leaving long-term unemployment.

Initially, while the scale of the job guarantee is small and the numbers of long-term unemployed very large, the job guarantee can be aimed at those least likely to leave unemployment unassisted (that is, the very long-term unemployed). But as the job guarantee becomes more comprehensive it must start to substitute for, rather than add to, the existing numbers of 'off-programme' placements of the long-term unemployed into work. In fact, the job guarantee could completely displace 'off-programme' recruitment, for example if it were to offer each person a job on the 366th day of their unemployment, and take-up were complete. In this case, long-term unemployment would be completely eliminated, but the job guarantee programme (together with the Community Programme) would still need to provide a million places a year to cater for the million new entrants to long-term unemployment in each year.

Our specific proposal for a job guarantee would start with 250 000 places in work or in training schemes in the first year, and build up to 500 000 places in the second year and to 750 000 places in the third year. In the first two years the programme would be aimed primarily at the very long-term unemployed whose prospects for leaving unemployment are otherwise very low (Figure 9.6). Thus we think that the bulk of the new jobs offered in these first two years would be additional to the existing 'off-programme' outflow. These new places would thus have the effect of reducing long-term unemployment on an almost one-for-one basis. Within two years long-term unemploy-

Table 9.9 The build-up of the job guarantee programme (millions)

Year	*0*	*1*	*2*	*3*	*4*
Long-term Unemployment (beginning of year)	1.35	1.35	1.10	0.75	0.60
Inflow	1.00	1.00	1.00	1.00	1.00
Outflow					
'Off programme'	0.75	0.75	0.60	0.15	0.00
'On programme' (incl. C.P.)	0.25	0.50	0.75	1.00	1.00
Total outflow	1.00	1.25	1.35	1.15	1.00

ment would therefore fall from its present level of 1.35 million to around, say, 750 000 (see Table 9.9).

From the third year, places on the job guarantee programme would be available to all the long-term unemployed, and it is clear that the programme would substantially reduce the numbers finding work outside the programme. Indeed, given that the programme includes a general financial incentive for recruitment (see below) there seems little reason why anyone should take a job outside the programme when, by taking the same job as part of the programme, they qualify for financial support. Thus, once the job guarantee is made generally available to all the long-term unemployed, the numbers of job placements outside the programme would fall to a trickle.

In practice, the number of places needed to deliver a job guarantee would almost certainly be smaller than these figures suggest. Many employers would prefer to avoid the paperwork associated with claiming financial incentives to which they would be entitled. Some of the long-term unemployed may leave the labour force, become self-employed or may not be prepared to take work of any sort. None the less, a job guarantee implies a commitment to find a place for all the long-term unemployed and it is essential to estimate the maximum scale of programme such a commitment might entail.

PROPOSALS

We have documented the human and economic cost of long-term unemployment and shown why we believe the solution requires special measures, over and above the existing programmes to help the unemployed, with the specific aim of bringing the long-term unemployed back into normal work. What is required is a job guarantee, that is to place an obligation on government to offer every person who has been continuously unemployed for a year or more a job, or a place on a training programme for a year. The thinking behind this proposal is that the long-term unemployed are currently at a disadvantage in the labour market because of the length of time for which they have been unemployed. A year of work or training would remove that disadvantage, reintegrate the long-term unemployed into the labour market and allow them thereafter to manage unassisted.

We now examine the form such a job guarantee might take. There are two major practical issues: the overall scale of the programme and the types of scheme of which it could consist. While we have considered these questions carefully, our conclusions are necessarily more speculative than those of earlier sections.

We have estimated that at 1986 levels of long-term unemployment and escape rates the job guarantee programme would need to build up to the provision of 750 000 places a year. We consider four schemes: the three suggested by the House of Commons Select Committee on Employment in its Report on Special Employment Measures (1986) and additionally a scheme for the extension of training opportunities for the long-term unemployed. Our conclusions are that these schemes appear feasible and cost-effective and that they merit further discussion with interested parties and investigation with regard to detailed implementation.

Criteria

In subsequent sections we outline a number of specific policy proposals. But it is first worth discussing briefly the criteria according to which they were chosen. The purpose of the job guarantee is to bring the long-term unemployed back into work as regular members of the labour force. The current extent of long-term unemployment is without historical parallel, and there is every reason to think that, in normal times, most of those now long-term unemployed would have been in normal work. As we have already seen, the long-term unemployed constitute a reasonably broad cross-section of the labour force as a whole: they are not concentrated in particular sectors, regions or age groups, although, as is true of unemployment generally, most are manual workers.

Both because of the variety amongst the unemployed and because of the scale of the programme it is desirable that it should involve as wide a range of activities as possible. For this reason we would wish to maintain all the programmes provided by the government including the original Community Programme. (In practice, we imagine the Community Programme would remain the main route back to work for young people – say under 21 – while the new programmes would cater primarily for adult workers.) The new programmes would be targeted to reach those of the unemployed for whom existing measures are least appropriate, in particular adults with few skills or with obsolete skills. For such people we would want to provide, as far as possible, regular jobs with regular employers providing a work environment of the type to which they were previously accustomed. The job guarantee would be a guarantee of a full-time job, but given the growth of part-time and irregular hours working in the economy as a whole, anyone preferring such a job would be allowed to take one.

The first criterion is to find work of a suitable kind. The second is to find such work at a sufficiently low cost. An appropriate measure of this cost is the 'first-round' net effect on the government budget. This is the gross public expenditure cost of the project less savings in unemployment or supplementary benefit, in other government outlays such as housing benefit, and less additional 'first-round' receipts from income tax and national insurance contributions. This measure is appropriate because it indicates the increase in taxation necessary to finance the programme (assuming no increase in government borrowing). Alternatively, if the programme is financed by borrowing, it indicates the additional borrowing required, since we are assuming that (with short-term unemployment remaining constant) there are no second or further round effects on unemployment.

In evaluating individual schemes, however, we focus only on estimates of gross costs. Our method for estimating the reduction in unemployment from the programme as a whole was set out earlier, and we do not attempt to estimate the contribution of the different schemes to the overall reduction in unemployment. In qualitative terms, we do, however, allow for differences in deadweight in determining the relative scale of the different schemes. Within each scheme, individual projects will have to be chosen on the basis that, consistently with the overall effect of the programme, for each long-term unemployed person taken on, the government saves a year of benefit payments. We assume no savings of benefits in respect of people employed on a project other than the long-term unemployed. To do so would be to make the assumption that one can achieve an overall reduction in unemployment by increasing government spending without risking an increase in inflation. In this chapter we are arguing that the case for the job guarantee does not rest on any particular macroeconomic assumptions so that we do not wish to base our estimates of cost on a specific view about the scope for fiscal expansion.

Our third criterion is economic efficiency. In addition to taking on long-term unemployed people, the schemes we discuss will produce various outputs which have economic value and employ other inputs which have economic costs. Clearly we would prefer schemes with the most favourable benefit-to-cost ratios. With a private sector scheme producing marketed output, the value of the output and the costs of other inputs are automatically taken into account by the employer. But on most projects in the public sector the output is not sold and hence its value will not affect the net financial costs of a scheme. Given the scale of the programme we propose it is clearly important that the resources are put to best use. This means public sector projects which are, or are close to being, economically viable but fall just below the margin given current public expenditure constraints. We turn now to the specific proposals.

Building Improvement Programme

Building improvement work is a clear priority. It is evident and has been well documented that much of the nation's infrastructure, in particular in public housing, schools, hospitals and roads is in decay and there is a huge backlog of repair, maintenance and improvement work. Some estimates of the scale of the problem are given in Table 9.10. The cause of this backlog is largely the cuts in public expenditure, and in particular in local authority budgets and capital allocations, since 1979. In consequence the bulk of such work will be in the public sector.

The second reason why building improvement is a priority is that much of the work requires skills that many of the unemployed already have or can relatively easily acquire. Table 9.11, which is derived from the 1983 *Labour Force Survey*, shows the previous industry of long-term unemployed people. A relatively high proportion are from the manufacturing sector and allied activities (such as transport workers), and most (see Table 9.1) are manual workers. Clearly people with previous experience of manual work in manufacturing industry are likely to have more immediate aptitude for

Table 9.10 Maintenance and construction needs for the infrastructure

Sector	*Maintenance backlog*		*New construction need*
Roads			
Motorways	being eliminated[1]	£4 bn over ten years[3]	£6–8 bn over ten years[4]
Other trunk roads	at least £0.2 bn over five years[2]		
Local roads	very substantial[1]		
Water supply			
Sewers	£1.7 bn[5]	£0.2 bn increase over five years[3]	
School buildings			
Secondary	£0.5 bn[6]		
Primary			
Hospitals (NHS)	£1.7 bn[7]		
Houses (Local Authority)	£18 bn[8]		£1 bn[3]

Notes:
[1] *Investment in the Public Sector Built Infrastructure*, NEDO, 1985.
[2] National Audit Office, 1985.
[3] Policy Studies Institute, 1984.
[4] From plans and calculations proposed by the CBI, PSI and British Road Federation.
[5] Water Research Centre, 1984.
[6] *Capital Expenditure Controls in Local Government in England*, Audit Commission, 1985.
[7] DHSS, 1985.
[8] Department of Environment, 1985.

Source: O. Simon, 'Investing in the Infrastructure', *National Westminster Bank Quarterly Review*, May 1986.

building improvement work than, say, for clerical or service sector employment.

The largest single component of the Building Improvement Programme would be repairs and improvements to council housing. According to the Audit Commission, no less than 85 per cent of the local authority housing stock is in need of such work and they estimate the average cost of the work needed per dwelling at £5000. While work of this nature is required throughout the country, the bulk of it will be concentrated in the bigger towns and cities, where unemployment rates tend to be highest. The maintenance of schools, hospitals and roads has also frequently been cut back by local authorities or health authorities as a short run response to financial cuts. Again the backlog of necessary repair work is greatest in the cities.

Table 9.11 Long-term unemployed by occupation

Length of unemployment	*less than 1 year* %	*1–2 years* %	*2–3 years* %
Professional (administrative)	2.1	1.1	1.2
Professional (health, education)	3.6	3.9	1.9
Literary, artistic and sports	0.7	0.8	0.4
Professional (scientific, engineering)	2.8	2.9	2.4
Management	7.2	4.9	3.5
Clerical	11.2	8.9	8.0
Sales	5.4	4.8	3.4
Security	1.8	2.2	1.3
Catering, personal services	8.6	8.0	7.7
Agriculture	1.6	1.4	2.1
Materials processing	10.1	11.8	11.3
Metal/electrical processing	16.8	16.7	18.3
Assembly work	6.8	8.3	7.6
Construction, mining	7.3	8.3	11.0
Transport	10.1	11.2	14.0
Miscellaneous	3.8	5.0	5.8
	100	100	100

Source: *Labour Force Survey*, 1983. The occupations are those of the person's last employment prior to becoming unemployed.

There is also a great deal of poor quality housing in the private sector. There may be scope for Building Improvement Programme work on property owned by housing associations, but it is more difficult to extend the Building Improvement Programme to owner-occupied or privately rented property. Improvement work would add to the value of a property and it is doubtful that the government would be prepared to allow private property owners to enjoy such financial gains without any provision for recovery of costs. While there are many in the private sector, particularly pensioners, who are too poor to afford even minimal repair work, experience with the Housing Improvement Grant programme shows that, however clear the intention of directing resources to those in need, the outcome is very often the opposite. Under the Building Improvement Programme no money would be paid out to owners, and opportunities for fraudulent misappropriation would therefore be less. While it would be desirable to include private housing, it would be necessary to limit the size of the programme to prevent abuse.

It would be particularly valuable if the Building Improvement Programme could make some contribution to improving labour mobility. One of the major obstacles to greater mobility is the availability of housing. Those areas of natural job growth often have 'tight' markets for accommodation and are inevitably expensive. Consequently, many potentially mobile people, particularly the young, cannot afford to move and search for work. The recent changes in housing payments in respect of social security claimants have made this situation worse. Plainly the current situation is unsatisfactory from both a social and economic point of view. One way to ameliorate this would be to use Building Improvement Programme resources in conjunction with housing associations and hostel groups to provide sheltered housing for unemployed people looking for work. The initial step on the ladder would be simple accommodation such as the YMCA which would allow individuals to stay in areas to pursue a job search for a reasonable period of time. The second stage would involve the provision of low cost flats as housing associations do now so that successful job searchers could make the transition into the local housing market. While this approach could not be undertaken on a massive scale it would make a valuable and helpful contribution to improving the labour market.

There is also some scope for Building Improvement work in the private sector other than in housing. The criterion here would be that, though under private ownership, the project would be of public benefit. The restoration of historic buildings in private ownership, the landscaping of a factory or the improvements of rights of way across private land are examples.

The essence of the Building Improvement Programme is that the individual projects would be run by commercial building contractors, rather than by government-approved project managers (as happened with the Community Programme run by the Manpower Services Commission (MSC)). The long-term unemployed would receive the same pay and be subject to the same work disciplines as other workers. The use of outside building contractors ensures that the unemployed people taken on would get experience of regular work subject to normal commercial pressures. But it requires careful procedures for cost control.

The projects would be administered in the following way. A government agency would invite suggestions from local authorities and other bodies for suitable projects. It would then, in consultation with the local authority and other sponsors, select projects according to the criteria set out in the previous section. The agency would then invite tenders from building contractors who would be obliged to commit themselves to taking on some given number of people from long-term unemployment. In the first two years of the programme, the agency would give priority to contractors, or projects, taking on the very long-term unemployed. The tenders would be assessed by the local authority for quality and cost standards.

The building contractor would be required to pay the rate for the job to the long-term unemployed taken on to the project but, in their cost estimates, would not be allowed to include overtime hours (paying for overtime could significantly increase the cost of a project without creating more jobs). The building contractor would pay the long-term unemployed taken onto the project a weekly wage (net of tax and national insurance) in the normal way.

The whole cost of the project would be met by the agency which would pay the contractor in stages as the work proceeded, again in the normal way except that the agency would need to ensure that the contractor was employing the numbers of long-term unemployed specified.

We come now to estimates of the exchequer costs per job on the Building Improvement Programme. The key issue is the relationship between the number of long-term unemployed people taken on and the number of other workers (and other costs) on a project. For simplicity we focus on a project employing five long-term unemployed people (but all the numbers can be scaled up or down for bigger or smaller projects). We assume that a project employing five people from long-term unemployment might typically also employ one skilled building worker and one supervisor. The gross operating cost of the project in 1986 prices is taken as £1200 per week, of which 10 per cent goes on materials, nearly 20 per cent on overheads and profit and the remainder on labour.

We are aware that most current building work involves a much higher ratio of skilled to unskilled labour than in the above example. However, we think the ratio we propose is not as outlandish as it may appear. First, many of the long-term unemployed have skills relevant to building work. In the northern cities in particular, where much of the greatest need for Building Improvement work is concentrated, there are significant numbers of skilled building workers amongst the long-term unemployed. Second, there are many successful examples of building work on the Community Programme at much less favourable ratios than those we envisage. Finally, we think it possible that

Table 9.12 Building improvement programme

	Gross cost in 1986	*Flowback £ p.w.*	*Net cost*
1 Supervisor	190	–	190
1 Skilled worker	165	–	165
5 Programme workers	525	400	125
Materials	120	–	120
Management overheads	200	–	200
	1,200	400	800
		£ per year	*£ per year per programme worker employed*
Gross cost of project in 1986 prices		60 000	12 000
Net cost of project in 1986 prices		40 000	8 000

the high skill ratios in existing work may be as much the product of existing working practices as of the technical requirements of the work to be done.

It is clear that allowing a higher ratio of skilled workers would greatly ease the task of the building contractors in operating the projects. The Building Improvement Programme is, however, already by far the most expensive (in terms of cost per job) of our proposals, and unless schemes can be operated at the ratio suggested it is simply not financially viable. We would stress, however, that we are assuming some relevant building skills among the long-term unemployed taken on.

The first column of Table 9.12 shows the breakdown of the gross cost per job. It implies that the agency would require a budget of about £12 000 a year for each long-term unemployed person taken off the register through the Building Improvement Programme. The employment of those workers reduces expenditure on income support, housing benefits and the like which in 1986 might have averaged around £60 per worker per week.[9] The government also collects income tax and national insurance which, on a gross wage of £105 per week might amount to £20 per week. Thus, of the gross wage of £105 per week the flow-back to the Exchequer amounts to £80 per week. Given the methodology we have adopted there are no flow-backs from the other inputs. The net cost of the project is thus as set out in the final column of Table 9.12, and the net annual cost per job amounts to £8000.

This calculation assumes that the Building Improvement Programme project goes ahead in addition to all the building work which would have been carried out in any case. It might seem that, if the agency is to meet in full the costs of Building Improvement Programme projects, local authorities or other sponsors would have a very strong incentive to put forward to the agency work that they would wish to do anyway, but otherwise would have to pay for from their own funds.

While it is impossible to prevent this substitution altogether, two factors lead one to think it would be quite limited in practice. First, most local authorities are very conscious of the need for more expenditure on repairs and improvements and thus would be very glad to add to their total volume of work rather than simply substitute one source of funding for another. Secondly, one can envisage a number of 'mixed' projects being put together where part of the work is undertaken on the Building Improvement Programme and paid for by the agency, and part undertaken by the local authority on its own budget. The opportunity for mixed projects might encourage additional local authority financed expenditure which could offset any substitution effects.

If substitution does take place, the overall effect depends on what the local authority does with the money it saves. If it returns the money to the ratepayers (that is, charges lower rates) the net cost per job may well become negative, since one must then include the reduction in rates as one of the savings from the project.[10] If it uses the money for other building projects, the substitution is irrelevant in terms of the cost per job calculation. But if it uses the money in some 'unproductive' way, there would be an additional resource cost to be added.

We believe it would be possible to provide, once the scheme was in full operation, 200 000 places a year on the Building Improvement Programme. This number is somewhat lower than that suggested by the House of Commons Select Committee. We regard the lower figure as more realistic, given the constraints imposed by the high ratio of long-term unemployed workers on a project.

Recruitment Scheme

Outside the construction sector it is difficult to identify specific projects which might qualify for support as 'free-standing' ventures. The only alternative approach is to encourage firms to take on long-term unemployed people in addition to their existing workers. Thus the proposal is that any employer who was prepared to add to their existing labour force by taking on a long-term unemployed person would receive a financial incentive of, say, £40 a week for the first year of the person's employment. As with the Building Improvement Programme, the people taken on would normally be employed full-time and would be paid the rate for the job. The recruitment scheme perhaps tackles most directly the labour market problem identified earlier: it prices the long-term unemployed back into work by compensating employers for the perceived risks of taking them on.

Some people doubt whether such a programme would have a large effect on recruitment in practice. Many employers are sceptical about the influence of financial incentives for recruitment on their employment decisions. A survey carried out on behalf of the EEC found that, in most member states, employers took the view that temporary employment subsidies would have a positive, but relatively small, effect on their recruitment decisions (*European Economy*, March 1986). On the other hand a survey conducted by the *Financial Times* found that tax concessions for hiring new workers would be the most effective policy for expanding employment (*Financial Times*, 1986).

Turning to other evidence, most serious econometric studies have found a significant effect of relative labour costs on the employment of different types of labour (for a useful survey, see Hamermesh and Grant, 1979). These studies attempt to estimate the actual change in employment associated with a given change in relative labour costs and thus may perhaps carry greater weight than possibly hurried responses to surveys and questionnaires.

While the £40 per week financial incentive lasts for a year, the intention is that many of the employers would retain people taken on for a longer period. We envisage the situation depicted in Figure 9.9. A firm, which might be, say, a large retail shop, a hotel or a fast food outlet, employs, say, 100 staff. As a result of the recruitment scheme it decides to increase employment to 105, taking on five long-term unemployed people each year. Before the scheme, as a result of labour mobility and natural wastage, it lost about 20 people a year, and replaced them with new recruits. The idea is that the long-term unemployed person, having received a year's apprenticeship as a low-cost worker, may at the end of the year move into normal employment with the same firm. Of course there would be no obligation on the firm to take him or her on because any such obligation might discourage the firm from taking on long-term unem-

Figure 9.9 The recruitment scheme

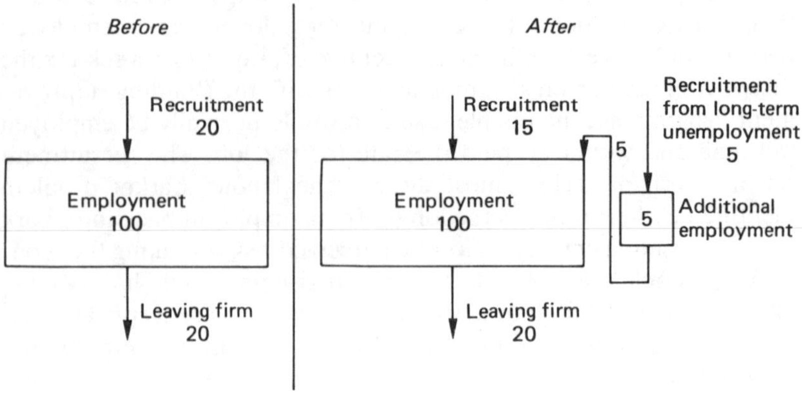

ployed people in the first place. The recruitment scheme would therefore raise overall employment and tilt firms' recruitment policy in favour of the long-term unemployed.

The problem with the recruitment scheme, as we have already noted, is that if such a scheme exists inevitably almost all recruitment of long-term unemployed people will qualify for financial support as part of the job guarantee programme. (Firms would not, however, be allowed to claim financial support for recruitment in any year in which they declared redundancies.) In the standard terminology, the deadweight cost of the scheme could be quite high. We have already discussed this issue at some length. The upshot is that, in the initial years of the programme, the recruitment subsidy should be restricted to the very long-term unemployed. This would very substantially reduce the extent of deadweight, as few of the very long-term unemployed find work unassisted. By the third year of the programme, the recruitment scheme would cover all the long-term unemployed. But by this stage their numbers are in any case fewer. In our costings we assume that 400 000 jobs a year receive support through the recruitment scheme, of which, on the basis of the examples discussed earlier, a large proportion represent hirings which might have taken place anyway.

The substantial element of deadweight is an important issue in evaluating the recruitment scheme in isolation. But in evaluating the cost of the job guarantee programme as a whole what matters are the gross costs of the individual programmes and the overall effect on the level of unemployment, which we have set out in Table 9.9. The gross cost of the recruitment subsidy is £2000 per job (at £40 per week).

Training Scheme

The importance of improving the effectiveness of the United Kingdom's education and training systems is now widely accepted across all political divides. The degree of training enjoyed by our labour force seems to be significantly less than in other major industrial countries (for instance see *Competence and Competition*, Manpower Services Commission, 1985). This in turn is widely seen as having a direct result on our relatively weaker economic performance. Moreover, where there are reasonably buoyant areas of the labour market and jobs are continuing to be created there appears to be an inadequate supply of skills to meet this demand fully. Consequently more people are unemployed than need to be.

Discussion of training, skills and economic performance understandably tends to focus on the need to develop the most advanced skills related to the emerging new technologies. No-one could deny the importance of this area nor the need to improve our performance here. However the relevance of improved training goes far wider than just these advanced skills. Looked at as a whole, our economic performance cannot be improved by simply concentrating on a relatively small number of potential workers in the most advanced areas. The quality of the entire workforce needs to be continually upgraded so that all economic functions can be performed more effectively and efficiently so helping in the generation of greater total added value. Possibly the gravest failing in the United Kingdom has been the widespread attitude that training is an idea relevant only to craftsmen or the educationally advanced. Everyone should be encouraged initially to seek training, skills and qualifications and then to improve and update them over time.

The long-term unemployed are a particularly important group to encourage to become involved in training. Many of them have few skills or have worked in occupations where the aptitudes required are now less in demand. Moreover such long spells of joblessness can not only erode technical abilities but also the capacity to 'hold down' a job through a loss of confidence, motivation and self-discipline. Employers are as concerned about the general qualities of potential recruits as they are about the quantity of them or basic qualifications.

Such qualities can be instilled as effectively by appropriate training courses as by work experience.

Training in a combination of technical ability and general attitude to work will help open up the opportunities for jobs to more people. Sceptics will point out that there will be no guarantee of a job at the end of a training course. But such guarantees could never be given without changing our whole approach to economic decisions. Rather training is a matter of giving an individual more opportunity and more chance of securing a job. Without it their prospects of work would be bleaker.

The training scheme would provide individuals with a voucher worth, say, £40 a week which could be spent either on payment of fees of any training college or other institution running government-approved courses, or be paid to an employer taking on the individual and providing training for him (again subject to the approval of the relevant government agency). While plenty of places on such education or training courses are likely to be available over the next ten years or so, given the sharp decline in the number of 18–21 year olds, many of the long-term unemployed will not have either the entry qualifications or in some cases the motivation to go back to school. For this reason, we think there might be about 100 000 placements a year on the training scheme.

In addition to the £40 a week education voucher, the people on the scheme themselves would receive an allowance for expenses and so on of £20 a week over and above their benefit entitlement. We appreciate that there are administrative difficulties in this proposal, although we note that the Swedish Labour Market Board, which operates a rather similar scheme, has managed to overcome them. If the average benefit payment is £60 per week, the gross cost of the training scheme is £120 a week (£6000 a place per year).

Public Sector Scheme

There are obvious unmet needs in social services and health. The move to community care requires at least 50 000 more workers in the community, while the National Health Service is short of orderlies, cleaners, and laundry and catering staff. The solution is not just to provide more money, but to provide more money linked to spending it on the long-term unemployed.

Here it is relatively easy to monitor additionality, and it therefore seems worthwhile to try and get those concerned employed on regular employment contracts. Wages would be paid by a government agency in the first year – for a full week's work if that was what the individual wanted. It would be inefficient not to embed them in the regular occupational structure, as that would lead to inefficient working – and an interrupted relationship with clients. When the year was up, the worker would cease to be subsidised. But he/she would not necessarily change jobs, and one would hope that the worker could be kept on on an unsubsidised basis. For this reason, and because we think there are legitimate doubts about the suitability of many of the long-term unemployed for some of the jobs required in these sectors, we propose a relatively small public sector scheme. If 50 000 places were made available each year we imagine that perhaps half the long-term unemployed recruited would leave voluntarily or be found unsuitable, while the other half (25 000 a year) could be absorbed. The National Health Service currently employs over 800 000 people and personal social services just under 200 000. With over a million staff in post it should be possible to absorb 25 000 a year to counterbalance natural wastage without excessive strain.

Those taken on would be paid a gross wage of about £120 a week, so that, allowing for supervisory time and use of office space, transport and so on the gross cost per job might be about £160 per week (£8000 per year).

Administration

The objective is that a government agency like the Manpower Services Commission would become responsible for guaranteeing to find a job or a place on a training scheme for every long-term unemployed person. There are two elements in implementing such a guarantee. First the places must be found. We think it unlikely that sponsors will come forward in sufficient numbers, so that a major task of the agency, supported by its area management boards, will be to publicise the programme and to persuade employers to take part.

The second element is to allocate places as they become available. As we have already indicated, in the early years of the scheme the objective would be to start with the very long-term unemployed. The first task would be to ensure that, within a year or so of the programme being set up, every person who had been unemployed for more than three years would be offered a place on a job or training scheme. As the scheme built up, and after the recruitment scheme became available to employers of all long-term unemployed people

Table 9.13 Job guarantee programme – a summary of costings

Programme	*Annual intake (thousands)*	*Gross cost per job (£ p.a.)*	*Total gross cost (£ bn p.a)*
Building Improvement Programme	200	12 000	2.4
Recruitment Scheme	400	2 000	0.8
Training Scheme	100	6 000	0.6
Public Sector Scheme	50	8 000	0.4
	750		£4.2 bn
Public expenditure savings			
Unemployment falls by 750 000 people at an average saving of £3000 per year per person.			£2.25 bn
Tax flowbacks			
Employment increases by 650 000 people at an average wage of, say, £100 a week, leading to payment of national insurance and income tax of an average £1000 per year per person			£0.65 bn
Overall net cost of programme			£1.3 bn
Overall net cost per job			£1700

by the third year, it would become possible to guarantee the offer of a job or a place on a training scheme to all the long-term unemployed.

From an administrative standpoint, the job guarantee could be regarded as a logical extension of the Government's Restart programme. This already involves interviewing and 'counselling' *all* the long-term unemployed. The job guarantee naturally complements this activity by providing an array of job opportunities which the long-term unemployed can be offered, once their capacity and potential has been identified by means of the existing interviewing arrangements.

Summary of Costings

The overall cost of the programme, once in full operation, is set out in Table 9.13. The top part of the table summarises the estimates of gross cost per job as discussed in more detail under the different schemes. The overall gross cost of the programme comes to £4.2 bn a year at 1986 costs. The lower half of the table derives net costs. We estimate first the saving in social security (including housing) benefits assuming half the unemployed going onto the programme are single

Table 9.14 The build-up of programme costs and savings (illustrative numbers)

	(mid-year averages) 0	1	2	3	4
Long-term unemployed (millions)	1.35	1.225	0.925	0.675	0.60
Intake: Building Improvement Programme, Public Sector Scheme, Training Scheme	0	0.10	0.275	0.35	0.35
Recruitment Scheme (millions)	0	0.025	0.10	0.275	0.40
Gross cost (£ bn)[1]	0	1.02	2.87	3.95	4.20
Savings in benefits etc (£ bn)[2]	0	0.47	1.62	2.60	2.90
Net cost (£ bn)	0	0.55	1.25	1.35	1.30

Notes:
[1] Gross cost is calculated at the average cost per job in the case of the Building Improvement Programme, Public Sector Scheme and Training Scheme (i.e. £9700) and at £2000 for the Recruitment Scheme
[2] Savings are calculated as the reduction in unemployment (i.e. 1.35 million less the number in the top row for each year) multiplied by the saving in benefit plus the increase in employment (on the assumption that the training programme builds up at the same rate as the Building Improvement Programme) multiplied by the assumed tax and national insurance flowback.

and half married (without children). The average benefit is about £60 a week (£3000 a year), and unemployment is reduced, as discussed earlier, by 750 000.

We also deduct the 'first-round' tax flowback, that is the income tax and national insurance contributions paid by those who go into employment. (There are no tax flowbacks for the training scheme.) We assume that most of the jobs taken by the long-term unemployed on the recruitment scheme would be low-paid, and therefore that the average wage across all the schemes would be around £100 a week. Tax and national insurance would amount to about £20 a week (£1000 a year).

Taking into account these savings, but no further repercussions of the programme, the overall net cost is estimated at £1.3 bn, and the implied annual net cost per job £1700. To give some feel for the possible build-up of the cost, we give some illustrative figures in Table 9.14. Here we distinguish between the Building Improvement Programme, the Public Sector Scheme and the Training Scheme on the one hand and the recruitment scheme on the other. In the early years of the programme, with the recruitment scheme limited to the very long-term unemployed, the emphasis would be on building up the other programmes and the deadweight would be quite small. Once the recruitment scheme is made generally available, however, it would be likely to be the largest component of the job guarantee and deadweight would be much increased.

Table 9.14 is calculated on the basis of 'mid-year' estimates. Thus, the unemployment figures in the top row for each year are the average of the figures in Table 9.9 for the beginning of each year and the beginning of the following year. The Building Improvement Programme, Public Sector Scheme and Training Scheme are together expected to build up to 200 000 places by the end of the first year, and to 350 000 places by the end of the second year, thereafter remaining at this scale. The Recruitment Scheme is expected to provide 50 000 places by the end of the first year, 150 000 by the end of the second year, and 400 000 by the end of the third year (by which time it would be open to anyone employing a long-term unemployed person). The figures in the second and third rows are mid-year averages of these numbers.

Conclusion

We wish to stress that all our costings are necessarily tentative. The determinants of unemployment and its duration are only partly understood, but for the sake of clear thinking we have used an explicit set of assumptions about how the labour market works. In this sense our procedure aims higher than the *ad hoc* (and partial) procedures adopted in the usual calculations of deadweight, substitution and displacement. Though we believe we have asked the right questions, our estimates nevertheless depend on many assumptions and cannot therefore be regarded as precise (or even necessarily nearer to the mark than those of the Employment Committee). Further research will enable us to do better as time goes on. But, as a result of our calculations so far, we are reasonably confident that the Employment Committee's calculations are if anything an overestimate. We therefore urge the government to show its concern about long-term unemployment by implementing these proposals.

Notes

1. Richard Jackman is Senior Lecturer in Economics at the London School of Economics and a Trustee of the Employment Institute. The first version of this text was published in December 1986.
2. The 1985 Labour Force Survey found that of the claimant count of 3.13 million in Great Britain, 880 000 had not sought work in a reference week, 335 000 of whom were so-called discouraged workers who would have liked a job but believed no jobs were available. In addition 200 000 benefit claimants were in employment of some sort or another. On the other hand, 760 000 people not claiming benefit had looked for work in the reference week. Conservatively counting as unemployed only people looking for jobs and *self-confessed* discouraged workers we find that the claimant count understates the 'true' level of unemployment by 15 000. No statistics from the survey were published for different categories of duration. However, it would seem safe to assume that a similar story can be told for long-term as total unemployment. (See 'Preliminary Results from the 1985 Labour Force Survey', Department of Employment Press Notice, 23 April, 1986.)
3. Parasuicide can be defined as deliberate non-fatal self-harm.
4. An alternative possible explanation is that the more potentially suicidal of the unemployed find it more difficult to get work, and hence form a higher proportion of the long-term unemployed. This explanation does not explain the high initial risk, however.
5. While the unemployed person may get no financial support, he or she will normally be entitled to assistance for dependent relatives, particularly children. Support for dependent children is more generous in Sweden than in the United States.
6. The technical issues are dealt with by Borjas and Heckman (1980). For a less technical introduction, see Creedy and Disney (1985) chapters 7 and 8.
7. In practice there are also large flows into and out of the labour force, which we are having to ignore as we have insufficient data.
8. Men over 60 who have been unemployed for more than a year are entitled to a higher rate of supplementary benefit and are no longer counted as unemployed. Thus almost all men who become unemployed over the age of 60 'retire' after one year of unemployment and do not enter long-term unemployment. Men who become unemployed in their late 50s and become long-term unemployed before their 60th birthday will, however, retire from long-term unemployment when they reach the age of 60. There are few married women among the long-term unemployed since few are entitled to supplementary benefit, and it is mainly married women who leave the labour force for family reasons.
9. For example, if half the workers were single, half married and all were in receipt of supplementary benefit plus housing benefits.
10. If the gross cost of the project is the same whether funded by a local authority or by the government agency, but the agency funding entails employment of long-term unemployed people, shifting the project from the local authority to the agency entails a net reduction in long-term (and hence total) unemployment and therefore an overall reduction in public expenditure due to savings in unemployment benefits.

Bibliography

Armington, C. and M. Odle (1982) 'Small Business – How Many Jobs?', *Brookings Review*, Winter.

Armstrong, H. (1986) 'The Divisions of Regional Industrial Policy Powers in Britain: Some Implications of the 1984 Policy Reforms', *Environment and Planning C*.

Armstrong, H. and J. Taylor (1985) *Regional Economics and Policy*, (Oxford: Philip Allan).

Ashcroft, B., J. H. Love, and J. Scouller (1987) *The Economic Effects of the Inward Acquisition of Scottish Manufacturing Companies, 1965–1980*, Industry Department for Scotland, HMSO.

Ashenfelter, O. and P. R. G. Layard (1983) 'Incomes Policy and Wage Differentials', *Economica*, vol. 50, May.

Atkinson, J. (1985) 'Flexibility: Planning for an Uncertain Future', *Manpower Policy and Practice*, vol. 1, Summer, pp. 26–9.

Banks, M. and P. Jackson (1982) 'Unemployment and the Risk of Minor Disorder in Young People', *Psychological Medicine 12*, pp. 789–98.

Bean, C. R., P. R. G. Layard and S. Nickell (1986) 'The Rise in Unemployment: A Multi-Country Study', *Economica Supplement on Unemployment* (vol. 53) pp. S1–S22.

Berthoud, R. (1984) *The Reform of Supplementary Benefit*, Policy Studies Institute (Working Papers).

Binks, M. and A. Jennings (1986) 'Small Firms as a Source of Economic Regeneration', in J. Curran, J. Stanworth and D. Watkins (eds), *The Survival of the Small Firm*, vol. 1 (Aldershot: Gower).

Birch, D. (1979) *The Job Generation Process*, Programme on Neighbourhood and Regional Change (Cambridge, Mass.: MIT).

Birch, D. and S. McCracken (1983) *The Small Business Share of Job Creation: Lessons Learned from the Use of a Longtitudinal File* Programme on Neighbourhood and Regional Change, March (Cambridge, Mass.: MIT).

Blanchflower, D. G. and A. J. Oswald (1986) *Shares for Employees: A Test of their Effects*, London School of Economics, Centre for Labour Economics, mimeo.

Bolton, J. (chairman) (1971) *Report of the Committee of Inquiry on Small Firms*, Cmnd 4811 (London: HMSO).

Borjas, G. and J. Heckman (1980) 'Does Unemployment Cause Future Unemployment?', *Economica*, August.

Bradley, K. and A. Gelb (1986) *Share Ownership for Employees* (London: Public Policy Centre).

Brant, J. (1984) 'Patterns of Migration from the 1981 Census', *Population Trends*, OPCS.

Brittan, S. (1986) 'At Last a Plan for More Jobs With No Inflation', *Financial Times*, 4 August.

Brittan, S. and P. Lilley (1977) *The Delusion of Incomes Policy* (London).
Brown, W. (1985) *Facing up to an Incomes Policy*, Cambridge mimeo, April.
Bruno, M. and G. Sachs (1985) *The Economics of World-Wide Stagflation* (Oxford: Basil Blackwell).
Cabinet Office (1985) *Lifting the Burden* Cmnd 9571 (London: HMSO).
Cable, J. (1986) *Is Profit-Sharing Participation?* University of Warwick, mimeo.
Cable, J. and F. Fitzroy (1980) 'Co-operation and Productivity: Some Evidence from West German Experience', *Economic Analysis and Workers' Management, vol. XIV*, pp. 163–90.
Campbell, B. (1984) *Wigan Pier Revisited* (London: Virago).
Casson, M. (1983) *The Economics of Unemployment* (London: Martin Robertson).
Charter for Jobs (1985) *Faster growth is Possible*, Economic Report vol. 1 no. 2, November.
Charter for Jobs (1986) *Full Employment – A Lesson From Sweden?*, Economic Report no. 9, August/September.
Charter for Jobs (1987) *Declining Unemployment: A Statistical Illusion?*, Economic Report, vol. 2, no. 7, May.
Commission of the European Communities (1984) *Communication for the Council as the Standing Committee of Employment*, Boumel: EEC Com (84).
Conte, M. and A. Tannenbaum (1978) 'Employee-Owned Companies: Is the Difference Measurable?', *Monthly Labour Review*.
Creedy, J. and R. Disney (1985) *Social Insurance in Transition: An Economic Analysis* (Oxford University Press).
Curran, J. (1986) *Bolton Fifteen Years On* (London: Small Business Research Trust, September).
Curran, J. and J. Stanworth (1986) 'Worker Involvement and Social Relations in the Small Firm', in J. Curran, J. Stanworth and D. Watkins (eds), *The Survival of the Small Firm*, vol. 2 (Aldershot: Gower).
Daniel, W. (1974) *A National Survey of the Unemployed* (London: PEP).
Davies, G. (1986) 'The Pay Dilemma – A Proposal', *The UK Economic Analyst* (London: Goldman Sachs) August.
Defourny, J., S. Estrin and D. C. Jones (1985) 'The Effects of Worker Participation upon Productivity in French Producer Co-operatives', *International Journal of Industrial Organisation*, vol. 3, pp. 197–218.
Department of Employment (1985) *Employment – The Challenge for the Nation*, Cmnd 9474 (London: HMSO).
Department of Employment (1986) *Building Business. . . . Not Barriers*, Cmnd 9794 (London: HMSO).
Department of Trade and Industry (1983) *Regional Industrial Development*, Cmnd 9111 (London: HMSO).
Department of Trade and Industry (1988) *DTI – The Department for Enterprise*, Cmnd 278 (London: HMSO).
Doyle, J. and C. Gallagher (1986) *The Size Distribution, Potential for Growth and Contribution to Job Generation of Firms in the UK, 1982–1984*, Research Report no. 7, Department of Industrial Management, University of Newcastle-Upon-Tyne.

Employment Institute (1988) *Half a Loaf: The Government's Proposed Unified Training Programme*, Economic Report, vol. 3, no. 5, February.

EPIC Industrial Report (1986) May 12.

Estrin, S. and N. Wilson (1986) *The Micro-Economic Effects of Profit-Sharing: The British Experience*, London School of Economics, Centre for Labour Economics Discussion Paper no. 247.

Financial Times (1986) 'Special Report on Work', 24 July.

Fitzroy, F. R. and K. Kraft (1985) 'Profitability and Profit-Sharing', *Journal of Industrial Economics*,

Foreman-Peck, J. (1985) 'Seedcorn or Chaff? New Firm Formation and the Performance of the Inter-War Economy', *Economic History Review*, series 2, vol. 38, no. 3, August, pp. 402–33.

Freeman, R. B. (1976) 'Industrial Mobility and the Union Voice in the Labour Market', *American Economic Review*.

Gallagher, C. and H. Stewart (1986) 'Jobs and the Business Life Cycle in the UK', *Applied Economics*, vol. 18, pp. 875–900.

Ganguly, P. (1985) 'Business Starts and Stops: UK County Analysis 1980–1983', *British Business*, 18 January.

Gregory, R. G. (1986) 'Wages Policy and Unemployment in Australia', *Economica Supplement on Unemployment* (vol. 53).

Hakim, C. (1982) 'The Social Consequences of High Unemployment', *Journal of Social Policy II*, 4, pp. 433–67.

Hamermesh, J. D. and J. Grant (1979) 'Econometric Studies of Labor – Labor Substitution and their Implications for Policy', *Journal of Human Resources*.

Harrison, R. (1976) 'The Demoralising Experience of Prolonged Unemployment', *Department of Employment Gazette*, 84, pp. 339–48.

House of Commons (1986) *Special Employment Measures and the Long-Term Unemployed*, First Report from the Employment Committee Session 1985–1986 (London: HMSO).

Jackman, R. (1985) *Professor Weitzman and the Unions. Why Profit-Sharing is Just Another Form of Wage Tax: A Note*, London School of Economics, Centre for Labour Economics Working Paper No. 776.

Jackman, R. and P. R. G. Layard (1986a) 'The Economic Effects of Tax-Based Incomes Policy', in D. Colander (ed.) *Incentive-Based Incomes Policy* (Cambridge, Mass.: Ballinger).

Jackman, R. and P. R. G. Layard (1986b) 'A Wage-Tax, Worker-Subsidy Policy for Reducing the "Natural" Rate of Unemployment', in W. Beckerman (ed.) *Wage Rigidity and Unemployment* (London: Gerald Duckworth).

Jackman, R. and P. R. G. Layard (1986c) *Does Long-Term Unemployment Reduce a Person's Chance of a Job? A New Test*, Centre for Labour Economics Working Paper No. 883.

Jackson, P. and P. Warr (1984) 'Unemployment and Psychological Ill-Health – The Moderating Role of Duration and Age', *Psychological Medicine*, 14, pp. 605–14.

Jensen, M. C. and W. H. Meckling (1979) 'Rights and Production Functions: An application to Labour-Managed Firms and Co-Determination', *Journal of Business*, vol. 4, pp. 469–506.

Johannesson, J. (1985) *On the Composition and Output of Swedish Labour Market Policy 1970–1985* (Stockholm).

Johannesson, J. and I. Persson-Tanimura (1984) *Labour Market Policy under Reconsideration* (Stockholm: Swedish Ministry of Labour).

Johnson, S. (1986) *What Sort of Jobs do Small Firms Create?*, UK Small Firms Policy and Research Conference, Gleneagles.

Jones, D. C. and J. Svejnar (1985) 'Participation, Profit-Sharing, Worker Ownership and Efficiency in Italian Producer Co-operatives', *Economica*, vol. 52, pp. 449–66.

International Labour Review (1942) *The Impact of War on Long-Term Unemployment*, January.

Layard, P. R. G. (1982) *More Jobs, Less Inflation*, (Oxford: Grant McIntyre).

Layard, P. R. G. (1984) *Public Sector Pay: The British Perspective*, London School of Economics, Centre for Labour Economics, Discussion Paper No. 229.

Layard, P. R. G. (1986) *How to Beat Unemployment* (Oxford University Press).

Layard, P. R. G. and S. Nickell (1986) 'Unemployment in Britain', *Economica Supplement on Unemployment (vol. 53)* pp. S21–170.

Layard, P. R. G. and S. Nickell (1987) 'The Labour Market' in R. Dornbusch and P. R. G. Layard (eds), *The Performance of the British Economy* (Oxford: OUP).

Layard, P. R. G., D. Piachaud and M. Stewart (1978) *The Causes of Poverty*, Royal Commission on the Distribution of Income and Wealth, Background Paper no. 5 (London: HMSO).

Long, R. J. (1978) 'The Relative Effects of Share Ownership versus Control on Job Attitudes in an Employee-Owned Company', *Human Relations*.

McCarthy, Lord (1985) Freedom at Work: *Towards the Reform of Taxing Employment Laws* Fabian Tract No. 508.

McCormick, B. (1987) *Housing and Labour Mobility*, Employment Institute Economic Report vol. 3, no. 3, December.

McCrone, G. (1986) *Regional Policy in Britain* (London: George Allen & Unwin).

Mason, C. (1986) *New Firm Formation since the Onset of Recession*, UK Small Firms Policy and Research Conference, Gleneagles.

Mason, C. (1987) 'Venture Capital in the United Kingdom: A Geographical Perspective', *National Westminster Bank Review*, May.

Mason, C. and R. Harrison (1986) 'The Regional Impact of Public Policy Towards Small Firms in the United Kingdom', in D. Keeble and E. Wever (eds), *New Firms and Regional Development in Europe* (London: Croom Helm).

Meade, J. (1982) *Stagflation, vol. 1.: Wage-Fixing* (London: George Allen & Unwin).

Meade, J. (1986) *Different Forms of Share Economy* (London: Public Policy Centre).

Metcalf, D. and S. Nickell (1985) 'Jobs and Pay', *Midland Bank Review*, Spring.

Middleton, R. (1981) 'The Constant Employment Budget Balance and

British Budget Policy 1929–39', *Economic History Review*, vol. 34, May.
Moore, B., J. Rhodes and P. Tyler (1986) *The Effects of Government Regional Economic Policy*, Department of Trade and Industry (London: HMSO).
Moser, K., A. Fox and D. Jones (1984) 'Unemployment and Mortality in the OPCS Longtitudinal Study', *Lancet ii*, pp. 1324–9.
National Economic Development Council (1986) *Possible Tax Relief to Encourage Profit-Sharing*, NEDC (86) 24.
Normington, D., H. Brodie and J. Munro (1986) *Value for Money in the Community Programme*, Report by Department of Employment, Manpower Services Commission, March.
Payne, P. (1984) 'The Human Nutrition Studies Group', in *DHSS Research and Development Handbook 1983* (London: HMSO).
Platt, S. and N. Kreitman (1984) 'Trends in Parasuicide and Unemployment among Men in Edinburgh 1968–1982', *British Medical Journal*, 289, pp. 1029–32.
Rajan, A. (ed.) (1986) *UK Occupation and Employment Trends to 1990* (London: Butterworths).
Rajan, A. (ed.) (1987) *Special Studies in the UK's Employment Prospects* (London: Butterworths).
Richardson, R. and A. Nejad (1985) *The Impact of Financial Participation Schemes on Share Price Movements*, London School of Economics, mimeo.
Rona, R., A. Wainwright and D. Altman (1979) 'Surveillance of Growth as a Measure of Health in the Community', in L. Irwig and C. Florey (eds), *Measurement of Levels of Health*, World Health Organisation.
Rosenberg, R. D. and E. Rosenstein (1980) Participation and Productivity: An Empirical Study, *Industrial and Labour Relations Review*.
Short, J. (1981) *Public Expenditure and Taxation in the Regions* (Aldershot: Gower).
Shutt, J. and R. Whittington (1987) 'Fragmentation Strategies and the Rise of Small Units: The Case of the North-West', in *Regional Studies, Vol. 21, No. 1*, February 1987, pp. 13–24.
Stern, J. (1986) 'Repeat Unemployment Spells: The Effect of Unemployment Benefit on Unemployment Entry', in R. Blundell and I. Walker (eds), *Unemployment, Search and Labour Supply* (Cambridge University Press).
Storey, D. J. (1982) *Entrepeneurship and the New Firm* (London: Croom Helm).
Storey, D. J. (1986) *The First Step is To Spot the Winner, Guardian*, 31 January.
Storey, D. J. and S. Johnson (eds) (1987a) *Small and Medium-Sized Enterprises and Employment Creation in Europe*, Commission of the European Communities.
Storey, D. J. and S. Johnson (1987b) *Job Generation and Labour Market Change* (London: Macmillan).
Storey, D. J. and S. Johnson (1987c) 'Regional Variations in Entrepreneurship in the UK', *Scottish Journal of Political Economy*.

Storey, D. J., K. Keasay, R. Watson and P. Wynarczyk (1987) *The Performance of Small Firms* (London: Croom Helm).

Taylor, J. (1986) 'The Use of Unemployment and Vacancy Data in Analysing Unemployment' *Recherches Economiques de Louvain*, December.

Twomey, J. and J. Taylor, (1985) 'Regional Policy and the Interregional Movement of Manufacturing Industry in Great Britain', *Scottish Journal of Political Economy*.

United States Small Business Administration (1985) *The State of Small Business: A Report of the President*, Washington: USGPO, May.

United States Small Business Administration (1984) *The State of Small Business: A Report of the President* Washington USGPO, March.

Vanek, J. (1965) 'Workers' Profit, Participation, Unemployment and the Keynesian Equilibrium', *Weltvirtschaftliches Archive*, pp. 206–14.

Wadhwani, S. (1985) 'The Macro-Economic Implications of Profit-Sharing: Some Empirical Evidence', London School of Economics, Centre for Labour Economics, Discussion Paper No. 222.

Wadhwani, S. (1986) *Profit-Sharing and Employment: Some Doubts*, London School of Economics, Centre for Labour Economics Paper No. 857.

Warr, P., M. Banks and P. Ullah (1985) 'The Experience of Unemployment among Black and White Urban Teenagers', *British Journal of Psychology*, 76, pp. 75–87.

Weitzman, M. L. (1984) *The Share Economy* (Cambridge, Mass.: Harvard University Press).

Weitzman, M. L. (1985) *Insiders versus Outsiders: a Macroeconomic Externality and the NAIRU under Profit-Sharing*, Massachusetts Institute of Technology, mimeo.

White, M. (1983) *Long-Term Unemployment and Labour Markets*, (London: Policy Studies Institute).

Worswick, D. (1984) 'The Sources of Recovery in the UK in the 1930s', *National Institute Economic Review*, 110, November.

Zabalza A. and P. Kong (1983) *Pay Determination in the Public and Private Sectors*, London School of Economics, Centre for Labour Economics, Working Paper No. 574.

Index